Living Indigenous
Leadership

Living Indigenous Leadership

Native Narratives on Building Strong Communities

Edited by Carolyn Kenny and Tina Ngaroimata Fraser

UBCPress · Vancouver · Toronto

21 20 19 18 17 16 15 14 13 12   5 4 3 2 1

Printed in Canada on FSC-certified ancient-forest-free paper (100% post-consumer recycled) that is processed chlorine- and acid-free.

Library and Archives Canada Cataloguing in Publication

Living indigenous leadership: native narratives on building strong communities / edited by Carolyn Kenny and Tina Ngaroimata Fraser.

Includes bibliographical references and index.
Issued also in electronic format.
ISBN 978-0-7748-2346-3 (bound); ISBN 978-0-7748-2347-0

1. Native women – Canada. 2. Indian women – United States. 3. Indigenous women – New Zealand. 4. Community leadership – Canada. 5. Community leadership – United States. 6. Community leadership – New Zealand. 7. Indian leadership – Canada. 8. Indian leadership – United States. 9. Women in community development – Canada. 10. Women in community development – United States. 11. Women in community development – New Zealand. I. Kenny, Carolyn Bereznak. II. Fraser, Tina Ngaroimata.

GN380.L59 2012   305.48'8   C2012-905027-X

Canada

UBC Press gratefully acknowledges the financial support for our publishing program of the Government of Canada (through the Canada Book Fund), the Canada Council for the Arts, and the British Columbia Arts Council.

This book has been published with the help of a grant from the Canadian Federation for the Humanities and Social Sciences, through the Awards to Scholarly Publications Program, using funds provided by the Social Sciences and Humanities Research Council of Canada.

UBC Press
The University of British Columbia
2029 West Mall
Vancouver, BC V6T 1Z2
www.ubcpress.ca

Dedicated to

Dorothy Bell
   Matriarch of the Tsiits Gitanne (Eagle) Clan
   Haida Nation
   Born 11 November, 1915-2011
   In Old Massett Village, British Columbia, Canada

   and

Bella (Te Pera) Ranui
   Tuhoe, Ngati Haka/Patuheuheu Tribe
   Born 21 February, 1911-1977
   in Aōtearoa, New Zealand

   and

All who work tirelessly
   to build strong and healthy
   Native communities

Contents

Foreword

THIS IS AN INSPIRING book written by Indigenous women scholars from across Canada, the United States, and New Zealand who have successfully challenged mainstream education to secure the highest academic credentials institutions of higher learning can offer. While engaged in years of study, they have maintained a profound interest in Aboriginal thought and perspectives. In this volume, they explore leadership concepts appropriate to building strong Aboriginal communities. They embrace primary sources in their research as they engage our people – grandmothers, parents, Elders, youth, and even former gang members whose stories and experiences have shown that leadership is unbound. Leadership, they demonstrate, is not the purview of the educated or the elected. It is a time-honoured belief among Indigenous peoples that each person is born with innate strengths that can assist in the overall betterment of the community. The influence of Western thought has led us away from this concept. The research in this publication encourages us to rethink leadership, to give thought to the original philosophies and practices of our people and to give voice to these invisible leaders.

This is a unique publication in that the authors are mothers, grandmothers, and single women of all ages who are Choctaw-Haida, Māori, Cree, Anishinaabe, Tlingit-Haida, Mi'kmaq, Stó:lō, Paiute-Shosone, Opata and Tarahumara, Yakama, and Métis. They are employed in various fields that include education, health, social justice, and ethnic studies, either in the community at large or as professors and doctoral students at major universities. Although they represent diverse nations, they and their stories also exemplify the many commonalities of history, tradition, and cultural values shared by Indigenous people. An awareness of this reality leads to the knowledge that building strong communities can be a collective effort. These women are leading the way.

If you have the same reaction to this book that I had, you will want to read on and on until you have read the whole book, maybe in the same day. It is an inspiration to me, someone who has spent many years trying to advance Aboriginal education, to see the calibre of the scholars and the research they are providing today to those who are seeking knowledge of the worldview and perspectives of Indigenous people. After you have read the book, I know you will join me in acknowledging the work of these brilliant women who have provided for us timely food for thought.

Ekosani.

Verna J. Kirkness
Fisher River Cree Nation
Professor Emerita, University of British Columbia

Preface

Carolyn Kenny

ON A COOL SANTA BARBARA morning, sea fog rolls through the palm trees into my bedroom window. This is Chumash territory. And I can imagine the Chumash earth goddess, Hutash, helping my ancestors from my spirit home in the Haida Gwaii. Together, they send spirits across the many waters, over the Rainbow Bridge from the sea, through the Channel Islands off the southern coast of California, into the city of Santa Barbara, and through my bedroom window. These gentle breezes have their source in the north. Along with the moisture, they bring the smell of sweet grass. It embraces me, signifying the presence of my ancestors. They are here to greet me, to guide me through this day.

It is extraordinarily important for Native people to locate themselves spiritually. Our ecological, historical, and humanistic spirituality finds expression in the stories that help shape our lives and guide our days. There is also a sense of immediacy in our Native world for those who choose to feel it. Locating ourselves in the moment calls forth our past and our future in elegant and expansive perspectives that remind us of the interconnection of all things and an inclusive holism that permeates our worlds.

My ancestors are Native American and Ukrainian, with a little bit of Irish thrown into the mix. I am grateful for all. My Ukrainian Baba took good care of me when I was a small child. Speaking little English, she negotiated her new culture with elegance and grace as a true matriarch. Through the years, I became aware of a deep yearning to know something about my Native grandmothers and other Native ancestors I never knew – especially my Choctaw grandmother, who, out of desperation, abandoned her family when my own mother was only three years old. This was a story told in the shadows of our family – people wanted to move beyond the sad histories. But it was a story that haunted me. I was incomplete.

Thanks to the influence of her Comanche auntie, my mother did encounter and accept many Native values while she was growing up. So, she was able to instill some of these values in me. But she always told me, "Don't get involved. You'll only get hurt." This was her sorrow, not mine.

When I moved to Canada in 1970, I was embraced by Native people who were not of my blood tribe – first the Musqueam and Squamish and Tseil-Waututh, then, through the years, the Stó:lō, the Cree, the Anishinaabe, the Mik'maq, the Nis'ga, the Haida, and many more. Later, I came to know the Māori and the Ainu. My journey has been a joyful one. And through the years, I have developed a deep sense of belonging that eluded my mother. So now the circle is complete. One day, I, too, will arrive on the scent of sweetness through the morning windowpanes to greet my loved ones with the morning light.

I am particularly grateful to my Cree big sister, Dr. Verna Kirkness, who embraced me in that wonderful Indian, informal, adoptive way that is so natural, full of love, and intensely intelligent and humorous. And I am ever so grateful to my Haida mother, Dorothy Bell, who adopted me formally into the Haida nation as her daughter. My Haida name is Nang Jada Sa-êts or, in the original, Nangx'aadasa'iid.

Jo-ann Archibald encouraged me to launch this journey into unbound leadership, and Ethel Gardner worked with me in the earliest stages of the project, bringing several contributors along with her. She also helped me in the early stages of editing. I raise my hands in gratitude and respect to you both.

Tina Ngaroimata Fraser

"Ko Maungapōhatu me Hikurangi ngā Maunga" (my ancestral mountains), "Ko Ōhinemataroa me Rangataiki ngā Awa" (my ancestral rivers), "Ko Papakainga me Waiohau ngā Marae" (my place of gathering), "Ko Kourakino me Tama-ki-Hikurangi ngā Whare Tīpuna" (my sacred houses), "Ko Ngāti Koura, Ngāti Haka me Patuheuheu ngā Hapū" (my subtribes), "Ko Tūhoe te Iwi" (my main tribe), "Ko Mataatua te Waka" (my ancestral canoe), the canoe that brought my people Tūhoe, the Māori, from Hawaiki to Aōtearoa (the land of the long white cloud) New Zealand. It is respectful for Māori people to identify themselves through a *pepeha* (genealogy). The pepeha connects the individual geographically and genealogically to his or her history and kinship ties. These are my ancestors, and I share my lived experience of growing up Tūhoe and learning to respect all things, people, and places, both in Aōtearoa and North America.

I remain humble and particularly grateful for the *aroha* (love) and the *manakitanga* (care) of the Dakelh nation, which comprises twenty bands, communities, and tribal councils in northern British Columbia, Canada. Thank you for allowing me to journey alongside the struggles of colonization, to be a part of decolonization for thirty-seven years. Most notably, I thank those Dakelh Elders who have since passed. I am reminded of the many hours I spent sharing and listening to stories in the hospital, the clinic, and in your homes and communities. Now, I know why. I am teaching your descendants in First Nations studies, Indigenous women's studies, health science, nursing, and education ... Some of your descendants have never had the opportunity to meet you but have heard about the leadership roles each of you played in the community. They have often said to me, "You are so lucky. We never got to meet our granny or great-grandparents. Even though we don't know them, we miss them all."

Since my arrival in Canada in 1974, much of my time has been spent in northern BC, living among the people, the mountains, the forests, and the animals. I loved watching moose, bears, and grouse outside of our log home in the winter and birds flying across the calm waters of Stuart Lake in the spring. Although I am a visitor residing on the traditional lands of the Dakelh nation, the Dakelh and I share common threads of inter-connectedness: the rhythm of the land surrounded by beautiful mountains and a variety of native trees; the opportunity to look beyond the horizon for possibilities; the ability to envisage historical events through symbolic carvings; animals who graciously share their hides so we can survive or listen to the beat of the drum in order to remain connected spiritually, emotionally, physically, and mentally; and lakes, rivers, and the ocean, which help us to maintain our existence. I can see the images of our past, present, and future leaders carved in the Rocky Mountains, the glacier representing our ancestors' tears. But most of all, I can hear the evocative lyrical call of ... All Our Relations.

THE IMPETUS FOR THIS book was a panel presentation at the International Leadership Association Conference, held in Vancouver, British Columbia, in 2008. The session was titled "Teaching and Learning: Indigenous Perspectives on Surviving and Thriving." Five of the original six members – Gail Cheney, Tina Ngaroimata Fraser, Ethel Gardner, Raquel Gutierrez, and Michelle Jacob – wrote chapters for this volume. The project grew over time to include many others.

We particularly want to extend our thanks to the Native women who contributed to this volume. They all write in an unbound way without taking up dominating theoretical positions. They write about what it takes and whom it takes to build strong communities – women, men, children, grandchildren, Elders, and ancestors.

This collection of case studies and stories is a testimonial to the power of Indigenous women and others to build strong communities. And it is a testimony to the strength of our spirits as Indigenous peoples – to not only survive but also to thrive, sometimes against all odds. The source of our strength arrives in quiet moments at the dawn of a new day for all peoples.

We would also like to acknowledge the financial support for this project from the University of Northern British Columbia and Antioch University.

Living Indigenous Leadership

1

Liberating Leadership Theory

Carolyn Kenny

IN MY WORK WITHIN Native communities, I have had opportunities to interact with leaders from many Indigenous nations. I have seen leadership from behind the scenes, upfront, and everywhere in between. These leadership situations require character, tenacity, compassion, intelligence, courage, and imagination.

Over hundreds of years, the practice of leadership in Native communities has taken on different forms based on changing historical tides – autonomy, imperialism, colonization, resistance, and renaissance. As Native people, we live on shifting sands. For thousands of years prior to colonization, leadership in Indigenous communities was based on the character of the land and the needs of the people in their traditional territories. Today, Native nations strive for solidarity and the right to govern themselves once again. This solidarity, the state of being in which we govern our own lives in our own chosen places, is becoming a reality. Aboriginal women are at the forefront of change – politically, academically, educationally, and in every other way (see Ah Nee-Benham and Cooper 1998; Smith 1999; Voyageur 2008; see also Battiste 2000).

Aboriginal knowledge often finds its source in the challenges of complexity. The implementation of complex change is no small task. This book contributes to conversations about leadership by highlighting the situations and practices of Native peoples in Canada, the United States, and New Zealand. The stories contained in these pages reveal some of the faces of leadership in Native communities. Each chapter tells a story of leadership through collaboration and community action. The telling is woven into a tapestry of scholarship appropriate to an Indigenous style and point of view. Stories are a creative act of leadership through which we manifest our solidarity and strengthen our people to take their next steps in encouraging good and healthy lives. "Without addressing context, our theories of leadership remain incomplete, making it more difficult to offer practical guidelines to address the leadership demands of changing organizations in contemporary society" (Ospina and Foldy 2009, 876).

The stories of Native leadership presented in this volume are free from dominating theories. They are grounded in experience and represent specific contexts, particular tribes, diverse lands, inherent values and beliefs, a variety of protocols, a plethora of languages, and a tremendous variety of circumstances. Theorizing in this context is tough. We do not offer a general Indigenous theory of leadership. However, we do offer concepts that can be adapted to particular contexts (see Fitzgerald 2006).

I do not critique Native and non-Native leadership theories. Nor do I focus on the arguments contained in leadership theories and concepts.[1] Rather, I propose, along with all contributors in this volume, ideas that spring from experiences on the ground. On the one hand, these ideas are written in a declarative style that represents story. On the other hand, these stories are connotative rather than denotative in order to free the reader to interpret our stories and apply the concepts to his or her own context. I hope that you will recognize some of the concepts presented in this chapter and throughout the volume, that they will resonate with your spirit, heart, and soul, and that you will find a place to implement them in your own community. The stories gathered here reflect the innate strengths of the individuals who wrote them and the communities that they represent. The story begins ...

Let the Children Lead: Land, Ancestors, Elders, Story

Thank You, Earth

Thank you, Earth, for being here.
Thank you for your ruby sky.
Thank you for the rain
That hammers down on me
And ripens everything
Around me.

Thank you for your core
That burns like the sun.
Thank you for the pounce
Of nature all around me.

I will never regret
The keen blessing that dwells
All around us and sneaks
Upon me like tears
And a heart beat.

Without you,
We would never be here.

– Isabella Venable, Grade 4

I begin my theorizing with the words of a child (see Cohen 2001). Imagine my gratitude when I heard my ten-year-old granddaughter reciting her poem titled "Thank You, Earth" at the Santa Barbara Art Museum. Isabella's poem embodies important concepts. In the Indigenous world, there is a principle called the seven generations. It instructs us to reflect on our actions and to be aware of the consequences of these actions seven generations hence. As a grandmother, hearing Isabella's words, I felt confident that all was well in the world.

A sense of place brings coherence to Aboriginal people and suggests an aesthetic engagement with the land – an intimate spiritual commitment to relationships with all living things (Kenny 1998). As we create more virtual spaces, this intimate relationship with the land becomes even more important because we have to work harder to accomplish it.

To maintain this sense of coherence, we can accept the earth as our first embodied concept of leadership. We follow Earth. We respond to the guidance of the processes expressed in our home place. Many say we listen and respond to our Mother. Everything begins here. We mirror the patterns, textures, colours, sounds, and processes of the earth as embodied beings. As Isabella wrote: "Without you, we would never be here." This is an idea, a feeling, and a concept to embed in our leadership theories and practices.

We then look to our ancestors as leaders (Alfred 1999). Ancestors often guide us with deep respect for what they themselves have left behind. They communicate with us through dreams, through the teachings that have come down through the generations, through spirit. Our constant guides in our life journeys of spiritual discovery, our sense of wonder with the animation of the world, often arrive through the presence of our ancestors and Elders, who carry the knowledge that we need for continuity and integration. Traditional knowledge weaves its way into the contemporary context for our present and future endeavours (see Schaefer 2006; Sterling 1992).

Our Elders often bring these teachings to us through stories. Stories provide many of the guiding lights to show us our way on Earth – to lead truly good lives (Archibald 2008). These stories are embodied in oral traditions, in arts, in traditional practices of all kinds. Stories, especially in the oral tradition, provide powerful bridges that connect our histories, our legends, our senses, our practices, our values, and, fundamentally, our sustainability as peoples. The power of narrative knowing is not confined to the Native world (see Polkinghorne 1988; see also Gabriel 2004). Stories presented in the oral tradition provide an opportunity for immediacy – a direct and immediate relationship with listeners. The storyteller can make immediate adjustments in the elements of the story based on relational needs and contexts.

The road to leadership is paved with land, ancestors, Elders, and story – concepts that are rarely mentioned in the mainstream leadership literature. They are embodied concepts unique to Native leadership.

Walking between the Worlds

Contemporary leadership demands that Aboriginal leaders make bridges between many worlds. The dilemmas involved in this bridge-building are often referred to as "living between two worlds." There is plenty of leadership work to do in order to walk between Indian country and the mainstream societies in which we find ourselves today. Each context is different. In addition to walking between two worlds, we now must walk among many worlds. The global context and virtual contexts offer even more complexities. Many stories in this volume describe these dilemmas and reflect the specific circumstances, thoughts, and feelings of Aboriginal people who experience dualities that are incompatible in terms of values, beliefs, lifestyle choices, governance systems, child-rearing practices, educational pedagogies, and much more. Aboriginal activists and cultural workers in education, health, government, and a host of other contexts often find themselves caught between what they often call Western values and Indigenous values. In these dialogues and debates, one can observe that colonization still exists in the layers just beneath the surface of things.

One must resist the romance and seduction of a kind of fool's gold in which only surface issues are discussed and resolved. Well-intended beginnings cannot overcome the ongoing lack of mutuality and shared responsibility between the worlds. Examples are rampant in policies and procedures. Take, for instance, the push and pull between solidarity on the one hand and fiduciary responsibilities on the other. Aboriginal people strive for ethical transitions into self-governance while governmental agencies continue to dominate negotiations (see Kenny 2002).

Networks of Strength: Themes from the Indigenous Leadership Literature

Martha McLeod (2002, 11), quoting Barbra Wakshul's "Winds of Change," lists the ways in which Indian leadership differs from mainstream leadership: "(a) Indian leaders need to know both their own community (values and history) as well as the Euro-American community because they must function in both societies; (b) Indian leaders need to be holistic because Indian communities are small. Indians value interconnectedness, and Indians work on a wide variety of issues; (c) Indian leaders belong to communal societies that must accommodate both tribal values and Euro-American systems in which Indians and non-Indians coexist."

Most Aboriginal people are familiar with the phrase *the moccasin telegraph*. This concept refers to a tightly knit communications system and a communal attitude in which word travels fast through Indian country, through networks of family, friends, co-workers, Elders, tribal leaders, and others in the community or communities. Within these networks of affiliation, Native leaders often function with powerful influence and persuasion. In fact, Linda Sue Warner and Keith Grint claim that persuasion is more important than position for Indigenous leaders. Positions change based on changing circumstances (Warner and Grint 2006), but influence is garnered by gaining respect over time. Shifts in position and influence create a fluid state in many communities. Influential leaders are not always the ones in visible positions of authority. Miles Bryant (1998) agrees with Warner and Grint's impressions of Native leadership but adds the concept of context or situational leadership, a theme we emphasize here and elsewhere in the volume.

Jacqueline Ottman (2005) mentions spiritual leadership through the presence and guidance of family and Elders. This style of leadership is also implied in a great deal of literature that does not emphasize leadership in an explicit way (Alfred 1999). Spiritual leadership through family, Elders, and networks of connection is a recurring theme in any aspect of Native life.

Nonhierarchical leadership is another important theme in Indian country. In the literature, this theme is succinctly characterized by scholars such as Martha McLeod and Warner and Grint (McLeod 2002; Warner and Grint 2006). Canada's Indian Act stands as an excellent example of the discontinuities between traditional Native and Western-based governance systems. Before legislators embedded the Indian Act into Canadian law, First Nations did not, as a rule, function as elected democracies. They had sophisticated systems of governance commonly based on inherited succession, consensus, and accountability to a council of Elders. In many tribes, women were considered to be the final word in moral authority (see Kenny 2006). Men often held formal positions of power while the women created a strong circle of accountability around the more visible male leaders. The women were reluctant to be identified as formal leaders. The forced creation of hierarchies by the Canadian state destroyed traditional tribal governance systems, usually without positive outcomes. The governmental and Christian attitudes that led to the creation of residential schools for Native people around the world also reflected hierarchies of privilege that dehumanized Native youth while systematically decimating their attachment to their cultural contexts.

The majority of Indigenous scholarship emphasizes the spiritual principle of the interconnectedness of all things. This principle is important in most Indigenous societies and contained in Indigenous religious and spiritual belief systems. "All things are related" expresses this principle in many prayers and ceremonies. Native peoples are reminded of the significance of the principle of interconnectivity throughout their lifelong learning, including in contexts of higher education. McLeod makes this point in reference to leadership in Native higher education (McLeod 2002), and Ottman (2005) describes the importance of interconnectivity in a contemporary context.

Joyce Grahn and colleagues and McLeod describe the burden of Native leadership (Grahn et al. 2001; McLeod 2002). Often, communities choose leaders because of their integrity, their accomplishments, and their specific attributes and skills. These leaders serve because of their commitment to the community, not because of any desire to have position or power. There is a kind of modesty in this aspect of leadership. Bryant (1998) notes that the burden of Native leadership often results in decentralizing the authority of the group. In this sense, immanent or inherent value is a primary attribute of leaders who serve. Through networks of affiliation, leaders are chosen to play a role for a time. They are chosen through influence and persuasion.

Sometimes, charismatic tendencies are revealed through the power and beauty of oration. Charismatic leaders inspire people to act collectively when change is needed. Sometimes, being the best leader means stepping down, but it often means stepping up into a role that one may not be so happy to play for a time. Indigenous leadership is aesthetic in nature because it has its source in coherence. With the flow and flux of changing circumstances, Native leaders must constantly monitor the pulse of the interconnectedness of all things and gauge how these connections challenge our communities.

Miriam Jorgenson and Rachel Starks characterize Native leadership as an aesthetic engagement – one that brings us to the beauty of our lives – on the land, with each other, and in relationship to all living things. "Art and the relationships embedded in its creation provide the power to restore and transform people and communities" (Jorgenson and Starks 2008, 16). Art expressions are often how we maintain not only a sense of coherence but also our resilience and, ultimately, confidence and strength. Art expressions such as drumming, singing, dancing, carving, and painting are another way to communicate the principle of interconnectivity.

Last, but not least, is the ever-constant power of story (Archibald 2008). Narrative is a theme throughout Indigenous scholarship. All cultures are sustained through stories that integrate past, present, and future (see Gabriel 2004; Polkinghorne 1988). Stories are bridges that connect our histories, our legends, our senses, our practices, our values and, in essence, our sustainability as people.

Indigenous leadership literature is a slowly emerging field of study, yet there are many scholarly texts written by Indigenous scholars that contain implications for leadership (Alfred 1999). The ones discussed here outline the explicit territory of a type of Indigenous leadership that is fluid and liberating, a type of leadership that may overcome the disparities between the many worlds. At its core, Indigenous leadership is relational. In healthy tribal societies, individuals acted on behalf of others in the community. Their leadership was the glue that helped to keep the nation together.

Collaboration and Complexity: Themes from the Non-Indigenous Leadership Literature

When I began my job, in 2003, as a professor in the PhD in Leadership and Change program at Antioch University, I decided to reflect on my own memories and awareness of the concept of leadership. As a child, I was a member of a paramilitary family. Lockheed Aircraft Corporation was our "community." My mother, father, brother, and myself together clocked one hundred hours of service at Lockheed, working in different company departments. My knowledge of leadership began there. Our branch of Lockheed Aircraft Corporation was next door to Dobbins Air Force base in Marietta, Georgia, and, as a child, I heard the term *leadership* a lot in my parents' after-work conversations. Later, as a college graduate, I worked for the *Marietta Daily Journal*. Many of the stories in our newspaper mentioned the term *leadership* in reference to military personnel in our region. So, my earliest images of leadership were of warriors in uniforms who risked their lives to keep us safe.

As a professor in the Leadership and Change program, I observe Native students attempting to weave their way through the growing literature on leadership, attempting to locate concepts that will help them in their own leadership practices in Indigenous communities. Initially, one or two categories described in the massive *Encyclopedia of Leadership* (Goethals, Sorenson, and MacGregor Burns 2004) catch their eye. But after a more thorough exploration of numerous theories, most of which are not grounded in empirical data, the spark of interest fades. Why? My sense is that even though many of these theories offer useful information, the literature as a whole rarely fits with our experience as Aboriginal people.

The scholarly tradition in leadership studies is planted firmly in business and management. Perhaps this is why, in the end, these studies seem lacking. A quick perusal of types of leadership – adaptive, servant, transactional, transformative, reconstructive, tyrannical, charismatic, autocratic, visionary, spiritual, invisible, socioeconomic, democratic, implicit, authentic, complex, and so on – does suggest that the literature has some promise. The most recent entry in the encyclopedia is "narrative." Although the leadership scholarship developed over the last thirty years in the context of business and management, earlier scholars did attempt to have a broader approach. Most notably, Max Weber, the prolific interdisciplinary scholar, studied charismatic leadership (see Gerth and Mills 1946). More recent studies of leadership also contain some promising analyses that go beyond Great Man theories, which are based on highly individualistic notions of leadership; trait theories, which are also influenced by individualism; or theories embedded with semiotic historical implications such as servant leadership (Eicher-Catt 2005).

Unlike the canon in leadership studies, written primarily by men, women have formulated theoretical ideas of their own. As early as 1918, Mary Parker Follett advocated a type of relational leadership, and before the dawn of formal leadership studies, women wrote about scholarly themes that directly related to leadership. However, as is often the case, these women's works were marginalized. Follett (1868-1933), a social worker turned management theorist, developed the idea of lateral processes within hierarchical organizations, the importance of informal processes within organizations, and many other important concepts that led to theories of collaborative and relational leadership in the context of organizations of all types.[2] More recently, Joyce Fletcher, whose book *Disappearing Acts: Gender, Power, and Relational Practice at Work* (1999) offers empirical evidence about female engineers, has revealed the importance of emotional intelligence and relational behaviour (relational leadership) within organizational cultures. Her work emphasizes the important role of collaborative and shared leadership in organizations for the present and future generations.

Hans Hansen, Arja Ropo, and Erika Sauer (2007) provide a scathing critique of current leadership theory. They claim that leadership research in general waters down the rich phenomenon of leadership partly because of its lack of empirical findings and partly because of its complete denial of the body and the senses. They offer the concept of aesthetic leadership, which is oriented towards the senses and coherence.[3] Amanda Sinclair's book *Leadership for the Disillusioned: Moving beyond Myths and Heroes to Leading that Liberates* invites us to expand our thinking: "Leadership can liberate us from confining or oppressive conditions – imposed by structures, others and ourselves. Rather than being used as a means to compel compliance and conformity, to dominate or prescribe, leadership can invite us to imagine, initiate, and contest" (Sinclair 2007, xix).

In *Leadership and the New Science: Discovering Order in a Chaotic World* (2006), Margaret Wheatley applies New Science complexity theory to leadership and shows us how to reflect the natural world in our leadership practice. In addition to Fletcher's invitation to re-imagine and Wheatley's reminder of our connection to the natural world, Sumru Erkut suggests in her study *Inside Women's Power: Learning from Leaders* (2001) that we need entirely new language to discuss leadership. After interviewing sixty women from across the professional spectrum, she reports that her participants preferred using mothering metaphors to describe their type of leadership and mothering and sibling models in their leadership training. These women resisted using the masculine language commonly used in leadership studies (Erkut and Winds of Change Foundation 2001). Resistance to masculine and militaristic language such as *indefensible, argument, target, shot down,* and *attacked* as figures of speech is discussed by Gerri Perreault in "Rethinking Leadership: Leadership as Friendship" (Perreault 2005).

Finally, Barbara Kellerman, who has written extensively on women and leadership, suggests in her latest book, *The End of Leadership* (2012), that the leadership industry in the twenty-first century should investigate how to change patterns of dominance and deference. She also suggests that there are no simple solutions and emphasizes the complexities of cultures and contexts.

Themes of *Living Indigenous Leadership*

The leadership stories in this volume explore a rich tapestry of themes and serve as examples of exactly how to build strong Aboriginal communities. All of the contributors are Aboriginal women, and many of their stories are about women. However, some of their stories are about men.

A brief word about Aboriginal feminism is appropriate. Aboriginal women, as a whole, take diverse positions regarding feminist ideologies and theories. In this collection, however, not one contributor mentions feminist theories. This silence is interesting, given that the contributors are all women. In the 1970s, Indigenous women who were scholars in the academy began to address the issues of feminism and use feminist analyses in their research. They gathered empirical data about Aboriginal positions on feminism, and many authors of these early articles and books regarded the concept of colonization as the primary mode of critique and analysis. They did not want feminist ideas to water down social action to mediate the negative effects of colonization (see Oulette 2007).

Aboriginal women resisted feminist ideology for a host of other reasons. In a dialogue between Kim Anderson and Bonita Lawrence, Lawrence states: "And when it comes to empowerment, they [feminists] don't often support poor men. Feminism still sees even poor men as the enemy – a competitor for power. But where does that leave our men?" (Anderson

2011, 277). Native women do not want to be bound by dominant theories that limit their capacity to function well in the community in their own ways and informed by their own values. The conversation between Anderson and Lawrence reflects a desire to retain traditional values and resist ideologies that encourage inauthentic adaptation to contemporary theoretical opportunities. Aboriginal women often perceive Western feminism as a phenomenon created by white women who are intellectuals in the academy and who see the world through an individualistic lens, as opposed to a community-based lens. Indigenous women struggle to find their own places within dialogues on feminist theories.

In 2007, Joyce Green published *Making Space for Indigenous Feminism*. The book, the result of the "Aboriginal Feminism Symposium" at the Saskatchewan Institute of Public Policy, concluded that it was time for Aboriginal women to make feminist theories their own. Many of the critiques contained in the book reflected ongoing concerns about feminism, as a grand narrative that would compromise the voices of Aboriginal women. Yet participants agreed that there were many positive aspects of feminist thinking (Green 2007). Bonita Lawrence and Kim Anderson had offered this conclusion two years earlier: "Ultimately, we have found the arguments by Aboriginal women, which either attach or support feminism, to be less useful than the importance of Native women finding their own strengths from within their own heritage. Furthermore, like postcolonial theory, feminism in general may have both positive and negative aspects for Native women to work through, accept or discard" (Lawrence and Anderson 2005, 5).

I am, however, haunted by the words of Laura Tohe, who wrote in the philosophically oriented *Wicaso Sa Review:* "Within the Four Sacred Mountains of the Diné, lay the red canyon walls of Canyon de Chelly, carved by the strength of the wind and water, it is the same strength we see carved into the lives of the Diné women. There was no need for feminism because of our matrilineal culture. And it continues. For Diné women, there is no word for feminism" (Tohe 2000, 110). As Tohe implies, we can imagine that Native societies with strong traditions never had a need for something called "feminism."

Embodied Concepts

The themes in *Living Indigenous Leadership* crisscross with themes explored in the emerging literature on Indigenous leadership. The contributions include explicit and implicit references to the interconnection of all things, the power of influence, the burden of leadership, the role of persuasion, Native perspectives on position, the fluidity of situational leadership, examples of nonhierarchical community-based initiatives, the persistence of immanent value, the continuity of narrative and story, the efficacy of the arts, and spiritual principles. Some of the chapters' themes also overlap with those of the non-Indigenous leadership literature. This volume's uniqueness, however, lies in its introduction of foundational themes or concepts that serve to ground Aboriginal communities, themes that are rarely mentioned in mainstream studies of leadership. These concepts are embodied – they are premised on the idea that the parts of our being cannot be separated. We are whole. Our mental concepts are one with our bodies, hearts, spirits, and souls. Land, ancestors, Elders, stories, women, grandmothers, parents, language, education, community, performing arts, knowledge, relationships, friends, culture, collaboration, healing, and resilience – these are the concepts that unite our worlds. The notion of embodied concepts animates our leadership theories with a richness that keeps our worlds vital, integrated, and whole.

I hope that you will be inspired by our stories and will be tempted to interpret our embodied concepts and themes within the context of your own community.

Notes

1 Deborah Tannen (1999) objects to what she calls an argument culture in the United States. We often hear the language of this culture in the academy. I encourage my students to developed sustained arguments in their major papers and theses, but it never feels right. So, I try to use the concept of sustained thinking or logic instead.
2 See Pauline Graham (1995) for a thorough study of the life and works of Mary Parker Follett.
3 Within the philosophical discourse on aesthetics, we learn that sensory data cannot be adequately represented by nonpoetic words on a flat page. For example, music offers knowledge that words cannot express (Elliott 1991).

Works Cited

Ah Nee-Benham, Maenette K.P., and Joanne E. Cooper. 1998. *Let My Spirit Soar: Narratives of Diverse Women in School Leadership.* Thousand Oaks, CA: Corwin Press.

Alfred, Gerald A. (Taiaiake). 1999. *Heeding the Voices of Our Ancestors: Kahnawake Mohawk Politics and the Rise of Native Nationalism.* New York: Oxford University Press.

Anderson, Kim. 2011. *Life Stages and Native Women: Memory, Teachings, and Story Medicine.* Winnipeg: University of Manitoba Press.

Archibald, Jo-ann (Qum Qum Xiiem). 2008. *Indigenous Storywork: Educating the Heart, Mind, Body, and Spirit.* Vancouver: UBC Press.

Battiste, Marie, ed. 2000. *Reclaiming Indigenous Voice and Vision.* Vancouver: UBC Press.

Bryant, Miles T. 1998. "Cross-Cultural Understandings of Leadership: Themes from Native American Interviews." *Educational Management and Administration* 26, 1: 7-20.

Cohen, William. 2001. "The Spider's Web: Creativity and Survival in Dynamic Balance." *Canadian Journal of Native Education* 25, 2: 140-48.

Eicher-Catt, Deborah. 2005. "The Myth of Servant Leadership." *Women and Language* 28, 1: 17-25.

Elliott, David J. 1991. "Music as Knowledge." *Journal of Aesthetic Education* 25, 3: 21-40.

Erkut, Sumra, and the Winds of Change Foundation. 2001. *Inside Women's Power: Learning from Leaders.* CRW Special Report No. 28. Wellesley, MA: Wellesley Centers for Women, Wellesley College.

Fitzgerald, Tanya. 2006. "Walking between Two Worlds: Indigenous Women and Educational Leadership." *Educational Management Administration and Leadership* 34, 2: 201-13.

Fletcher, Joyce K. 1999. *Disappearing Acts: Gender, Power, and Relational Practice at Work.* Cambridge: MIT Press.

Gabriel, Yiannis. 2004. *Myths, Stories, and Organizations: Premodern Narratives for Our Times.* Oxford: Oxford University Press.

Gerth, Hans Heinrich, and C. Wright Mills, eds. and trans. 1946. *From Max Weber: Essays in Sociology.* Oxford: Oxford University Press.

Goethals, George R., Georgia Jones Sorenson, and James MacGregor Burns. 2004. *Encyclopedia of Leadership.* Thousand Oaks, CA: Sage.

Graham, Pauline, ed. 1995. *Mary Parker Follett: Prophet of Management.* Boston, MA: Harvard Business School Press.

Grahn, Joyce, L. Swenson, X. David, and Ryan O'Leary. 2001. "A Comparative Analysis between American Indian and Anglo American Leadership." *Cross-Cultural Management* 8, 1: 3-20.

Green, Joyce, ed. 2007. *Making Space for Indigenous Feminism.* New York: Zed Books.

Hansen, Hans, Arja Ropo, and Erika Sauer. 2007. "Aesthetic Leadership." *Leadership Quarterly* 18, 2: 544-60.

Jorgenson, Miriam, and Rachel Starks. 2008. *Leadership Development in the Native Arts and Culture Sector.* A report commissioned by the Ford Foundation. New York: Ford Foundation.

Kellerman, Barbara K. 2012. *The End of Leadership.* New York: Harper Collins.

Kenny, Carolyn. 1998. "The Sense of Art: A First Nations Perspective." *Canadian Journal of Native Education* 22, 1: 77-84.

–. 2002. *North American Indian, Métis, and Inuit Women Speak about Culture, Education, and Work.* Ottawa: Status of Women Canada.

–. 2006. "When the Women Heal: Aboriginal Women Speak about Policies to Improve the Quality of Life." *American Behavioral Scientist* 50, 4: 550-61.

Lawrence, Bonita, and Kim Anderson. 2005. "Introduction to 'Indigenous Women: The State of Our Nations.'" Special issue, *Atlantis* 29, 2: 1-8.

McLeod, Martha. 2002. "Keeping the Circle Strong: Learning about Native American Leadership." *Tribal College Journal of American Indian Higher Education* 13, 4: 10-13.

Ospina, Sonia, and Erica Foldy. 2009. "A Critical Review of Race and Ethnicity in the Leadership Literature: Surfacing Context, Power and the Collective Dimensions of Leadership." *Leadership Quarterly* 20, 6: 876-96.

Ottman, Jacqueline. 2005. "First Nations Leadership Development." Banff Centre. http://www.banffcentre.ca/departments/leadership/aboriginal/library/.

Ouellette, Grace J.M.W. 2007. *The Fourth World: An Indigenous Perspective on Feminism and Aboriginal Women's Activism.* Halifax: Fernwood.

Perreault, Gerri. 2005. "Rethinking Leadership: Leadership as Friendship." *Advancing Women in Leadership Online Journal* 18 (Spring). http://www.advancingwomen.com/.

Polkinghorne, Donald. 1988. *Narrative Knowing and the Human Sciences.* Albany: State University of New York Press.

Schaefer, Carol. 2006. *Grandmothers Counsel the World: Women Elders Offer Their Vision for Our Planet.* Boston: Trumpeter Books.

Sinclair, Amanda. 2007. *Leadership for the Disillusioned: Moving beyond Myths and Heroes to Leading that Liberates.* Crows Next, NSW: Allen and Unwin.

Smith, Linda Tuhiwai. 1999. *Decolonizing Methodologies: Research and Indigenous Women.* London: Zed Books.

Sterling, Shirley (Sepeetza). 1992. "Quaslametko and Yetko: Two Grandmother Models for Contemporary Native Education Pedagogy." *Canadian Journal of Native Education* 19, 2: 165-74.

Tannen, Deborah. 1999. *The Argument Culture: Stopping America's War of Words.* New York: Ballantine Books.

Tohe, Laura. 2000. "There Is No Word for Feminism in My Language." *Wicazo Sa Review* 15, 2: 103-10.

Voyageur, Cora. 2008. *Firekeepers of the Twenty-First Century: First Nations Women Chiefs.* Montreal and Kingston: McGill-Queen's University Press.

Wakshul, Barbra. 1997. "*Training Leaders for the 21st Century: The American Indian Ambassadors Program.*" *Winds of Change* 12, 2: 24-28.

Warner, Linda Sue, and Keith Grint. 2006. "American Indian Ways of Leading and Knowing." *Leadership* 2, 2: 225-44.

Wheatley, Margaret. 2006. *Leadership and the New Science: Discovering Order in a Chaotic World.* San Francisco: Berrett-Koehler Publishers.

PART 1

Leadership, Native Style

2

Learning to Lead Kokum Style

An Intergenerational Study of Eight First Nation Women

Yvonne G. McLeod

Ni T' Atchimowin (My Story)

ANIN SIKWA KIN! *Tansi n'totemak!* My name is Yvonne McLeod. I am a Saulteaux Cree member of the Peepeekisis Reserve, originally from the Muscowpetung First Nation. I begin my leadership story with the mindset that "the journey into the future envisioned by leaders inevitably involves learning" (Tinelli 2000, 2). I learn through a cyclical process of reflection, experience, and self-direction. Reflection enables experiences to be transformed into learning (ibid., 69). Likewise, reflection on my experiences enables self-direction. Self-direction stems from understanding our personal stories (Brayboy and Morgan 1998). This process of reflection, experience, and self-direction is foundational to learning to lead kokum-style, as this intergenerational study of eight First Nation women reveals.

Reflection

As I reflect on learning, I relate my personal experiences to promote better understanding of my leadership journey. I agree with Tina Ngaroimata Fraser, who writes in Chapter 7 of this volume, "I embody the lived experience of witnessing [my grandmother's] tireless efforts to build strong communities." The formative years of my education began under the care of my grandparents. My *kokum* (grandmother) had the greatest influence over me, along with family and community members of Pasqua and Muscowpetung First Nation. I received my elementary and secondary schooling sporadically at a federal day school, a residential school, and in a provincial school setting. Later, I received a bachelor of education degree (1987), a master's degree in educational administration (1995), and a doctorate in educational administration (2010). I also became a qualified psychometrist and am currently a member of the Saskatchewan Educational Psychologist Association.

Experience

In an attempt to understand learning and leadership through experience, I questioned how I had learned to be the educational leader that I am today. My research led me to understand that "experience is an attribute of learners" (Tinelli 2000, 54). I recognize that experience enriches learning by contributing to my world consciousness and that an archive of knowledge composed of systems, rules, and values forms a single narrative of one's world consciousness (Smith 1999, 42). As I reflected on this, I considered the two learning systems – First Nation and non-First Nation – that had influenced my world consciousness.

I had experienced a First Nation learning system that had originated from a Saulteaux Cree linguistic worldview. Within the system, I had three major influences. First, during my childhood years, I learned about the Saulteaux Cree way of life from my grandparents, family members, and community members. Second, my kokum established a foundational, holistic way of learning that was grounded and balanced through a process that was spiritually driven, emotionally supportive, physically applied, and mentally understood. Third, the Saulteaux Cree learning system handed down leadership information, knowledge, techniques, and insight from one generation to the next through storytelling. I gained my land-based identity, a lifelong strength, from this learning system.

I also experienced a non-First Nation learning system that originated from a mainstream societal perspective. I recall three major influences: residential school, mainstream societal teachings, and the religious structures of the non-Native world. During my residential school years, nuns, priests, and non-Native educators imparted mainstream societal teachings and the Catholic way of life. Other experiences included being separated from my family, abuse, and denigration of my First Nation beliefs, knowledge, language, and history. For example, teachers within this structured, linear learning system discredited my kokum's teachings, and I was made to feel ashamed of being a First Nation person. My kokum's teachings eventually helped me to adapt to the imposed mental, physical, social, and religious structures of the non-Native world. In time, I succeeded in gaining a mainstream academic identity; however, it came with issues, costs, and challenges.

Learning to function in the two world-systems presented a number of challenges. For example, I had to consider the issue of having a dual leadership identity, the costs of assimilation in engaging in dual discourse, and the challenges of establishing a leadership voice both First Nation and female. Willie Ermine (1995) defines *discourse* as a repository of thoughts, attitudes, values, ideals, and experiences. I use the term *dual discourse* in reference to my First Nation and non-First Nation leadership knowledge. I learned that dual discourse framed my leadership identity, which included costly assimilative experiences such as renouncing certain First Nation teachings and assuming certain non-First Nation teachings, or vice versa. Assimilative experiences caused me to question whose leadership knowledge system I was validating. Ultimately, this tension resulted in confusion, devaluation, and personal identity struggles.

Interestingly, the struggles and experiences I associated with dual leadership identity taught me to become a self-reflective leader. Cultural differences are believed to result in cultural clashes that, in turn, result in a cultural identity crisis (St. Denis 2002). Many First Nation women wrestle with learning white people's ways of doing things while continuing to learn as Aboriginal women (Monture-Angus 1999). As I grappled with being true to myself, I recalled simple phrases that my kokum would say, such as *Aw keyam* (Never mind. Don't worry. It will be all right). Kokum's phrases became powerful literacy devices, which I used to direct myself and reaffirm my cultural norms. The knowledge of previous generations is embedded in language and cultural norms, even if it is not experienced directly (Goulet 2005, 17). Reflection on kokum's words ultimately became a process of decolonization that sustained my cultural identity while I learned to function in both learning environments. I gained an advantage in that I developed a positive sense of being that included a strong dual leadership identity and voice, which included both First Nation and non-First Nation values.

The challenges associated with developing my First Nation, female leadership voice were many. Most research concerning First Nation women is bound by colonial constructions (Anderson 2000; Gunn 1989; King 1991; Klein and Ackerman 1995; Moss 1993). For instance, First Nation women commonly experience racism. Racism is enacted in the practices of mainstream society (Ng 1993), as in the oppression of leadership opportunities for First Nation females. Shauneen Pete-Willet (2001, 107) writes that determining self is an essential decolonizing step that encourages women to use their voices to tell their own story in a way denied them in the past. Establishing a leadership voice for First Nation females begins with daily family interaction and positive communication experiences. A people's philosophy, worldview, spirituality, and cultural ways of thinking and doing are built into the communicative structure of the First Nation language. This is why kokum's voice could not be silenced. Experiences such as the above create opportunities to develop a collective female leadership voice. This female leadership voice is gained through the example of role modelling, mentoring, and coaching. The tender nurturing of my kokum contributed to the development of my leadership voice, an important factor in becoming a self-directed leader.

Self-Direction

I understand self-direction as bringing about change for the good of all. It is the doing! I decided to do an intergenerational study of eight women in my family: three first-generation leaders, four second-generation leaders, and one third-generation leader. These women had been teachers,

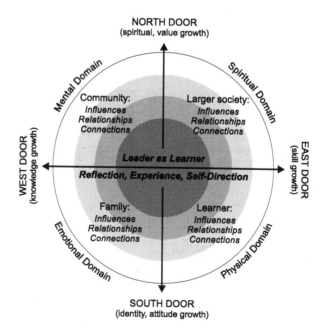

FIGURE 2.1   This intergenerational framework for female First Nation leadership is based on the medicine wheel, an appropriate conceptual framework for indigenous research. I designed the leadership framework as a result of this study.

Saulteaux Cree specialists, consultants, education counsellors, administrators, principals, university instructors, or directors of education at some point in their professional lives. Their experiences and stories affirm that First Nation leadership (Assembly of First Nations 1994) is a learned intergenerational process. The leadership framework outlined in Figure 2.1 emerged as the first-generation women engaged with the second- and third-generation women and identified the medicine wheel as a suitable model (see also Graveline 2000; Hampton 1995; Regnier 1995).

The women in this study influenced my decision to adapt the medicine wheel to better understand First Nation female leadership learning and development. The medicine wheel captures the physical, emotional, mental, and spiritual development of the aspiring leader. It encapsulates the reflections, experiences, and self-directive actions of the women, particularly as they relate to intergenerational influences, relationships, and connections. The framework organized my thinking and gave definition to what I learned from both the mainstream leadership literature and from First Nation storytelling. For example, kokum used the drum to teach that the medicine wheel "has four domains: physical, emotional, mental, and spiritual" and four circles that suggest the teachings learned from self, family, community, and the larger society (Stiffarm 1998, 91). The leader, as the learner, is situated in the centre of the first circle, where personal reflection on influences, experiential relationships, and connections start. The leader proceeds to the eastern physical quadrant and then moves clockwise, experiencing learning in all four cyclical domains. In the medicine wheel framework, learning includes integrating the processes of reflection, experience, and self-direction into the four domains (Tinelli 2000). Learning applies to "skills, attitudes, sensibilities, and values," which appear in the medicine wheel framework as leadership skills in the physical domain, leadership attitudes in the emotional domain, leadership sensibilities in the mental domain, and leadership values in the spiritual domain. Since learning influences all aspects of a person, it is supported by the Saulteaux Cree belief that all things are interrelated and interconnected holistically. The medicine wheel framework helps trace how the leaders in my family learned to be the leaders that they are.

The Leadership Learning Process
In the medicine wheel framework, the learning concepts of reflection, experience, and self-direction helped us to understand the leadership learning process in our family. They passed on leadership knowledge

through a cyclical, circular learning process. For example, the concept of reflection helped us understand the relationship between reflection and life experiences. The concept of experience enhanced our understanding of the relationship between experience and learning to engage in self-directed change. The concept of self-direction enriched our understanding of how the women in my family used their life experiences and stories as an active channel for learning from one another.

The learning process in this framework is reciprocal in that the learner triggers learning in others and vice versa. As Aunt Clara indicated, her ancestors followed "bloodline" leadership: the upcoming leader observed, respected, and preserved family and community input. Each of the eight women in my family continues to maintain a form of bloodline leadership that is transmitted from generation to generation. Aunt Clara influenced my leadership style by encouraging me to (1) see the positive results before they occurred (visioning), (2) take action towards positive results (modelling), (3) speak words of affirmation referencing positive results (coaching), and (4) share knowledge about how to get positive results (mentoring). Her wisdom, gained from experience, was imparted to me as she used the circular part of the drum to portray her life cycle, the four domains, and the influences of self, family, community, and the larger society. The hand drum creates a mental picture of leadership learning experiences that reinforces self-actualization in the learner. The learning process is described as "a process of internalization and actualization within oneself in a total way" (Lightning 1992, 243).

Aunt Clara used learning tools such as the drum to teach me cultural artifacts (Cole 1996, 117). Cultural artifacts may include legends, stories, metaphors, and visual descriptors from the culture in question. Cultural artifacts allow a person to have an understanding of the world that sense alone cannot provide (Goulet 2005, 18) because the artifacts facilitate the "intermingling of 'indirect, cultural' aspects of experience" (Cole 1996, 119). For example, I use geese and buffalo metaphors, the medicine wheel, the circle of life, the four domains, teepee teachings, the Teachings of the Seven Grandfathers, and the hand drum to shape an understanding of how kokum influenced my leadership development through experiential learning. According to Linda Goulet (2005, 18), our thinking is shaped by the tools, language, and people around us, such as kin, who influence how we interpret our experiences.

The concept of kinship, referred to as *wahkotowin* (Ermine 2000), is a fundamental First Nation principle relevant to understanding intergenerational female leadership (Weenie 2002, 44). The kinship relationships of the women in my family include a shared history and a common understanding of leadership issues and challenges. First Nation intergenerational leadership identity is transmitted through our family stories, visions, and collective memories. I offer an excerpt from each family member's story. These stories were transmitted to me during discussions in 2000.

CLARA PASQUA, FIRST GENERATION

I was born in 1924. I am an eighty-two-year-old Saulteaux Cree woman from the Muscowpetung First Nation Reserve. I married onto the Pasqua First Nation, and I lived there most of my life. My husband was the last of the hereditary chiefs on that reserve. I learned through experience, a traditional upbringing, boarding school, residential-school training, and provincial upgrading. At age fifty-four, I completed the Saskatchewan Indian Federated College university entrance program. Later, I completed four years of postsecondary education. I did not complete a degree. I had so much difficulty in math. After failing it three times, university policy prohibited me from taking it again. It was very hard for me and very discouraging. My discouragement was with the provincial educational system. It was not geared for us. I had a difficult time adjusting to university due to my experiences with residential school. I was not alone in this. We would sit between classes and share experiences: their generation and mine. I found it painful but healing and empowering to hear the young women's stories speak of their family members. We learned that the educational system was not ours. It was unjust and based on racism and ignorance. The white people didn't know, and we did not know! Each generation has to sort out the baggage of residential school effects. It is a difficult process.

My educational administrative career has been in the Treaty 4 area, near Fort Qu'Appelle, Saskatchewan. I worked for the Department of Indian Affairs, Pasqua First Nation Band, and for the Intergenerational Grandmothers program at the University of Regina. I held a political leadership term as the education counsellor on my reserve for a number of years, too. I worked towards self-determination as a reserve political leader under the direction of my chief – my husband. As leaders of our community, our focus was on the treaties and education. For years, Indian Affairs, especially during the sixties, operated on the belief that Indians were their wards and that only Indian Affairs could dictate what was best for us. As leaders, we worked towards changing this. If you have to deal with Indian Affairs, then be prepared to have a stormy relationship and to develop thick skin, because many of their representatives who come on the reserve make us feel like we are to forget the past, be thankful for what you got, and get on with life. No, that is not the way ... we have a job to educate society about the wrongs towards our people and leave a written history for our future leaders, especially about the learning of our treaties and the retention of our language. We have to learn both ways.

I have had firsthand interaction with the educational changes that involved a traditional education to higher-level education. Because of my involvement with my husband's role as chief, I kept up with the political changes to First Nation communities across the province. I am able to talk about the evolving history of organized "Indian resistance" in Saskatchewan. I believe that to be "truly educated," leaders must teach our future generations about the evolving traditional forms of government that contributed to our somewhat unified Indian voice. As women, historically, we had the role of giving voice in leadership situations. Traditional leadership goes back to the days of treaty, when we had good leaders such as Chief Piapot and Chief Cheekuk in the Treaty 4 area. Our children need role models like Andrew and Walter Gordon; they were not afraid to take a stand for our educational issues with the government. But, today, many of our male leaders have abused the system and our communities. I think that is why more women on our reserves are speaking out and taking over the leadership.

Francis Anaquod, First Generation

My name is Francis. I am a sixty-eight-year-old Saulteaux woman from the Muscowpetung First Nation Reserve. Originally, I came from the Fort Alexander Reserve in Manitoba. I married onto the Muscowpetung First Nation. After years of teaching in different provinces, I returned to my reserve. I was greatly influenced by the family that I married into. For example, two family members had teaching certificates, and they travelled to different provinces to teach. I took teacher training in Winnipeg so that I could follow their example. I worked in a number of provinces, but for years I served as the principal of the Piapot Federal School. The band school transitional years were a real challenge. Sometimes, we have to flow with the change, even though we may not agree with it. But I leaned to support the direction and decisions of the board and band.

I am a widow, and I am the mother of two boys and three girls. I came from a large family of twelve, of which there were three boys and nine girls. Years ago, I arrived in Saskatchewan to complete my high school at the Lebret residential school. Residential school was difficult, as I lost touch with my family for long periods of time. I felt disconnected when I did return home. The good thing is that I met my husband at the school. We married and eventually moved back to the Muscowpetung Reserve after many years of teaching in Alberta and in northern Saskatchewan. We were adventurous back then. In order to work, we travelled to different provinces. Along the way, during my career, there were people who influenced my leadership growth. If you have a good attitude, smile through the difficult times, and show yourself as a lifelong learner, you will find life as an educational leader to be much easier. Early in my career, I learned to deal with issues in a timely manner. I would smile, wait, listen, show interest, and express a deep concern. People read your behaviours, and they respond positively or negatively.

As I recollect, in my family, it was my parents who provided leadership so that I could make something of myself and care for my family by doing what I had to do. We were shown what hard work was, and we were also expected to work as a team. Our family was a team, and we shared the workload. There was a pecking order; if one member fell short, that person was dealt with. Values were important when I was growing up. It was part of life to share and care for one another; if you didn't – you would soon feel alone, left out, and shameful. Relationships are important, and our connection to the land and our language is so vital. Many young people do not know this. I think it is because of residential school that these connections are diminishing.

I love to share my Saulteaux language, and I enjoy teaching it too. It is the foundation of who we are as Indian people. I wish that more of our young people could speak and understand it. I try my best to pass it on. I learned from family that what we do today is important for the generations yet to come. For example, one of my faithful students is my daughter Sharon. She has learned a lot about her language and culture because she is very interested in who she is as a First Nation woman. As older women, we need to support our young women who are taking on leadership in our communities. They need to be encouraged that they are doing right for the people. I would say especially in the development and retention of our Saulteaux language. We have other family members who support our desire to retain the language and culture. The medicine wheel teachings and the teepee pole teachings are being taught in the teacher education programs now, so that helps. My daughter learned to use the wheel to incorporate our values and teachings into the curriculum.

Stella Ketchemonia, First Generation

My name is Stella. I am a sixty-six-year-old Saulteaux woman from the Keeseekoose First Nation Reserve located near Kamsack, Saskatchewan. I returned to live there later in my life. My husband, Leonard, and I worked and travelled in Alberta. I taught in that province for a number of years. My husband was the administrator of the schools where I taught. On a number of occasions, Auntie Francis and I would connect as our paths crossed from school to school. We were always happy to see one another, and we found it very encouraging to know that someone from back home was teaching close by. I learned that it takes an effort to stay connected and to reconnect with family.

Most of my career in education has been in Treaty 4, near Fort Qu'Appelle, Yorkton, and Regina, Saskatchewan. I also worked in Alberta as a teacher. I experienced being a school principal before the transition from a federal to a band-controlled school administration. Because of my teaching and leadership experiences, I am familiar with the need to teach both Aboriginal and non-Aboriginal perspectives, to understand our perspectives, and to find ways to integrate them into the curriculum and into our professional practice as Indian teachers. Having lived through the transitions from reserve life, day schools, residential schools, provincial school integration, university life, and different leadership roles, I realized that we need to lead in educational change. I have been the first First Nation woman to do a lot of firsts – for example, the first female bus driver on our reserve, the first female bus instructor on the reserve, the first First Nation female principal on the reserve, and the first Saulteaux instructor in our local provincial school.

So, I share my experiences to help others. Looking back helps to bring positive changes. We learn from the past and, hopefully, as educators we can transfer the learning process on to our children and then onto their children and the ones yet to be born. It is more important to learn how to do something rather than to learn a lot about everything and not know how we got there. Our First Nation history in this country is the result of the government leaving out the important aspect of learning. How? Like our parents and grandparents taught us. Once our children learn the process of learning, then they are able to learn anything that they want. Another thing, as the principal, I have always encouraged my staff to acknowledge their influence on the emotional development of our children. Touching the heart of the child is so important in teaching them to learn. I remember hearing you say, "If we can touch the heart of a child and quicken that child's spirit, then that child is able to be physically involved in learning what has to be learned." In our family circle, the old people made the children feel good, and they cautioned not to hurt the spirit of the child. Nowadays, knowledge comes first and then physical involvement, and most times the heart and spirit of the child are left behind in the learning process. Some of us are wounded, so we need to learn to love ourselves and move on. It is up to us to make the changes – to influence for the good for all.

As First Nation women in education, we have to be willing to risk and challenge change. The old people would say to us, "Do something and try." So I tried. For example, I was a nurse and a dietician. I became the first female to take on different leadership roles in my home community. I was a bus driver; bus driver instructor; Saulteaux instructor; Saulteaux curriculum writer; professor; cultural consultant; author and producer of the Ketchemonia, Innu of the Land, Manitoba Association for Native Languages (KIM) international language program kit; and a principal. At times, different men from back home who sat on committees would ask why I wanted to take on these jobs, and I would say, "There is nothing that says a woman is not allowed to do any type of job she wants to do."

On a personal note, I am a mother, auntie, kokum, and a foster mother. My husband and I have raised ten children and numerous foster children. We are actively involved in contributing to the raising of my grandchildren. My greatest struggle has been to overcome the grief of losing five children and one grandchild, all in infancy. My family taught me to respect our loved ones, from the youngest to the oldest in our family. Respect means to learn to value life and look to the next generation, especially through the losses that we experience. We, as family members, must never give up on what the future holds for us. We must continue to share our successes and challenge and build one another up.

My early years of schooling were in several residential schools in Saskatchewan. It was these experiences that made me realize that our educational system needed to be changed so that our future generations would benefit from what we consider "quality education." In order to set the example, I knew that I had to return to school and get a university degree. I had to do this for myself, my children, and my grandchildren. I noted that our history books provided limited leadership models for our children, so higher-level education became my mission – so get a PhD!

ANGIE REDMAN, SECOND GENERATION

My name is Angie. I am Yvonne's sister. I am a Dakota First Nation woman from the Standing Buffalo First Nation Reserve. I was married, divorced, and now I am a single parent who works and studies. Juggling home life, family needs, studies, and career is very challenging and demanding. Like everything else in my life, I know that if I want peace of mind, I have to work towards a good sense of "balance," especially in my career life. My career is how I support my family. My career has been within the Treaty 4 area, near Fort Qu'Appelle, Saskatchewan. I worked as a teacher in Regina, Saskatchewan, a principal on my First Nation reserve, and also at the University of Regina, Saskatchewan Indian Federated College (SIFC), for a number of years as a professor and as a field experience supervisor in the Department of Indian Education. Later, I returned to the University of Regina to complete my master's degree in curriculum and instruction.

One thing that I have noticed is that the women in my family have been very influential in who I am today. I watched other First Nation women move ahead in their careers, and this led me to believe that I, too, could probably further my education. As a family, we women tend to readily share our stories, experiences, and successes. I know that through observation, listening, and mimicking I have learned a number of leadership strategies that work. Especially, being a single parent, I look to other women who model successful careers. I was encouraged by the Aboriginal women who were in leadership at the Department of Indian Education at SIFC. My sister was one of these women who had a leadership position in that department. I applied for a part-time teaching position as the professional studies instructor with SIFC. I taught for two years at the university, during which time I recollected many of my traditional teachings. I found that working as a team player contributed to the good of all, especially in adapting the teacher education curriculum to meet the needs of our First Nations students. I was taught that we all have a "gift" and that we should use that gift for the benefit of others – it is not a self-gratifying endeavour but an opportunity to do some good for everyone involved and to leave something for the future generations.

I was born on Standing Buffalo Reserve and was raised there for the first six years of my life. And then I went to Lebret residential school. Residential school had its challenges. First Nation language loss is an example. I notice that in many of our First Nation communities the people most committed to language revitalization are young parents who would like their children to be raised with greater language abilities than what the young parent had. These young parents may have had little or no exposure to their language growing up and, as a consequence, they feel like they have missed out on important First Nation knowledge and teachings. Because

I had a desire to learn my language at university, and I had a desire to have the university provide greater opportunities for other students, I worked at ensuring that my language would be offered at the university. That was my first experience with doing research with effective results – my language is now offered at the university.

Back to my story. My mother brought me back to our reserve, but I went through a lot of internal discrimination. I was told by reserve kids to go back to Lebret and that I did not belong on the reserve any more. Later, I realized that what I experienced was "discrimination" at the residential school and then on my own reserve by my own people. This left me feeling unsure about who I was and my purpose in life. Reflection is a good thing; it brings some clarity to past issues and opens one's mind to better solutions while providing an opportunity to do something or change.

Yes, there were many other challenges that I experienced as a young girl. Later, my mother got sick and was hospitalized so we moved to a small town nearby. Again, I faced racism but this time from white kids who told me to go back to the reserve – "You don't belong here." I became very angry, and I struggled with not knowing how to deal with this type of behaviour. I learned to fight to survive in the white society as a child – after all, we seemed to get the blame when trouble in school happened because we were never believed. By the time I reached Grade 7, I had a lot of anger within me. It got so bad that I would fly into rages, and the male supervisors would have to come and wrestle me down. But, you know, nobody followed up or questioned why I behaved the way I did. Instead, I received punishment after punishment. So, eventually, I quit school after Grade 10.

Later on in life, I have learned I needed inner healing. So, I focused on learning to love myself, find a sense of balance, and maintain positive relationships. Leaders need to know who they are and what they need to be strong influential leaders able to work through systemic racism. A good leader is not afraid to ask for help. Sometimes, what people perceive as being weak is actually being strong. After my mother got sick and left to live in the city, I was thankful for my aunt and uncle who took me in as their daughter – in the Indian way. In addition to this, there were four other community women on the reserve who took me under their wings – they took on the role of mother, sister, auntie, and grandmother.

They showed me how to care for myself and how to manage on my own as a young mother and parent. I learned to find my place in the work world and to establish a positive identity.

ANN MARGARET OBEY, SECOND GENERATION

My name is Ann Margaret. I am a forty-one-year-old Saulteaux woman from the Keeseekoose First Nation Reserve. I married onto the Pasqua First Nation Reserve near Fort Qu'Appelle, Saskatchewan. I live on this reserve with my husband and family. My husband is a political councillor on this reserve, too. He is very supportive of my role as the principal. Because I have four children, I find that balancing the responsibilities of home and school is a real challenge. I was fortunate to be a principal on my husband's reserve for a number of years.

Later, I became the principal of another band-controlled school. I had to move away from home and live in a motel for a year while my family remained on our reserve. I would go home on weekends. It was a difficult time for all of us. The job of principal was challenging in the sense that I worked for three bands. The politics were horrendous. At the beginning of the year, the chief and council maintained an "arm's length" involvement with the school, but by November the political leadership changed for two bands. By January, the leadership in all three bands was new. The school board members were also changed, and by February the political leadership was no longer at arm's length regarding school issues and business. My aunt was the director, my cousin was the special education coordinator-teacher, and I was the principal at that time. We learned to support, encourage, and team together to complete the school year in good standing. It was a trying experience, and we learned what job commitment was all about. Our family contributed support by listening, sharing ideas, suggesting options for decisions and action plans, and mentoring by example and experiences. We can laugh about the hard times now because we learned a lot. We are stronger leaders because we walked through the challenges.

I am amazed at how my mother did what she had to do during her training and career, and still managed to be a wonderful mother and parent. Managing family and work can be very demanding. The stress of being away from home and not being in direct control of my own family needs was a challenge. I would reflect on my mother's ability to balance the family needs, her studies, and her work performance. This encouraged me to do what I had to do. I reminisced on the days that Mom drove from the reserve near Kamsack, Saskatchewan, to Saskatoon on a weekly basis for her university training. She was a good family planner and a great organizer. Many times, both Mom and Dad would split us kids up for the week, and we would all get together on the weekends. They shared the family responsibilities. We adjusted to this and accepted it as normal. I learned that both Mom and Dad believed education to be a priority.

A great majority of my career has been in Treaty 4 near Fort Qu'Appelle and near Kamsack, Saskatchewan. I worked as a classroom teacher in Keeseekoose and Cote First Nation schools. In the last three years, I served as the principal of the Pasqua First Nation School. It is an elementary K-9 level school with a population of approximately 120 students.

My latest endeavour is to serve as principal for both an elementary and a high school. I really appreciate the training that Pasqua First Nation has given me. I appreciate the fact that I was able to work with my aunt Yvonne and my cousin Rachel. Rachel is a woman of great ability. My aunt was my supervisor-mentor; she was the director of education. We talked a lot about work and supported one another. We try! That's the key – the will to do something even when things don't go as planned. We encouraged each other that giving up would not be an option.

As a principal, I continue to learn by working in collaboration and participation with staff. I believe that we learn from one another. For example, I learned commitment to the community from my mother, but I also learned from my cousin that it is all right to be deeply moved by school circumstances yet portray inward strength and a good sense of humour. My aunt taught by example. She modelled a flexible leadership style that thrived on the nature of the job and community. In her life, she endured a lot, but she is a survivor, and her work ethics demonstrate her gift – a capable, highly educated director. As I reflect on my mother, my aunt, and my cousins, I am given the courage to venture where others might choose not to lead.

One last point with regard to family influences on my leadership as a principal, I have to say that my aunt Yvonne contributed a lot to my development and self-identity as a leader. I had the opportunity to work as her principal for one year. During that year, I learned a lot about communicating with people in a good way. I knew that I could count on her to help me organize myself with the administrative duties. This was a weakness that I had as a new principal, and she was there to help mentor me, even though I was her supervisor. In the following year, our roles switched: she became my supervisor as the director of education. In that situation, I had the opportunity to work with my cousin Rachel. It was quite an experience working together. I know that we learned a lot from one another. Rachel completed her master's during that time, and Yvonne continued to work on her doctoral studies while I contemplated a master's degree.

SHARON ANAQUOD, SECOND GENERATION

My name is Sharon. I was born in 1965. I am a forty-three-year-old Saulteaux woman from the Muscowpetung First Nation Reserve. I am like Rachel: I grew up with a mother who was a principal and a teacher. I saw my mother put in long hours at the school as the principal. I saw my mother interact with our band membership with regard to many school issues because she was the principal for a long time. I became aware of school-funding issues with the Department of Indian Affairs. I learned that school connections did not start at 8:30 a.m. and end at 4:30 p.m. The role of principal that my mother portrayed reflected daily contacts that entailed early-morning and late-night commitment.

I have lived on or near our home reserve for most of my life. Presently, I live in Fort Qu'Appelle, and I drive to work on the Muscowpetung Reserve. I am a principal, and I know that I have a great influence on my students. I was taught to give back to my community, and I am privileged to do so as an educator. Muscowpetung is my home reserve. I have had a number of people influence my learning and development, and most of them were family members, some of whom are uncles. Uncle Glen has taught me to be a visionary person and to be a spiritual person. On the other hand, Uncle Bob has taught me the love of learning and that as an adult it was never too late to learn. As a result of their influence, I strive to educate myself at every opportunity, and I gained a degree in education.

My kokum had quite an influence on me because I spent a lot of my younger years with her. One of the most important things I learned to value was her cultural connections. Cultural connectedness helped me develop a good self-concept about who I was as an Indian. It also gave me a strong sense of direction and a tenacity to deal with difficult life experiences such as racism. Both my mother and kokum influenced my development as a Saulteaux woman. Some of the things that I remember are beading, sewing, powwows, singing and drumming, ceremonies, feasts, and give-away gatherings. I was taught to respect my Elders, grandparents, family, and community members. We learned to greet and shake hands.

More recently, I have focused on learning about my First Nation history, culture, and language through many discussions with my mother and my Uncle Glen. This is an ongoing thing since I have become a teacher. I learn by listening to my Elders, reflecting on what I hear, see, feel, and do while with them – like when I watched my mom while she worked at the school. I stayed at one job for a long time until circumstances forced me to make a decision to go back to school. I had a strong will to do something with my life and to help young people. I worked as a supervisor of summer students, a youth community worker, a Saskatchewan Justice data enterer, a File Hills Qu'Appelle Touchwood Tribal Council receptionist, a federal school administrative assistant, a clerk, and an administrative assistant. Presently, I am a first-year principal on my home reserve.

For nine years, I worked as the education administrative assistant to the first Indian principal of the Lebret residential school. I learned a lot through that work experience. I especially appreciated the guidance counsellor, who modelled a great way of working with our youth. She was a compassionate, giving, and considerate person. She influenced the students to have a strong sense of belonging to their home communities, even though the students were away from their homes. The students responded to her ways. It is memories such as these that encourage me to try some of "her ways" in dealing with students. She shared stories and history with our students. The values she lived by include caring and sharing. At university, we learned about the teepee pole values, too. Now, I have the opportunity to be like her and make a difference in someone else's life as a teacher and principal. I was taught that life is about "giving back," and I believe that, as a teacher and principal, I am able to do so.

Presently, I am a teacher-principal at the Muscowpetung First Nation band school. My mom is our cultural language instructor and Head Start teacher. She is also my mentor, as I am in my second year as a principal. I have many aunts and cousins to look up to as educational leaders. They are my trailblazers, and now I take the same role as a trailblazer, too. I am encouraged that they are available if I need help. When I was learning to teach, I recognized my mother's behaviour in my teaching style, and now that I am in a leadership role, I see myself modelling what she modelled for me when she was a principal. I am becoming a "mini Francis," and it scares me, but it is a good thing. After all, she has been a great leadership model for me and many other family members.

RACHEL CLARKE, THIRD GENERATION

My name is Rachel. I am Saulteaux Cree. I was born in 1970. I am a thirty-eight-year-old First Nation woman originally from the Muscowpetung First Nation Reserve. I say "originally" because, when I was born, my mother and father were not married, so I became a registered Muscowpetung First Nation band member. After my mom and dad married, within a month, both my mother and I were transferred to Peepeekisis First Nation. My mother had no input into this decision, as INAC (Indian and Northern Affairs Canada) sent an eighty-one-dollar cheque with new treaty numbers, which indicated that both my mother and I were now Peepeekisis members. That was my first lesson on how INAC deals with First Nation women. Later, I learned INAC did not recognize my mother and I as having any rights to the certified-possession land that my father inherited, as it was land to be passed down to the male child. I learned that the INAC system is unfair and unjust to First Nation women. This makes me more determined to bring about change.

As a young teen approaching the age of majority, I realized that I had decision-making power. I could make my own choices in life. My parents were very controlling during that time, but they eventually respected my wishes and let me go my way. As a young unwed mother, I experienced a lot of trials. One day, as I looked at my baby son, I realized that I had to do something to care for my child. I reflected on my mother's life, and I saw a mother's example of love for her children. My mother could not read fluently at age thirty-four, but she made a point to return to school and get an education – she now has her PhD. I saw her example, and I knew that it was not too late and that I could do something with my life, too. If she could be committed to an education for the benefit of her children and grandchildren, then I believed that I could do the same. We all benefit from the good that family does.

My dad was my greatest moral support, and my mom was my greatest example of resiliency. Dad assisted in fundraising to allow me an opportunity to celebrate my sixteenth birthday in Israel. I worked for two months in Israel to help build an orphanage. Years later, I travelled to Mexico and Latin America to work as the coordinator of a youth leadership placement program that was affiliated with the Saskatchewan Indian Federated College. Dad has always been an influence in my life – during my university studies, he was my proofreader and academic monitor. On the other hand, Mom influenced me in a different way. She modelled a lot of her expectations because that was the way that she learned from her kokum. She talked about kokum's "old ways" of doing things and how we are all interconnected and that I had special gifts. I always said that I never wanted to be a teacher like my mom, but here I am – a teacher, a principal, and a director, just like she was.

I married a wonderful northern Cree man who is very support-ive of my career and personal educational goals. He speaks fluent Cree and taught me many important traditions while helping me learn the Cree language. His teachings only add to my experi-ences – from British Columbia to Ontario – as a school adminis-trator. My teaching career has been mainly in the Treaty 4 area near Fort Qu'Appelle, Saskatchewan, as a classroom teacher, special educator, early-childhood adult lecturer, curriculum developer (in Regina, Saskatchewan), and adult educator (across this province).

I am the oldest of a family of two siblings. Being the only girl, I spent a lot of time with my mother, who was a teacher and principal. I learned about teaching and school organization at a young age through her example. It was a common experience to have to spend hours at the school with Mom. She taught me to file, type, and organize – even when I did not want to. She had a gentle way of persuading me into things and making me feel good about it.

I have two children, a boy and girl. My son lives with my brother, and my daughter is still in our home. Like my mother, teaching has become a calling where I am able to share my Saulteaux Cree teachings with the next generation. My kokum Clara instilled within my mother certain values, traditions, and cultural teachings, and I have become the beneficiary of those teachings, as demonstrated in my leadership. As I reflect on my leadership experiences, I naturally think, what would Mom do, or what would Kokum Clara do? If I was really desperate, I would question, what would Dad do? [*laughs*] and then act accordingly. My dad has been the positive male influence in my life, along with my grandfather. I learned to build on their leadership ideas, especially in the area of instructional leadership. I enjoy developing First Nation curriculum and adapting Western ideas to accommodate the "two world" educational philosophies. This is our challenge – to pass on what we have learned to the next generation and on to the seventh.

Discussion of Themes

The women in this book agreed that they had learned leadership behaviours, resiliency, knowledge, and the ability to vision through a process of personal reflection, experience, and self-direction. For example, they learned leadership behaviours by observing family members in leadership positions, by listening to family leadership stories, and by doing what had worked for the generation before them. They learned leadership resiliency by watching, experiencing, and following through during many difficult situations. They learned leadership knowledge by listening to family stories, Nanabush life lessons, and legends, and through family networking. Nanabush is a character in Saulteaux worldview stories and legends who teaches life lessons. They learned leadership visioning through active involvement with Elders and spiritual advisers. One important aspect of their learning was that they were given opportunities, choices, ownership, options, and the time to make informed decisions.

Clara, Francis, and Stella, the first-generation women in this study, agreed that they had learned to lead within the context of their language and culture by watching, listening, doing, and asking the question, How do I ...? They shared a foundation in First Nation language, culture, trapping, fishing, hunting, and daily sustenance and in the good work ethic of living off the land. They indicated that everyday life lessons established that First Nation culture and language are essential to children's lifelong learning. After studying the tacit knowledge of children, Robert Sternberg and colleagues (2001) concluded that the knowledge learned in everyday life may be distinct from that which leads to success in school. The first-generation women understand and have experienced the intense responsibility associated with learning educational leadership and leadership relationships within First Nation communities. Francis pointed out that "our children are our future and, as educational leaders, our focus is the child."

Stella explained, "We learned by example ... what our parents, grandparents, and elders taught us, such as our ceremonies, rites of passage, and celebrations. We learned at a young age to be responsible, to respect people, and to value relationships. Our grandmothers taught us this." According to Henry Sims Jr. and Charles Manz (1996, 59), a superleader leads others to lead themselves: "Give a man a fish and he will be fed for a day; teach a man how to fish and he will be fed for a lifetime." The First Nation grandmother can be considered a superleader. She is highly regarded in a powerful role that greatly influences within the network of community relationships.

Clara, Francis, and Stella agreed that they had learned the importance of sharing life disappointments, challenges, and successes with one another. They were very supportive and connected to one other. Lightning (1992, 237) emphasizes that learning to be whole also means being "connected to others in compassion; love." Francis reported, "I learned about having a sense of balance when listening to the legends, stories, and humour made by the old people during celebrations and ceremonies. This connected us to the land. As young girls, we saw how our family used humor, teasing, and laughter as meaningful ways to learn. The teasing made us tough-skinned."

Clara mentioned that certain cultural "object lesson" tools were important in her learning. She learned to use the medicine wheel, the teepee,
and the drum to reflect purposefully on her experiences so that she could
practise self-direction in a positive way. Stella agreed, "We had the drum,
the teepee, and the medicine wheel teachings plus many other traditional
ways of learning about life and our place in society." For example, Clara
shared leadership stories, concerns, and lifestyle options by referring to
animal survival behaviour in a metaphorical way. The first-generation
women were able to make the transitions in their learning and relationships from situation to situation. At times, Clara jokingly shared how she
had learned from stories about Nanabush. Francis shared that when the
three women met one another at various community functions, they would
ask, "How do you deal with ...?" At other times, they watched one another's
leadership performance from a distance. Each of these women learned
that it is all right to laugh, cry, and sometimes be embarrassed about their
leadership flaws together.

Clara, Stella, and Francis agreed that they learned leadership behaviours
from a combination of traditional teachings, residential school experiences, and provincial school programs. They were adamant that their
learned negative behaviours were a result of low self-esteem and a lack of
First Nation identity. This needs to be changed. They agreed that learning
effective leadership behaviours begins with self-love, which in turn contributes to positive change and growth. Stella said, "I learned to do what
had to be done without question. Change comes easy when you are motivated by heartfelt concern for the future generations." In the medicine
wheel philosophy, there is a cyclical interconnectedness that has its roots
in the land. Likewise, these women learned to emphasize their connection
to the land through the Saulteaux language and cultural worldview.

Yvonne, Angie, Sharon, and Ann Margaret, the second-generation
women, agreed that they, too, had learned to lead in the context of their
culture by watching, listening, doing, and asking certain questions such
as How do I ...? and When do I ...? but rarely Why do I ...? According to
the women, learning good leadership behaviour begins by respecting
the Elders, extended family members, and the First Nation community.
Yvonne said, "I learned that 'why' questions were a form of disrespect. I
learned to spend more time listening, watching, and doing, utilizing the
two eyes, two ears, and two hands learning process." Angie indicated that
asking too many questions put her off balance. She said, "Learning to

question situations is easier off the reserve because you're a loner, and that is the way things are done out there. But on the reserve, well, things are done differently – it is community-driven. If you want to lead effectively in today's world, you have to learn both ways." As Afsaneh Nahavandi (2006, 155) explains using the analogy of geese, "Whenever a goose falls out of formation, it suddenly feels the drag and resistance of trying to fly alone and quickly gets back into formation to take advantage of the power of formation." The second-generation women agreed that they had learned to rely on the leadership knowledge, strength, and wisdom of family members who were involved in educational administration.

The women of the second generation indicated that a sense of balance, self-love, and cyclical interconnectedness within their relationships and life experiences was important to their learning process. Angie, Sharon, and Yvonne learned this lesson while in the First Nation teacher education program, where they used the medicine wheel as a learning tool in a number of ways: for reflection, for recording experiences, and for organizing thought processes. Ann Margaret indicated that her immediate family had taught her to learn from ceremonies and traditional teachings. Because all of the women struggled to maintain contact with Elders from their home communities, they depended on the coaching and mentoring of older women in their immediate family.

The second-generation women affirmed that balancing the four medicine wheel categories was an important aspect of learning to be strategic leaders. The medicine wheel taught them to see the big picture of where they came from, who they were, and where they wanted to be. Ann Margaret said, "In order to be a strong leader, I need to know who I am as a First Nation woman and my sense of place and how I hope to influence the next generation. I need to follow up with my personal and professional leadership goals." All of the second-generation women felt it was important to learn where they came from, to establish where they are today, and to determine where they wanted to be as leaders of tomorrow. They learned leadership behaviours that promoted their values, vision, and educational philosophies.

The second-generation women also agreed that acknowledgment through the use of humour was another important element in the learning process. Yvonne said, "I learned to deal with life situations through teasing and encouraging words from my grandmother, and later in life, my aunt took over that role. Teasing and humour from family members helped me learn to be tough-skinned and more accepting during difficult, tiresome situations." Nahavandi (2006) explains, "When the lead geese gets tired, it rotates back in the wing and another goose flies point. The back geese honk from behind to encourage those up front to keep up their speed." This analogy of the geese illustrates how relationships and verbal encouragement are important factors in developing leadership skills.

Learning to be an educational leader requires knowledge of First Nation governance, treaties, and First Nation women's historical role. Sharon, Ann Margaret, and Angie appreciated what they had learned at university in their Indian studies classes and in their First Nation language courses. Language acquisition meant that they had a role in the protection of their language as an inherent right, a treaty right, a constitutional right, and an Aboriginal right (Kirkness 1998, 107). Currently, they all hope to learn their First Nation language. In the language, they find support for women holding a strong position in First Nation society. For example, they agreed that the grandmothers and aunts had influenced their role as supportive, caring, and sharing leaders. Nahavandi (2006, 115) alludes to this supportive, caring leadership style: "When a goose gets sick and falls out, two geese fall out of formation with it until it is either able to fly or it is dead. They then launch on their own or with another formation, to catch up with the group." As good leaders, these women learned to value and support relationships in the workplace by teaming together, mentoring, and coaching. In essence, they learned by watching, listening, and doing and by asking specific questions while maintaining respect for the people involved in either on-reserve or off-reserve work environments. They all learned through some form of cultural activity influenced by community relationships. Angie explained, "I continue to learn in ceremony and in traditional teachings." Ongoing collegial collaboration and reflection on experiences that produce necessary change were critical aspects of their leadership development.

Rachel, the only third-generation participant in this study, agreed that she, too, learned by watching, listening, doing, and questioning in a respectful manner. She proclaimed, "I do not speak for all third-generation First Nation women in leadership, but only for myself." Therefore, the following discussion is not representative of all women (hooks 1989). Rachel began by saying, "I learned through sharing and celebrating. Mom and Dad always made sure that each educational milestone in my life was acknowledged, shared through storytelling, and then celebrated with family. My grandpa died just before I received my master's degree – we celebrated this milestone at his gravesite." My kokum, Clara, had modelled the importance of acknowledging the "spirit" of the child and respect for the Elder. She taught Rachel that stories bring one's work to a place of centring (Cajete 1994) by connecting the soul and the heart of people engaged in the process. Rachel reminisced about her mother's words, "If we do not touch the heart and spirit of the child, we will have failed in providing a safe, caring learning environment where the child willingly becomes physically involved in what has to be learned." The conceptual framework of the medicine wheel requires empathy and an intuitive response of emotional and social intelligence (Goleman 1998). Rachel was taught to view leadership learning first as a heart and soul activity and then as a physical and mental process. For example, she learned to use stories about the legendary trickster Nanabush to bring humour to life lessons and social relationships. Rachel recognizes both the trickster tales and medicine wheel philosophy as learning tools that help the leader to think from the heart.

In addition, Rachel explained, "Mom talked a lot about leading in two worlds, but my learning process involves three worlds: the world of my First Nation traditional family teachings, the changing world of today's teachings, and the world of my mainstream teachings. The greatest challenge in the way that I learn is to validate my First Nation ways of knowing in a changing world." Rachel noticed that her learning process differed from her mom's in the sense that "I did not hesitate to ask questions. I was made to feel assured that I could learn by watching, listening, doing, and asking as many questions as I wanted, providing that I show respect. My learning opportunities are different from those of my grandmothers', my aunts', and my mother's time." She elaborated, "My learning systems included grandparent teachings, family teachings, traditional teachings, federal school, provincial school, band school, First Nation business management, First Nations University, SUNTEP teacher program, SIAST [Saskatchewan Institute of Applied Science and Technology], and the University of Regina." Rachel's learning experiences are summed up well by Sims and Manz's quote on leadership. Rachel herself concluded that she had learned "how to from her mother who learned how to from her aunt who learned how to from her mother who learned how to from her grandmother!" First Nation leadership is an intergenerational learning process.

Rachel shared how difficult it was to maintain her First Nation female identity while learning in an assimilative university system. "As a student in high school and at university, I felt like I did not belong. I had to learn to overcome the same feeling when I returned to the reserve to work, too." The situation that Rachel describes here is similar to James Belasco and Ralph Stayer's (1993) metaphor of the lead buffalo. If the lead buffalo is killed, then the herd will stand and become easy targets for hunters. Rachel viewed assimilation as a systemic process of cultural genocide, and she did not want to be an easy target. She concluded, "If my grandmother, my aunts, my mother, and my cousins can rise above issues, then I, too, can learn to move on and be the leader that I was meant to be."

A Female and First Nation Leadership Voice

First Nation female leadership knowledge is grounded in a sense of caring and sharing. Shirley Sterling (2002) indicates that, as female leaders, grandmothers model "caring and sharing" and helping others. Kokums, aunties, cousins, and sisters naturally and understandably communicate through family networks on a regular basis. This type of communication fulfils the leadership's function of bringing together, or connecting, the generations within First Nation communities. The women in this study also credited their leadership success to other influential persons such as husbands, uncles, brothers, and community members. The women of my family are of the mindset that the good they do is not just for today but for the generations to come.

Leadership is "doing, feeling, knowing, and seeing"; it is offering a servant-type service for the good of all. By capturing intergenerational First Nation leadership learning from a Saulteaux Cree perspective, this study fulfils a number of objectives:

- creating awareness of intergenerational learning and leadership practices such as resiliency
- developing a learning process that uses cultural artifacts to pass on First Nation cultural identity, values, and norms
- creating a learning environment to gain practical knowledge gleaned from living within a two-world system
- creating a holistic learning system that incorporates the seventh-generation rule.

Such are the elements of an intergenerational leadership model that incorporates a holistic methodology for aspiring leaders. Figure 2.2 provides an overview of this model, beginning with the domains, aspects, dimensions, and circles of influence and concluding with the developmental stages.

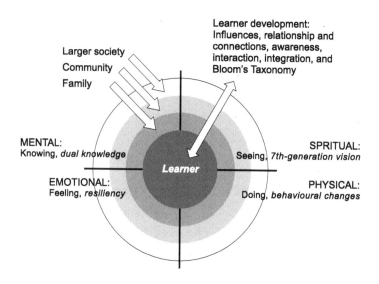

FIGURE 2.2   An intergenerational First Nation leadership model

The First Nation, intergenerational leadership model consists of the following:

- four *domains* of human development: the physical, emotional, mental, and spiritual
- four *aspects* of intergenerational philosophy: doing, feeling, knowing, and seeing
- four *dimensions* of leadership: behavioural change through leadership preservation, resiliency through two-world leadership struggles, dual knowledge through intergenerational circular leadership awareness, and seventh-generation visioning through reliance on the foresight of intergenerational leaders
- *four circles* of influence: self, family, community, and the larger society.

Awareness, interaction, and mastery are developmental stages within the model.

The four philosophical domains teach human relations that prepare learners to look inward and to work with others in a good way. The work of Marge Scherer (1992) lists conflict resolution as a top priority, and Mary Katherine Deen (2000) suggests that conflict has the potential to be productive, a necessary part of positive interpersonal relationships, creative problem-solving, and group cohesiveness. The leadership constructs of James Kouzes and Barry Posner's (1995) research reveal that effective leaders focus on the following practices: challenging the process, inspiring a shared vision, enabling others to act, serving as role models, and encouraging the heart. Getting along with others, managing conflict effectively, communicating, restoring relationships, and maintaining relationships are also aspects of intrapersonal and interpersonal leadership skills.

I conclude my story of family leadership by emphasizing that the next step is to formally introduce the First Nation, intergenerational leadership model into a curriculum for leadership education. The curriculum will determine the worldview, attitudes, knowledge, and skills that aspiring leaders gain. John Gardner (1993) suggests that educational institutions have been ineffective in producing effective leaders. This study identifies the lack of intergenerational learning and leadership processes as the problem. The First Nation, intergenerational leadership model presented here offers a learning process geared for leadership success for the next seven generations.

I am grateful to the women in this study for sharing their reflections, experiences, and direction. As Tina Ngaroimata Fraser observes, they are the women who played a significant role in my life, and they taught me the fundamental principles of life, cultural survival, retention, and sustainability. I am a seventh-generation product of my ancestors. I am my kokum's legacy.

SEVEN GENERATIONS – YET TO COME!

We are First Nation women who reach back and reach forward between
  generations.
We bridge past, present, and future success,
through a learning process of reflection, experience and self-direction.
We present our family stories and teachings to our children.
In turn, our children extend them to their children.
In doing so, we continue to pass on valued learning and leadership
traditions
to the seven generations yet to come.
As long as the sun shines, the grass grows, and the rivers flow.
We are forever learning!

Works Cited

Anderson, Kim. 2000. *A Recognition of Being: Reconstructing Native Womanhood.* Toronto: Second Story Press.

Assembly of First Nations. 1994. *Tradition and Education: Towards a Vision of Our Future.* Ottawa: Assembly of First Nations, 1994.

Belasco, James A., and Ralph C. Stayer. 1993. *Flight of the Buffalo: Soaring to Excellence, Learning to Let Employees Lead.* New York: Warner Books.

Brayboy, Mary E., and Mary Y. Morgan. 1998. "Voices of Indianness: The Lived World of Native American Women." *Women's Studies International Forum* 21, 4: 341-54.

Cajete, Gregory. 1994. *Look to the Mountain: An Ecology of Indigenous Education.* Durango: Colorado Kivaki Press.

Cole, Michael. 1996. *Cultural Psychology: A Once and Future Discipline.* Cambridge, MA: Belknap Press of Harvard University, 1996.

Deen, Mary Katherine. 2000. "Differences in the Solution-Oriented Conflict Style of Selected Groups of 4-H Youth Development Volunteers." *Journal of Extension* 38, 1: http://www.joe.org/.

Ermine, Willie. 1995. "Aboriginal Epistemology." In *First Nations Education in Canada: The Circle Unfolds,* edited by Marie Battiste and Jean Barman, 101-12. Vancouver: UBC Press.

Gardner, John W. 1993. *On Leadership.* New York: Free Press

Goleman, Daniel. 1998. "What Makes a Leader?" *Harvard Business Review* (November-December): 93-102.

Goulet, Linda. 2005. "Creating Culturally Meaningful Learning Environments: Teacher Actions to Engage Aboriginal Students in Learning." PhD diss., University of Regina.

Graveline, F.J. 2000 "Circle as Methodology: Enacting an Aboriginal Paradigm." *Qualitative Studies in Education* 13, 4: 361-70.

Gunn Allen, P. 1989. *The Sacred Hoop: Recovering the Feminine in American Indian Traditions.* Boston, MA: Beacon Press.

Hampton, Eber. 1995. "Towards a Redefinition of Indian Education." In *The Circle Unfolds,* edited by Marie Battiste and Jean Barman, 262-87. Vancouver: UBC Press.

hooks, bell. 1994. *Teaching to Transgress: Education as the Practice of Freedom.* New York: Routledge.

King, Cecil. 1991. "Indian Worldview and Time." In *Time as a Human Resource,* edited by E.J. McCullough and R.L. Calder, 183-87. Calgary: University of Calgary Press.

Kirkness, Verna J. 1998. "The Critical State of Aboriginal Languages in Canada." *Canadian Journal of Education* 22, 1: 93-107.

Klein, Laura, and Linda Ackerman. 1995. *Women and Power in Native North America.* Norman: University of Oklahoma Press.

Kouzes, James M., and Barry Z. Posner. *The Leadership Challenge: How to Get Extraordinary Things Done in Organizations.* San Francisco, CA: Jossey-Bass/Pfeiffer, 1995.

Lightning, Walter. "Compassionate Mind: Implications of a Text Written by Elder Louis Sunchild." *Canadian Journal of Native Education* 19, 2 (1992): 215-53.

Monture-Angus, Patricia. 1999. *Journey Forward: Dreaming First Nations Independence.* Halifax, NS: Fernwood Publishing.

Moss, Maria. 1993. "We've Been Here Before: Women in Creation Myths and Contemporary Literature of the Native American Southwest." PhD diss., University of Hamburg.

Nahavandi, Afsaneh. 2006. *The Art and Science of Leadership.* Upper Saddle River, NJ: Prentice-Hall.

Ng, Roxana. 1993. "Racism, Sexism and Nation Building in Canada." In *Race, Identity and Representation in Education*, edited by Cameron McCarthy and Warren Crichlow, 50-59. New York: Routledge.

Pete-Willet, Shauneen. 2001. "Kiskinawachihckana." PhD diss., University of Saskatchewan.

Regnier, Robert. 1995. "Warrior as Pedagogue, Pedagogue as Warrior: Reflections on Aboriginal Anti-Racist Pedagogy." In *Anti-Racism, Feminism, and Approaches to Education*, edited by Roxanna Ng, Pat Staton, and Joyce Scane, 67-86. Westport, CT: Bergin and Garvey.

Scherer, Marge. 1992. "Solving Conflicts: Not Just for Children." *Educational Leadership* 50, 14: 17-18.

Sims, Henry P., Jr., and Charles C. Manz. 1996. *Company of Heroes: Unleashing the Power of Self.* New York: Wiley.

Smith, Linda 1999. *Decolonizing Methodologies: Research and Indigenous Peoples.* London, UK: Zed Books.

St. Denis, Verna. 2002. "Exploring the Socio-Cultural Production of Aboriginal Identities: Implications for Education." PhD diss., University of Saskatchewan.

Sternberg, Robert J., Catherine Nokes, P. Wenzel Geissler, Ruth Prince, Frederick Okatcha, Donald A. Bundy, and Elena L. Grigorenko. 2001. "The Relationship between Academic and Practical Intelligence: A Case Study in Kenya." *Intelligence* 29, 5: 401-18.

Sterling, Shirley. 2002. "Yetko and Sophie: Nlakapamux Cultural Professors." *Canadian Journal of Native Education* 18: 4-10.

Stiffarm, Lenore, 1998. *As We See ... Aboriginal Pedagogy.* Saskatoon: University of Saskatchewan Extension Press.

Tinelli, Archie. 2000. "Leaders and Their Learning: What and How Leaders Learn as They Transform Organizations." PhD diss., Virginia Polytechnic Institute/Virginia State University.

Weenie, Angelina. 2002. "A Study of Resilience in First Nations Post-Secondary Education Students." Master's thesis, University of Saskatchewan.

3
Elders' Teachings on Leadership
Leadership as a Gift
Alannah Young Leon

STRONG INDIGENOUS LEADERSHIP is developed by empowering people to reclaim cultural values through the investigation of local, living genealogies, oral histories, and reflexive praxis. They should be allowed to do so within an environment that supports self-determined change. This chapter focuses on Elders' perspectives on the role of culture in Indigenous leadership, a pedagogical frame that informs my research and application of Indigenous knowledge to leadership in postsecondary institutions. The Elders I interviewed worked with First Nations House of Learning (FNHL) programs and provide narratives that continue to inform my leadership education. I learned that Indigenous leadership includes knowing and sharing your history by introducing yourself, your family, and your nation when you begin speaking.

I am a member of Opaskwayak Cree First Nation (Treaty 5), and I live on the unceded territory of the Coast Salish, XwMuthkwium (Musqueam) in Vancouver, British Columbia. From 1995 to 2009, I worked at the FNHL at the University of British Columbia. As an Aboriginal female education leader, I developed the student Longhouse Leadership Program, which ran from 2000 to 2009. In 2006, I completed a master's thesis that summarized FNHL Elders' recommendations about Aboriginal leadership. My doctoral studies continue to explore Aboriginal leadership through storywork with Elders in rural Manitoba. In this chapter, I focus on the four pedagogical components of an Indigenous leadership program: (1) land interaction, (2) cultural practices, (3) community service, and (4) and language and genealogy. As Figure 3.1 outlines, these components can help open leadership discussions and develop leadership goals

Promote life experiences and places as pedagogy

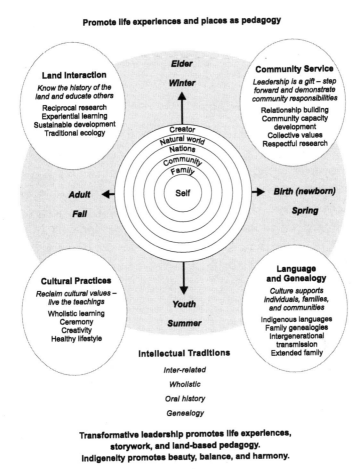

Land Interaction
Know the history of the
land and educate others

Reciprocal research
Experiential learning
Sustainable development
Traditional ecology

Elder

Winter

Community Service
Leadership is a gift – step
forward and demonstrate
community responsibilities

Relationship building
Community capacity
development
Collective values
Respectful research

Creator
Natural world
Nations
Community
Family
Self

Adult

Fall

Birth (newborn)

Spring

Cultural Practices
Reclaim cultural values –
live the teachings

Wholistic learning
Ceremony
Creativity
Healthy lifestyle

Youth

Summer

Language
and Genealogy
Culture supports
individuals, families,
and communities

Indigenous languages
Family genealogies
Intergenerational
transmission
Extended family

Intellectual Traditions

Inter-related

Wholistic

Oral history

Genealogy

**Transformative leadership promotes life experiences,
storywork, and land-based pedagogy.
Indigeneity promotes beauty, balance, and harmony.**

Figure 3.1   Indigenous leadership: Core components program

Background

The First Nations House of Learning was established in 1987 with a mandate to ensure that university resources are made accessible to First Nations students and communities and to improve UBC's ability to accommodate the First Nations community. Since 1993, the FNHL has been housed within the First Nations Longhouse, an award-winning building based on Coast Salish architecture that serves as a home away from home for UBC's Indigenous community. The FNHL is committed to three principles: (1) heightening awareness about Aboriginal issues, (2) promoting Indigenous leadership on campus, and (3) providing a positive environment founded on First Nations cultures and philosophies. These principles are based on the longhouse teachings of respect, responsibility, reverence, and relationship. These cultural values guide work at the FNHL and are the core components of the First Nations House of Learning's Longhouse Leadership Program.

The Longhouse Leadership Program

The Longhouse Leadership Program was developed as a noncredit student program specific to Indigenous contexts and perspectives. It consists of three core seminars, four elective workshops, and a six-hour service-learning component. The program was established in 2000 because the academic training offered to students did not adequately provide the leadership training required to work in Indigenous contexts. During its first three years, funding for the program came from the UBC Equity Office's Equity Enhancement Fund, and the FNHL continued to fund the program until 2009.

The Longhouse Leadership Program provides Indigenous leadership training necessary for promoting leadership on campus, and it introduces skills for working in and understanding Indigenous contexts. In collaboration with FNHL student services, UBC's various faculties, and UBC student services, the program offers workshops and opportunities for service learning. To facilitate teachings on leadership, cultural protocols, and ceremonies, the program meets two or three times a month during lunch hour and has a six-hour service-learning component. The latter requires students to work towards positive change in communities by applying the cultural values of respect, relationship, responsibility, and reverence and to report back to the program. The program also offers workshops that introduce non-violent communication skills, respectful research strategies, and respect for human rights and values. The workshops promote strength in diversity, political leadership for contemporary contexts, inclusive relationships, identity and belonging, and values as a foundation for leadership. Although the program promotes relevant values, its cultural aspect requires further development to articulate how cultural teachings can play a significant role in Indigenous leadership and, more specifically, to take Elders' perspectives into account within the FNHL community (Young 2006).

Elders

In many Indigenous contexts, Elders are considered leaders, consultants, and teachers. Elders, as a collectivity, are considered an authoritarian body because of their combined expertise and wisdom. Not all old people are Elders: Elders are those who know the protocols associated with cultural teachings and demonstrate them in appropriate ways. Elders are chosen by the people in their community (Archibald 2008). They are accepted, listened to, and are usually good speakers and storytellers. Elders are the historians, philosophers, and teachers of tradition and heritage. They teach us how to make meaning out of history, to connect the past to present conditions, and they indicate safe directions to pursue so that the people's history can be sustained and advanced. Wisdom is a virtue that Elders demonstrate by example so others can learn from their lived experiences. They also teach adherence to core spiritual values and demonstrate complex understandings in a variety of situations. Not all Elders are cultural leaders and storytellers, and not all Elders live good lives. An Elder can be someone who is not yet old but who understands and lives a good life according to cultural values and teachings.

Cree Elders define leaders as *skabayos* (helpers) who remember core cultural teachings, which contain community values and embody the good life path (Young and Nadeau 2005). The core values of the good life path include thinking the highest thought, which embodies the utmost integrity for one's family, nation, and environment (Cajete 1994). Elders who live and embody core cultural teachings influence the actions of both individuals and the community. The cultural teachings are located in stories and include living a life that is respectful, wholesome, and spiritual. Larry Grant, a XwMuthkwium Elder, describes the leadership journey as individuals working together with one heart and one mind. In visiting with the Elders, I learned that leadership benchmarks include cultural engagement, interaction with the land as stewards, and perpetuating good lifeways or cultural teachings so that seven generations will benefit.

Reanimating Leadership through Storywork

Storywork, as described by Jo-ann Archibald (2008), brings together Indigenous ways of knowing and leading. Storywork teaches us how to remain connected to the land and to one another. Storywork is the teacher transmitted through specific Elders and educators. The storywork framework is based on the principles of respect, responsibility, reverence, reciprocity, holism, interrelatedness, and synergy. Storywork is an appropriate vehicle for the transmission of Indigenous intellectual traditions and Elders' knowledge and thus provides an additional guiding framework for leadership. The Elders' lived experiences, oral histories, and storywork provide interconnected cultural teachings about leadership that fall naturally into components or themes. The exploration of these themes animated my own storywork process and demonstrates my own leadership-learning process.

Land Interaction: Know the History of the Land and Educate Others

It is late spring 2005, and my daughter, partner, and I are travelling to the BC Interior to meet with my Elders to discuss leadership. It is sage- and bitterroot-picking season. These plant medicines are the helpers required for the annual summer ceremonial season. The two Elders I plan to interview are our adopted parents in the traditional Indigenous way. They serve as role models through their interaction with the land, which includes performing the seasonal work that needs to be done to ensure the transmission of Indigenous knowledge.

We must first get the sage and bitterroot from the mountainside – the medicines are the leaders in this situation. We set up outside, and as we prepare the medicines, the Elders talk to us about leadership and transmit knowledge to the four generations present. We hear trains in the background, and the wind and dry mountainous desert surround us. The storytellers talk to us about the local mountains. The stories that the mountains contain remind us to listen to our Elders. The stories, ceremonies, and languages are held within the land, and along with them are the teachings.

Learning about the land includes experiential learning outside the classroom, teachings on traditional ecological practices and protocols and developing conscientious reciprocal relationships with local Indigenous peoples (Dergousoff 2008; Pidgeon 2010). As Michelle Jacobs states in Chapter 12 of this volume, Native people are working to reclaim educational institutions that sit on Indigenous homelands. This educational endeavour benefits all peoples and requires lifetime commitments from institutions and community leadership stakeholders to engage in true power-sharing partnerships. Systemic cultural change must go beyond "sweet words" and superficial representations so that students can receive relevant leadership education for this country.

Leadership education includes learning about local histories, sustainable development, and Indigenous land management practices. The FNHL Elders described history as crucial to understanding the present context and providing a foundation for respectful relationships. The storytellers shared personal narrative accounts of internalized racism and its continued impact today. Their stories and life experiences help us to decolonize our leadership education and practice.

In general, both students and the Elders felt that the cultural value of restoring respectful relationships was missing in leadership training. In Chapter 12 of this volume, Michelle Jacob calls us to move beyond visions of diversity and multiculturalism that cater to "white" interests and curiosities. We should instead embrace a vision that honours and includes Native peoples and cultures as true partners in institution-building, a vision that demonstrates structural commitment to reversing the trend of institutional racism. Larry Grant, a XwMuthkwium Elder, explains:

> We are a contributing factor in the formation of this country, which is denied by not having our culture recognized, regardless of how diverse our cultures were and are. We played a major, major role in the structure of Canada. A systematic exclusion of the existence of Aboriginal culture and languages demonstrates a lack of respect for our cultures. The culture brings about ceremonies, language, geography, history, and medicines. On the West Coast, we have marine engineers who built the canoes; the structural engineers built the big houses, all of that. Cultural curriculum would identify how industrious, self-sufficient, reliable, and intelligent we were and are. (In discussion with author, 2006)

The Elder storytellers also identified the need to reclaim holistic health through cultural training that resists the oppression of the past. Gary Oleman, Saa Hiil Thut, stated:

> Racism, religion, reservations, residential schools, and RCMP. I started talking about these five *R*'s and how important the teachings about how to live and where we come from [are] today. We lasted through five hundred years of oppression and oppressive communication. This is how we got here. This is how I described it was the five *R*'s, because I saw them as the core reasons or indicators about why we are the way we are today.
>
> Now, if I was going to talk about the traditional teachings that you are talking about – the four *R*'s, the longhouse teachings – they bring about awareness, and we have cultural ways that people can look at themselves. In our language, to say *sweat lodge*, we say *K'ul'za*. It means "to look at yourself." And so, when you go to the sweat lodge, you are actually going there to look at yourself, and if you see something wrong, then work towards changing it.

So, that would probably be one of the first steps I would do if I was going to train leaders – have a way for them to look at themselves. You were showing me a diagram before, and that's a good way of doing it. Physically, ceremonially, it would be more like the importance of having a spiritual way of life. People don't even think of that today. That means to me they are disconnected from the spiritual realms. (In discussion with author, 2006)

Norma Rose Point (traditional name, Papet), XwMuthkwium and Seabird Island Nation, reflected on the importance of knowing your own histories, the history of the land where you live now, and sharing this knowledge as part of leadership development:

> It is important to convey and to provide an understanding of their history – what it means, how it developed – by interpreting what is being taught to them and to take what is necessary to carry on with life ... For example, the Coast Salish big house or longhouse culture has four direction witnesses. Calling witnesses (because, traditionally, there were no written histories), they always called two witnesses to pass on the information to verify the facts. The reason you leave two witnesses is because one person only sees one side and the other person sees the other half. My aunt and uncle say, "Only believe half of what you see. You can only ever see one side of a story and not the whole thing." Also, one verifies the other. (In discussion with author, 2006)

This statement has implications for leadership. It demonstrates the importance of acknowledging the diversity of multiple voices to arrive at the whole story. Knowing their history can help leaders make informed decisions that move us beyond decolonized educational spaces into places of transformation (see Chapter 12, this volume). Indigenous cultural practices with community collaboration will continue to inform innovative leadership models, as they did for millennia.

Cultural Practices: Reclaim Cultural Values and Live the Teachings
Cultural teachings provide us with leadership principles, foundations, and understandings. In spring 2006, I reflected on a series of dreams I'd had during the fall and winter of 2005-06. In the dreams, I am in the city, and I hear the Sundance songs. I cannot see the ceremonial grounds, and I am worried that I am late and that the ceremony has begun without me. Along the way, I encounter Judge Point, a Stó:lō Elder, cultural leader, and lieutenant-governor of British Columbia, in a downtown eastside

school playground. A group of us gather in the playground and listen to the ceremonial songs. The songs teach us how to enact our leadership – our relational responsibilities to our spirit, the people, the community, and the lands. The songs express our connection to all of creation and reflect the teachings of all my relations.

The Longhouse Leadership Program introduces the protocol of acknowledging the XwMuthkwium territory on which UBC is located to demonstrate respect for the original peoples of the area. The program teaches learners about the local Indigenous language and about the importance of cultural values to leadership practices. Facilitators in the program demonstrate the cultural aspects of using the XwMuthkwium greeting "*i 'uh 'ch'ew 'ey'al*" and encourage learners to sing "Teswanic Slolem," a public song that belongs to the George family of Tsleil-Waututh First Nation, during each session.

Indigenous knowledge, intellectual traditions, and cultural expressions such as the Sundance and Mediwiwin (Grand Medicine Society) provide teachings that inform both my leadership genealogy and educational roles. For me, the Sundance ceremony connects us to the land and our genealogies and expresses the values and collective leadership vision needed for a better future. Each Indigenous culture has its own version of the good life path: Anishinaabe have *Bimaadziwin* (the good life path), the Cree of the northern Prairies have *miyowicehtowin* (having good relations), the Iroquois have *Skennen'kowa* (maintaining peace between peoples), the Navajo have *hózhǫ́* (walking in beauty, with a sacred manner, or with a peaceful heart), and the Yupiat have *Yuluni pitallkertugluni* (living a life that feels great). These different versions of the good life path have one thing in common: the lived values of relations, community, and balance (Young and Nadeau 2005). Members of the Longhouse Leadership Program explore aspects of the good life path and cultural practices and values, and they frame their reflections at the end of the program.

Providing relevant cultural content is essential in Indigenous leadership education. Exploring cultural values through Elders' teachings can provide the foundation for building strong, effective leaders. Lee Brown, of the Ani-Waya (Wolf Clan) of the Tsalagi (Cherokee), stated: "The role of culture is that it teaches us how to be related, related first to ourselves, related to the spiritual realm, related to the family, the community, and the world around us, and the environment. So, culture teaches. It holds our values, and it holds our knowledge. It holds the accumulated knowledge and wisdom of our ancestors" (in discussion with author, 2006). Brown talked about the importance of developing self-awareness by exploring cultural values. He believes that individuals who have the opportunity to explore their values and how their values inform their thoughts and actions will also develop a deeper understanding of how other forms of leadership operate. Cultural processes give leaders in training opportunities to explore how cultural knowledge and leadership are transmitted in particular contexts. Indigenous leadership training should teach leaders to listen respectfully to Elders' teachings and engage with the wisdom of cultural practices.

The Longhouse Leadership Program and the core components of an Indigenous leadership program (see Figure 3.1) contain elements of an Elders' pedagogy based on cultural teachings and values. It is up to the individual to describe their own leadership journey and apply the elements. For those planning to develop a leadership program, these pedagogical components can be addressed in workshops in collaboration with relevant Indigenous stakeholders.

Community Service

I want my research story to demonstrate that I have learned the leadership values of reciprocity and responsibility to my relations and of providing relevant service to the community. Mediwiwin cultural teachings require us to go home and check in with our home communities – to be of service to them. My inspiration for exploring graduate work is part of my leadership story. Peguis First Nation Education Authority supported my first academic degree by paying my tuition in the Bachelor of Arts program at the University of Winnipeg. To demonstrate reciprocity and serve the community, I am now exploring in my doctoral work how to document the Elders' pedagogy used at the Peguis Medicine Camp.

The Aki Mashkiki Na Na Da Wii li Way Wiin Earth Medicine Program or Medicine Camp is a community-based service in existence since 1992. The camp's story demonstrates that, despite colonialism, Indigenous knowledge education endures and persists. Elders serve as role models, and their experiential interaction with the land stands as an example of holistic pedagogy. Edna Manitowabe and Kathy Bird are Elders and primary teachers of the Medicine Camp Programs. Doris Young, Edna, and Kathy are Cree and Anishinaabe and are considered Elders, teachers, and spiritual leaders of the Mediwiwin Medicine Society. Doris and I were in Edna's trailer when we began discussing how my academic work might give back to the community – in effect, how the story of the Medicine

Camp and the Elders' narratives could be instructive to those in educational leadership positions.

During the conversation, Doris told me a story that she had heard from her father, John Young. Doris believed her dad had told her the story to explain why he hid her mother's knowledge of plants from outsiders. In the mid-twentieth century, he told her, an Indian Agent from the Department of Indian Affairs had imposed patriarchal domination on First Nations communities, overturning matriarchal leadership. The Indian Agent destroyed a year's worth of harvests, which resulted in the matriarchs' going underground and hiding their knowledge from outsiders. That the matriarchs continue to transmit traditional knowledge through land-based education at the Medicine Camp demonstrates the persistence of an Indigenous educational and leadership ethic, one that provides relevant community service in spite of the pressures imposed by the Canadian state.

I believe the burnt harvest story is the reason I was given an audience with the matriarchs, who agreed to consider my request. The story clarifies that our histories make the leadership work we do relevant both in the present and beyond. Using the authority of the Indian Act, the Canadian state interrupted the intergenerational transmission of Indigenous knowledge, especially through the residential school system and the loss of Indigenous languages. However, this knowledge is not lost. Instead, Indigenous leadership practices continue to be transmitted in new ways, mobilized through our stories and those of our Elders, stories that re-establish links to the land (Marsden 2005). I have since graduated from the land-based health education program known as the Medicine Camp and plan to document the stories and narratives as examples of Elder leadership teachings in practice and to demonstrate my leadership through community service.

Many of the Elders agreed that to serve the community is a gift and a responsibility. To transmit Indigenous knowledge and culturally relevant leadership skills, Indigenous communities must focus on building community through intergenerational learning. The Elders view culture as a healthy resource for community and family living. Leadership skills develop through community-based cultural processes and through protocols that require collaboration. Norma Rose Point shared her views on the importance of collaboration by demonstrating through example: "I am living with seven generations of my family alive today. I grew up with midwifery and culturally appropriate child-rearing as a form of women's leadership in our community. I worked in the hospitals and schools for most of my life. I also provide leadership by educating and collaborating with peoples about the medicinal plants in my neighbourhood." On intergenerational leadership Lee Brown stated:

> I am with the Institute of Aboriginal Health and Vancouver Coastal Health's Aboriginal Health Practice Council, and I like what they do in committees. They not only have the administration and faculty here, but they also have students as part of the committee, which is also a form of leadership. Sometimes, as leaders, we pigeonhole ourselves – this is the way things are done. Whereas you get the new blood in, [you] get new, fresh ideas, because the world is always changing. Intergenerational leadership is how I think about sitting on advisory committees. Everyone gains when we put our minds together.

Intergenerational and lifelong learning are persistent leadership concepts, and collaboration is indispensible for developing leadership programs. Listening to and respectfully honouring Indigenous perspectives are required if we hope to overcome the possibility of perpetuating historical injustices through our leadership.

Doris reminds me that we did not come this far, carrying and preserving the ancestors' leadership knowledge, to just leave it behind. Many Elders continue to persevere, listen, learn, and enact the ancestors' teachings as part of their leadership. Their perseverance can be heard in their introductions, stories, songs, languages, and cultural protocols. N'kixw'stn James, a Nlaka'pamux Elder in residence at the FNHL who holds a master's degree in education, discussed the importance of listening to the Elders and including cultural teachings and practices as part of a holistic approach to leadership education:

> I was the third generation of all females, so I was selected to be the hunter. And when I was going through life turmoil, my grandfather decided he was going to take me away from that type of life ... He put me into the sweat and then into an isolated fast, where I went into the mountains, and when I came back down – thirty days clean of alcohol and drugs. It was back in those days where we listened to our grandfather. He said, "I want you to see the world. Find out a way to see the world." And I joined the military, and then I saw the world. And, so, he said, "When you see the world, you come back here to the community and tell the children about it." And that's what I am doing.

I was in college and came to university, and now I am teacher, and I teach in school. I am doing exactly what he told me to ... I believe in teaching our spirituality to women and children ...

Don't stop having sweat ceremonies. Don't stop having warrior [wellness] talking circles and Elders' programs. You know, don't stop doing those traditional things, because they show leadership, and they help students to lead from a cultural foundation, if they want to. So, it's not one or the other. They need to know there are options and choices. I would say culture is really important, like observing the protocol that acknowledges that we are visitors on XwMuthkwium Musqueam territory because the university stands on XwMuthkwium Musqueam unceded territory. And they should always be honoured. (In discussion with author, 2006)

The sweat lodge teachings are a part of the Longhouse Leadership Program. It is thus important to continue them even though they are ceremonial practices from outside the local Nations because these cultural ceremonies are open to all peoples, whereas many of the local ceremonial practices have restricted membership requirements. In order to transmit this teaching practice, this ceremony is a good way members of Longhouse Leadership Program can learn local protocol. FNHL received permission from Elder Tsimilano (*xwmuthkwey'um* Musqueam) to perform the sweat lodge ceremony in their territory. The monthly sweats, the cultural ceremonies such as burnings, smudges, and wellness talking circles, were available to students outside of the Longhouse Leadership Program.

Leadership means supporting the reclamation of cultural knowledge and values, which will inform both the activism and the healing required for change. Safe, healthy individuals, families, and communities need to collaborate and develop decolonizing and self-determined consciousness to mobilize communities when under threat (Graveline 2002). We can learn from the Elders' stories because the stories teach us about the changes required to transform our selves, our families, and our communities.

White Cloud, a health care professional, demonstrated her teachings as she shared her life experiences:

I am an Anishinaabe Metis grandmother. "Wabish Quanoquot Iqwauy, Nezibiquay, Hialoqtinot, nideshnikaush mihegan nidodem" (My name is White Cloud Woman and Two Feathers of the Anishninaabe). Hialoqtinnot is the name I was given when I was adopted into the Nielson-Elliot family on

Vancouver Island. The name translates roughly into "a friend of the family."
My great-grandmother was the midwife, and she worked with medicines and
healing around the Selkirk area, St. Peter's. What we did when I was chief ...
we used our spiritual activities with pipe ceremonies and the sweat lodges. I
brought to them the full moon ceremony, and they practised that long after
I left. The Elder that took it over, she started remembering how their people
did it ... Because some don't know any better, and it's up to people like you
and I to share – so they don't have that fear. That fear stems from the church
and government and residential school. We are still left with that legacy. So,
the cultural values and principles can teach us how lateral violence can be
defused using culture, spirituality, and the protocols ... We take that responsibility, and then we also have choices ... What are we going to do? ... and how
we are going to work on our healing. The good parts about that last seven
generations – there was a lot of our elder and spiritual people that passed
our teachings and ceremonies, kept them alive, went underground. You know
that is the positive part. Our people are flocking to that like a thirst. So, there
is lots of positive that we need to balance out, but we still have to face reality
on what is going on. Yes, there is a lot of sad things going on, and what are
the positives? Maybe there are a lot of people that are working for the good
of the whole in that community. (Doreen Sinclair, White Cloud, in discussion
with the author, 2006)

Indigenous leadership requires living healthy lifestyles and interacting
with cultural knowledge and principles that can provide a foundation for
safe and sober living, paving the way for sovereignty in the future.

Language and Genealogy

The Longhouse Leadership Program recognizes the intergenerational
transmission of decolonizing knowledge as leadership education. Culture
supports individuals, families, and communities through Indigenous
languages, family genealogies, and extended families. Hopokeltun – a
traditional XwMuthkwium speaker, resource person with the Vancouver
School Board, and cultural consultant for events at the FNHL – stated:
"*Indian* is an objectification word formulated by the Canadian government in 1876 when they formed the Indian Act. So, those are Indians.
Indians are objects and subjects of the Canadian government. *Wholmulk*
are people who are Aboriginal who know language and culture unbroken
from time immemorial ... I am in agreement with educational institutions

to respectfully make use of the protocols, language, and the culture of the people whose territory they are in" (Shane Point, in discussion with author, 2006).

The cultural harm and brainwashing that occurred in residential schools still affects social, political, educational, and leadership conditions today. Elders advise leaders to explore their cultural values and practices in collaboration *with* Indigenous communities. Students in the Longhouse Leadership Program reported that listening to the Elders' stories of local lands and learning local Indigenous peoples' genealogies, which reflect a holistic episteme, enhanced their leadership knowledge and skills. I attribute my leadership skills to the Elders' stories and the wisdom they shared.

Indigenous identities have been under threat and affected negatively by pervasive colonial attitudes. Indigenous peoples and communities require appropriate Indigenous leadership models to build relevant and effective relationships. Supporting the unique leadership needs of each individual requires flexibility and time, and individual attention is crucial to Indigenous leadership programs. John O'Leary (Sahnbadis), a Mi'kmaq cultural ceremonialist and Elder in residence at the FNHL who also holds a master of arts degree, shared his thoughts on leadership and identity:

Cultural teachings can inform various aspects of identity, but not everyone will be a cultural leader. Leadership is unique to the individual. By looking into different aspects of a person's existence, for example, we have a spiritual existence, we have a locational existence, we have an educational existence ... we can develop and use some criteria like that for leadership development ... So, once you establish that leadership tool or map, a way of assessing where you stand, then ask the person, "Are you comfortable with where you are, or is there something you need to add or change?" And go from there. That's why I call it a diagnostic tool, because you begin a leadership plan to help people get to where they want to be ... Again, deciding what's in the new and what is in the old is involved in whatever activity. They have to map their own leadership development. (In discussion with author, 2006)

Developing a cultural identity tool to assist people to move towards their leadership gifts and to respect their cultural integrity is a common theme discussed by Elders in the FNHL programs and the medicine camps. The Elders insist that we maintain leadership based on cultural values and address contemporary challenges. I designed the core components diagram to assist those who are interested in developing contemporary Indigenous leadership models.

The Elders' stories and narratives also expressed interrelated and intersecting visions of Indigenous leadership. These visions take into consideration the holistic well-being of individuals, families, communities, and the land and recognize the cultural expressions of these value orientations as critical features in Indigenous leadership. Strong Indigenous leadership is developed when institutions create an environment that empowers students to reclaim cultural values by investigating local living genealogies, oral histories, and reflective practices.

Conclusion

Elders associated with the First Nations House of Learning and the Peguis Medicine Camp point to the importance of fostering respectful relationships with the land, language, cultural ceremonies, and holistic experiential leadership education in a manner consistent with Indigenous knowledge and intellectual traditions. The Elders discussed the role of culture in leadership development and how culture and storywork had informed their own leadership development. Their stories and experiences challenge colonial historical narratives and highlight the need to develop a critical consciousness among Indigenous leaders, one that moves beyond the agendas of assimilation or decolonization. The Elders' narratives demonstrate the power of stories by conveying their worldview and leadership skills directly. Their knowledge stands as a testimony to the existence of a holistic Indigenous theory. Their teachings show that storywork can be used as a method to develop Indigenous leadership without reference to Western models.

Teaching protocols and cultural values, even when applied within a limited time frame, enhance students' experiences as they begin to develop their own leadership potential. Meeting student needs can be facilitated by encouraging different interests and by being flexible. The Elders' storywork constitutes responsible, respectful, and relevant research, by and for Indigenous researchers. It contributes to a deeper understanding of the social, cultural, and spiritual dimensions of Indigenous holism, Indigenous leadership theory, and practice at the local level. The persistence of systemic inequalities in societal attitudes, beliefs, and actions, however, demands broader educational approaches that make transformative antiracism and action strategies a priority. The core components of an Indigenous leadership program outlined here, when delivered within such a framework, will help foster leaders who understand that leadership is both a gift and a responsibility, leaders who will step forward and empower the people to reclaim cultural values through the investigation of local, living genealogies and oral histories. The end result will be the transformation of our communities.

Works Cited

Archibald, Jo-ann. 2008. *Indigenous Storywork: Educating the Heart, Mind, Body, and Spirit.* Vancouver: UBC Press.

Cajete, Gregory. 1994. *Look to the Mountain: An Ecology of Indigenous Education.* Durango: Colorado Kivaki Press.

Dergousoff, Debbie. 2008. "Ethnobotany, Institutional Ethnography and the Knowledge of Ruling Relations." *Canadian Journal of Native Education* 31, 1: 162.

Graveline, Jean. 2002. "Teaching Tradition Teaches Us." *Canadian Journal of Native Education* 26, 1: 11-29.

Marsden, Dawn. 2005. "Indigenous Wholistic Theory for Health: Enhancing Traditional-Based Indigenous Health Services in Vancouver." PhD diss., University of British Columbia.

Young, Alannah E. 2006. "Elders' Teachings on Indigenous Leadership: Leadership Is a Gift." Master's thesis, University of British Columbia.

Young, Alannah E., and Denise Nadeau. 2005. "Decolonizing the Body: Restoring Sacred Vitality." *Atlantis: A Women's Studies Journal* 29, 2: 13-22.

4

Parental Involvement in First Nations Communities

Towards a Paradigm Shift

Evelyn Steinhauer

In Mankato, Minnesota, I walked down the stairs to a little con-
venience store. I stood in the aisle hesitating over the choice of
soups when an old man confronted me, "Do you have time?" I
looked at him ... "Yes, I have time." "Wait here," he said, and
walked away ... He came up the aisle with a large cardboard box.
It seemed empty and I was puzzled until he thrust it forward,
holding it in front of my face ... His question came from behind
the box. "How many sides do you see?" "One," I said. He pulled
the box towards his chest and turned it so one corner faced me.
"Now how many do you see?" "Now I see three sides." He stepped
back and extended the box, one corner towards him and one
towards me. "You and I together can see six sides of this box," he
told me. Standing on the earth with an old white man, I began to
understand. (Hampton 1995, 41-42)

I BEGIN WITH THIS story because I think it is a good reminder that things
are not always what we believe them to be. We believe them to be what we
think they are because we have consulted with a wide variety of sources,
and these various sources – media reports, governmental studies, and
scholarly papers – have convinced us that this is in fact the truth. For instance, these sources have told us that Aboriginal parents "lack interest
in their children's education and fail to engender in them an appreciation
of its value" (Mackay and Myles 1995, 166); therefore, this is what we
believe. We have come to believe that Aboriginal parents simply do not
care about their children. Have we not? We have probably all heard comments such as "They never show up," "They are so unreliable," "Those
people just don't care." Am I right?

In this chapter, I will argue otherwise. In fact, I will go so far as to say that most Aboriginal parents care about their children, and like any other parents in Canada, they want their children to graduate from high school and become self-sufficient adults. And many of them are involved in the education of their children. They may not be physically present in the school, but they are actively involved; they are simply not involved in the traditional way that school administrators and educators have come to see as signs of parental involvement.

To demonstrate this involvement, I use data from interviews I conducted to investigate parental school choice in First Nations communities. Every participant addressed the issue of parental involvement in great detail. They recognized that all aspects of schooling are interconnected, and because they knew this, they gifted me with much valuable information about parental involvement. It is their words that I share.

About the Participants

The participants in this study were all First Nations who lived on-reserve (Saddle Lake Cree Nation and Goodfish Lake First Nation) at the time of the study, in 2005-06. In total, I interviewed nineteen people – fifteen parents and four youths.

The following sections present our voices – my voice and the voices of the participants – as we "trouble" the issue of parental involvement. A great deal of literature exists on parental involvement, and I decided that the most effective way to discuss this literature was within the text, in direct connection with the voices of the participants. I thus use the literature to show that the experiences and issues presented in this chapter are not individual in nature or limited to a particular First Nation but rather represent patterns of experiences for many Aboriginal parents in Canada.

Why Did I Want to Write about Parental Involvement?

Research does not support the widely held assumption that Native families do not have the same goals for their children's education that non-Native families do (Abele, Dittburner, and Graham 2000; Auger 2006; Kavanagh 2002; Makokis 2000; Steinhauer 2008). "Like their parents and grandparents, today's parents want their children to succeed" (Castellano, Davis, and Lahache 2000, 253); they want their children to graduate from high school and become self-supporting individuals. Statements such as these are often troubling for those whose only frame of reference for Native people is what media reports have fed them. Because "stereotyping has long been a feature of media coverage of Aboriginal people in Canada, it is not surprising" when people shake their heads in disbelief (Harding 2005, 312). From these stereotypical responses, it is obvious that much of what Native people do and do not do is judged against what the mainstream considers the "proper way." "All cultures operate with this myopia, it seems, not even suspecting that others have developed very different rules" (Ross 2006, 5).

I am often called upon by the Faculty of Education at the university where I am employed to make presentations to various undergraduate and graduate student groups, and I commonly hear comments such as "I am having a hard time believing what you just told us. If Aboriginal parents do care about their children, why then are they not involved in their children's education? Why is it that there is still a huge disparity in graduation rates?"

These questions never come as a surprise to me; in fact, I expect them. But, as much as I expect them, I don't like them because they cast doubt on the ability of Native people to successfully manage their children's lives and schooling experiences. Furthermore, I don't like them because they exhaust me. The following journal entry, which I wrote after a recent presentation that I gave on Native education, provides a better picture of what I mean when I say they exhaust me:

I can't believe I just did that! I walked away today without answering those dreaded questions. I don't know what possessed me to do that, but I did. I love talking about Native education but I dread the question period, not all of it, but the part where someone in the crowd feels obliged to challenge me. This time the "condescending questions" didn't come until the end. Everything was going so well, and then she shouted in a tone I have come to hate, "*If First Nations parents do in fact care about their children, then why aren't they involved at the schools? Why do their children miss so much school? I have yet to see a Native parent attend parent-teacher nights! I am having a hard time believing that they do care.*" It doesn't matter how many times I hear these comments, the result is always the same. I feel as though I have just been punched in the stomach; but I can't stay with the pain, I must defend my people! Why, why must I always have to qualify our existence? What is it about us that you don't like? Well today, I did something that I have never done before. I walked away from the question. I didn't mean to, it just happened. When the questions came, I couldn't respond. I opened my mouth, but the words didn't come.

Why did I walk away from the mike without responding to her? Was it because my spirit and my heart couldn't take this "crap" anymore or was it that my mind simply was too tired – tired of qualifying and defending my "Indianness"? I need to think about this. What can I do to better prepare myself to respond to these kinds of questions?

I don't know how many people can relate to this story, but I suspect that many Native people might have at least a small inkling of what I mean when I say "I am tired of qualifying my Indianness." It is a sad reality that so many of us continue to have to do this every day of our lives. I wonder how different this world would be if we all understood that everything we see and hear is interpreted through our own culture lens. Rupert Ross (2006, 4) suggests that until we do so, we "will never be able to see or hear things in any other way." Like the old man in Eber Hampton's story, I invite you to pick up the box and take a look at it from different angles. With open minds and open hearts we will collectively discover the different ways that Aboriginal parents are involved in their children's education.

Defining Parental Involvement

Most Aboriginal parents want their children to graduate from high school and become self-supporting individuals. As Halee, a parent participant, stated, "Although all of my children didn't graduate, [that] doesn't mean that this wasn't what I wanted for them. I wanted them to finish school so they could go out on their own and be completely self-sufficient" (interview with Halee, 1 May 2006, Saddle Lake Cree Nation). Every parent in this study wanted the same, and Pamela asserted, "I want to raise independent children" (interview with Pamela, 13 February 2006, Goodfish Lake First Nation).

Despite low graduation rates, it is my belief that most Aboriginal people value education. All of the contributors in this volume make mention of this in one way or another. In fact, many share stories about how their own parents wanted them to succeed or how, as parents, they too want the best for their children and other youth in their communities. "My mother ... had visions for me," shares Tina Fraser. "My mother's vision was [for me] to succeed academically, which required me to attend school" (see Chapter 7, this volume). Michelle Jacobs's story (see Chapter 12, this volume) is not much different: "I was taught by family members and tribal leaders about the importance of rising to one's potential to make the best contribution possible to our people as a collective." Getting a good education was important to her family and, equally, to her community. This is un-mistakably evident in her story:

When I was a child, tribal youth who had good attendance or good grades were honoured each year by tribal leaders. The leaders paid for a special field trip to our tribal headquarters. A ceremony and meal honoured our achieve-ments. Family and community members beamed with pride as they helped to honour the next generation of Native leaders. At each of these special occasions, tribal leaders reminded us that our work as students was a reflec-tion on our tribal nation. We had a responsibility to do our best work so that our people would be represented in a good way, to reach our potential as students and, ultimately, to become leaders within our community.

But what is parental involvement? All of the participants in this study agreed that it was important for Aboriginal parents to be involved in their children's education, but what they did not agree on was the definition of parental involvement. As one parent (Halee) put it, "What the heck is parental involvement, anyway" (interview with Halee, 1 May 2006, Saddle Lake Cree Nation)? Some parents' definitions or understandings of par-ental involvement were similar to the definition offered by Carol Ascher (1988, 109):

Parental involvement may easily mean quite different things to people. It can mean advocacy: parents sitting on councils and committees, participating in the decisions and operations of schools. It can mean parents serving as class-room aides, accompanying a class on an outing, or assisting teachers in a variety of other ways, either as volunteers or for wages. It can also conjure up images of teachers sending home notes to parents, or of parents working on bake sales and other projects that bring some much-needed support. In-creasingly, parent involvement means parents initiating learning activities at home to improve their children's performance in school: reading to them, helping them with homework, playing educational games, discussing current events, and so on.

Others assigned a definition similar to that proposed by Tracy Friedel (1999, 139): parental involvement is about "teaching their children values, priorities, and how to make sense of things."

In the interviews, some parents defined involvement as participation in formal ways, such as on parent advisory committees, fundraising committees, and sports committees. Others referred to more informal activities at home such as reading to their children or ensuring that they do their homework or practise spelling words. Still others defined involvement as providing nurturance; ensuring that children are fed, bathed, and well rested; and instilling cultural values. It appears, then, that parental involvement can be defined much as Ascher (1988) describes it, as the diverse activities, either at home or at school, that permit parents to share in their children's educational process.

In their research, Ron Mackay and Lawrence Myles (1995) found that educators often have a narrow definition of parental involvement and, as a result, are quick to conclude that Native parents are not interested in the education of their children:

> One indicator that educators use to judge parental interest is the extent to which parents participate in parent/teacher nights organized by the school. By and large, it was reported that Native parents do not attend these meetings. Both Native and non-Native educators recognized that many parents are uncomfortable coming to school ... Many educators used the presence or absence of parental support to explain a student's decision to remain at or drop out of school ... Such an apparently cogent explanation can enormously comfort educators because it placed responsibility for a student's behavior firmly with the parents and released the school system from blame and remedial action. (Ibid., 168)

Nadine explained: "I know that teachers think we are not interested in our children's education if we don't show up for parent-teacher interviews, but they are wrong. I don't go to these any more because, as far as I am concerned, they are just a waste of time" (interview with Nadine, 13 February 2006, Goodfish Lake First Nation). When I asked her to elaborate, she complained that all that the interviews did was made her feel inadequate. In her view, the interviews were all one-sided, especially during a year when her children were having some academic difficulties: "It was like the difficulty that my children were having was all my fault." There was pain in her voice as she spoke about these interviews. It was clear in her case that when the interview became more about her, the parent, and everything that she was doing wrong as a parent, it was easier to stay away.

Halee stated, "You do your best as a parent, but they don't see that. Instead, they tell you everything that you are doing is wrong" (interview with Halee, 1 May 2006, Saddle Lake Cree Nation). Although she continued to attend the parent interviews, she admitted that she hated going because it meant hearing about all the things that she was not doing right: "It just bugs me when they [teachers] tell me, 'Well, you should be helping your children with their homework. You should read to them.' When the heck do I have time to read to them? What the heck do they think I am doing all day – nothing?" Even prior to Halee's formal interview, I sensed that this was a hot topic for her, so, in the recorded interview, I asked her about it:

> *Interviewer:* So you really do have a problem with that phrase *parental involvement*, don't you?
>
> *Parent:* Yeah, because of the way it is interpreted – with the teachers' interpretation. They need to be educated about what parental involvement is, and that's to provide a stable, nurturing home for the kids while *you* teach them! I hate it when they try to put a guilt trip on me, and they say, "Well, how much of this did you do, and how much of that did you do?" when you go for the parent-teacher interviews. Or you will get a report once in a while. Once in a great while they will ask you to work more with the student in this area or that area. I hate it when it reflects on you as a parent. It is not your job. Your job is already there for you.

I decided to include this portion of the interview because it reveals Halee's frustration clearly. Although the inflections in her voice cannot be heard, the resentment is apparent in her words.

Halee agreed with Nadine's assessment: "I don't know if it is their training, but teachers present themselves as almighty!" Both of these parents were very much aware that teachers had prejudged them, and they resented it. Mackay and Myles (1995) concur that parents are often prejudged, and the judgments are based on direct conversations between educators and Aboriginal parents in very few cases. They found that prejudgment occurred even when "the vast majority of teachers ... never visited the reserves, and few had personal conversations with the parents of their Aboriginal students" (ibid., 166).

I agree with the participants in this study. Parents are involved in their children's schooling.

I used to tell people that my mother was not involved in my schooling because she never attended the parent-teacher interviews, never came to school events, never asked me what I was learning in school, never went through my books to see whether I had actually completed my homework, and never looked at my report card when she signed it. It was only recently that I began to appreciate how much she had been involved in other ways. She provided my siblings and me with the stability that we needed. She was there when we left for school in the morning and when we got off the bus in the afternoon. We always came home to a spotless house, our clothes neatly washed and ironed, and full-course meals complete with fresh bread awaited us daily. She was there to guide us. She told us when to get up, when to go to bed, and when to do our homework. We had a stable home in which she taught us the basics of hard work and the values of love, caring, sharing, honesty, and determination. Today, I realize that this was parental involvement at its best. She had a Grade 7 education and knew little about modern schools. She went to school in a one-room schoolhouse, where all the children from Grades 1 through 7 shared the same teacher. My mother did not attend parent-teacher interviews because she did not feel that there was a place for her there.

Although the parents in this study were noticeably more involved than most Aboriginal parents – in other words, many of them attended parent-teacher nights and participated in many of the activities mentioned by Ascher (1988) – most of them described their parental in-school involvement as being limited in much the same way that mine had been. Halee explained:

> Our home was as stable as it could be ... We always had food, and we were given a lot of responsibility on our parts, but my mother never once went to the school. My mother believed that her job was to take care of our basic needs, while it was the school's responsibility to take care of our academic needs. I believe this, at least to a certain extent ...
>
> That's why I told that one teacher, "Okay, you come to my place and do some of my work for me, and I will do some of your work for you," because it is their job. They went to school for that, and they are being paid to teach your kids. It just bugs me when they told me, "Well, you should be helping your child with their homework. You should read to them," when they were younger. (Interview with Halee, 1 May 2006, Saddle Lake Cree Nation)

"Even though the teachers think parents are not involved, that they don't care, I know they care. They care and support their children in many different ways," Veronica said when she shared her views (interview with Veronica, 8 February 2006, Goodfish Lake First Nation). Pamela added, "Parents buy books for their kids from the Scholastic book club. They are encouraging them to read. This alone should prove their involvement" (interview with Pamela, 13 February 2006, Goodfish Lake First Nation). Although most educators do not usually consider these actions involvement, Veronica disagreed. She shared a story about her mother's involvement in her learning:

> My mom, though she wasn't educated – she only had a Grade 8 education – saw the importance of education ... I used to just love to read. I used to just pick up and read a novel, and I would pick real interesting and exciting ones, and I would read. I would say, "Oh, this is a good story," and then my mom would say [in Cree], "Well, tell me about it." And you know what? I would have to tell the story in Cree to her. I didn't speak English because we just spoke to her in Cree all the time ... I must have really had to comprehend the story in order to relay the story in Cree to Mom, and she would just make me read. I would end at the exciting part because I knew that maybe I could get away from work a little bit if she made me read on. So, I would read to the exciting part, up to where I knew she would want me to read some more. [In Cree she would say,] "Go and read some more so you could come back and tell me more!" I think I used that a few times. *[laughs]* My mom didn't know it, but she helped me with reading and comprehending, even though, when I look back now, that was a big task to try and translate what I read, because I really had to have a good understanding of what I was reading. My mom helped me a lot, and I don't think she knew that.

Florence perceived parental involvement as occurring along a spectrum: "I think involvement can be described in different ways, and there might even be a spectrum of involvement from a person who hasn't even opened a report card to a person who is there practically every day checking up on their kids. So, there are different ranges and kinds of involvement" (interview with Florence, 26 June 2006, Saddle Lake Cree Nation).

The participants' comments reveal a variety of views and activities related to parental involvement in their children's schooling. The following quotations show some of the different ways they described involvement:

> I help them with their homework, and if there are issues, I phone the school ... I am more aware ... Kids need structure, and I grew up with structure, so my kids have that too. It's homework time, and that's when they do homework; and when it is bedtime, they go to bed. (Interview with Marleen, 23 September 2005, Saddle Lake Cree Nation)

I used to do lot of volunteer work with the school because I am on the Parent Advisory Committee. That is where I sit, too. They are always into sports, too, so I help out with the school program. I do volunteer work, like work bingos and stuff like that. (Interview with Louise, 24 October 2005, Saddle Lake Cree Nation)

Others also explained their involvement:

I think it helps the child when they know they have supportive parents ... and that includes being [involved] with their after-school activities, with their sports. (Interview with Dakota, 26 September 2005, Saddle Lake Cree Nation)

I do everything I can to help her get along in this world that much better. Fundraising for hockey – that's all I did all year. Drive her to practice, drive her here, and drive her there. (Interview with Alexis, April 20, 2006, Goodfish Lake First Nation)

It starts at home, like ... getting him involved in the Cree language, listening to music, taking him to events or ceremonies, just exposing him to that. (Interview with Bernice, 13 February 2006, Saddle Lake Cree Nation)

Challenges to Parental Involvement

"While almost all parents want to contribute to their children's positive experiences in school, levels of satisfaction with parental involvement are not yet perceived as adequate" by formal educators (Kavanagh 2002, 12). Most teachers believe that Native parents are not doing enough for their children, and they often misinterpret this perceived lack of involvement as a lack of caring (Friedel 1999; Mackay and Myles 1995; Silver et al. 2002). However, my interviews revealed that parents do care very much about their children's education. As Morton Inger (1992, 1) suggests: "Many school administrators and teachers misread the reserve, the non-confrontational manners and the non-involvement of ... parents to mean that they are uncaring about their children's education – and this misperception has led to a cycle of mutual mistrust and suspicion between ... parents and school personnel."

The participants in this study contended that parents do not go to the schools, even reserve schools, because they are uncomfortable. They feel intimidated by school personnel, especially if principals or teachers use a condescending tone when speaking to the parents. "I can see that intimidation might be a contributing factor, especially with our principal. He is very intimidating," one parent reported. Another participant agreed and explained that she had, in fact, taken it upon herself to talk to the principal:

> I said to him, "You are not listening to the people."
>
> "I listen and I give them time to talk," he said.
>
> "No," I said. "While they are talking, you are interrupting them. I heard the parents. You need to really, really start practising effective listening, where you really listen to what they are saying, what they are feeling. Just listen. Don't say a word and just hear them out. Once they finish, then you can speak, but don't try and interrupt them as they are talking because they get really angry. They don't want to be interrupted. They want their voices heard, too. And the other thing, don't smile like what they are saying is funny." I know he does that, because he does that to me, too. It is like he is laughing at someone. I said, "You know what? You make people feel, hey, he is laughing at me." And I said, "You can't do that."
>
> He will do that to me, and then he will explain, "I'm not laughing at you. I am thinking about this." And then he will repeat what he is thinking of right at that very minute.
>
> And I said, "I have no problem [with your] doing that to me, because you will explain it to me, and I will stop, and you will have to explain it to me. But don't do that with my people. You can't, because you make them feel like they are not valued, like the statements they are making are just not important and you are just laughing at them. That is what they feel. Don't do that to them."
>
> He said, "Okay." (Interview with Veronica, 8 February 2006, Goodfish Lake First Nation)

Not all parents will take the direct approach when speaking with authority figures. Most parents will let things go unchallenged for diverse reasons. "Parents will react to the paternalistic attitude of teachers or administrators in two ways. They will do nothing, or they will overreact by yelling and screaming," George suggested (interview with George, 20 April 2006, Goodfish Lake First Nation). Another participant had witnessed this latter extreme in his school and described it as "over-involvement," sometimes as a result of the frustration that parents feel at not being heard or listened to. If overreaction and a display of anger occur, the schools view the parents as too aggressive. I knew what George meant when he said that parents "will overreact by yelling and screaming," because, as a parent, I have reacted to the school principal in a similar manner on more than one occasion, as my journal entries reveal:

March 16, 2003

[Daughter's name] always seems to be in trouble this year. I don't know what it is, but I dread having to go and talk to [the principal] again. I hate going to see him, because he frustrates me. He patronizes me and makes me feel inferior. When I go in there, I immediately regress. I am just a dumb Indian again. My power is sucked out of me immediately. I know when I go in there again, he is going to get to me.

March 17, 2003

Well, as expected, our meeting escalated to yelling again. He doesn't listen to me. When he says something, I automatically get defensive. He is so condescending. I walked in there today thinking I was going to try my best to be calm, but his voice just irritates me. I can't stand his "I am the authority" voice.

Today when I walked into his office, I tried to be conscious of how and when this happens. I realized our discussions turn bad almost immediately. He starts off by telling me what he has to tell me, and I give him my opinion. He doesn't like to hear my opinion. He thinks I am trying to defend [my daughter], but I am not. I am only trying to get him to see something from my point of view. I am trying to tell him why I think these two girls are fighting. But he doesn't want to hear it, so he begins to elevate his voice, trying to prove to me that his theory is right. I elevate my voice. Next thing you know, we are screaming at each other. We are not hearing each other. I can't take this any more. I think I am just going to leave things from now on; I'm not going to go to the school any more.

Reflecting on these journal entries helped me to put things into perspective. When parents such as Nadine say, "I hate going to the school because I always walk out feeling inadequate," I can understand fully. However, as a researcher and an educator, I have to continuously question and critically assess the source of these feelings of inadequacy, which seem to consume us as First Nations people. I believe that we have allowed ourselves to be consumed by such feelings because we have unconsciously internalized the distorted images of racism. Even though we know better, we have internalized the stereotypical and racially derived image of "the

Indian" that permeates Canadian society. We see ourselves as inadequate and inferior because the society in which we are immersed perpetuates that image in multiple and continuous ways. Our response to those feelings of inferiority, which we know are not true, is aggression or silence. Paulo Freire (2001, 56) suggests that when this happens, we are suffering from the "duality which has established itself in [our] innermost being." We want to be free, but we cannot let go. When we react with aggression, we are trying to take on the role of oppressor, but we cannot fully succeed because this is not our way. Freire (ibid., 48) explains this phenomenon: "They are at one and the same time themselves and the oppressor whose consciousness they have internalized. The conflict lies in the choice between being wholly themselves or being divided; between ejecting the oppressor within or not ejecting them ... between speaking out or being silent, castrated in their power to create and re-create, in their power to transform the world. This is the tragic dilemma of the oppressed."

We have been oppressed since birth, and we have had few, if any, opportunities to understand, articulate, own, and release these learned feelings of inadequacy. In our adult minds, we know the truth, and we understand the sources of these feelings. However, the opportunities are few for most of us to address these feelings of inadequacy, and we therefore watch as our children and our grandchildren enter the same cycle, often with the school providing the initiation fire.

When I hear parents talking about their feelings of inadequacy in dealing with authority figures in schools, I see again how a lack of power contributes to their anger and defensiveness. As parents and as Indians, we accept responsibility for our children's education and, ultimately, their survival. But throughout our histories we have lived without any power or authority to act on that responsibility. Our power to act on our own behalf as peoples and societies has been and is continually being stripped away from us. This is an undeniable Indigenous reality in Canada.

Some parents were reluctant to become more involved in their children's education for numerous reasons, particularly when it involved going into the schools. In addition to experiencing feelings of intimidation and guilt, the participants suggested that parents do not engage with schools in the formal education of their children because their expectations of how the school will show them respect and offer them space as parents differ from those of the school. Their personal educational attainment levels are not considered, and this lack of consideration is obvious in the manner in which school personnel relate to them. Their own past experiences with schooling were negative and personally debilitating. Social and familial issues and needs can inhibit or determine their involvement.

Parental versus School Expectations

Parental involvement is commonly cited in the literature and in government-sponsored studies and reviews as a huge concern for public schools. "But in all honesty, do they really want us to be involved?" Alexis asked (interview with Alexis, 20 April 2006, Goodfish Lake First Nation). She wondered about this, because whenever she volunteered to assist the teacher in the classroom, she was always turned down or relegated to menial tasks. She would be told, "Oh, Mrs. so-and-so is volunteering this month. How would you like to come and assist us when the children go skating? You can help tie skate laces." Another parent had a similar response from school staff when she offered to assist in art classes. Instead of being invited to participate, she was asked to make playdough, a job that could be done at home. These parents interpreted the responses that they had received as "You are not capable of assisting in the classroom because you're not bright enough, but you can tie shoes because even a child can do that." This paternalistic attitude from school personnel was enough to deter these parents from ever offering to assist or being involved at school again.

Public schools often begin the school year by inviting Native parents to sit on the Parent Advisory Committee. Some parents go to the first few meetings, but their attendance drops off quickly because they cannot find a place for themselves at these meetings. The parents reported feeling uncomfortable and silenced, and a few referred to themselves as "token." Pamela shared her own experience of attending these meetings:

I went to a couple of PAC meetings. They had called me and invited me, so I thought, here is an opportunity. I did go, but you know, I felt uncomfortable. They didn't acknowledge me, and they didn't even connect me with my child, other than the one parent who knew me ... and she was the one who invited me and wanted me to be a part of it. But you know what? They went yakking away. They talked, and I just sat back and listened. They didn't ask me about my opinions, and I thought, what is the sense of coming back to another meeting? ... Even if they would have said, "Who is your child, here?" They must have just thought, who is this woman? But you know what? They will never understand that [parents do not feel welcome]. They will never understand that ... it is a waste of time. I have always said that: What for? They still think, bottom line, we are still spit on the ground. (Interview with Pamela, 13 February 2006, Goodfish Lake First Nation)

Educational Attainment Levels

Schools expect parents to help their children with their homework, but some parents find that they cannot because of their own lack of education. They become ashamed and try desperately to hide the secret from others. They will avoid situations in which the truth might be revealed (Friedel 1999; Makokis 2000; Morrisseau 1998). "I think that is why my parents weren't involved," Alexis suggested, because "my mom only had Grade 6, and I think my dad was higher than her, but not much more" (interview with Alexis, 20 April 2006, Goodfish Lake Cree Nation). Another participant acknowledged that this might have been why her parents were never involved either: "My mother and father had very low education, maybe Grade 7, so they could not really help us with our homework. I used to think that they didn't care, but now I know that I was wrong to even think that. Even if they wanted to help, they wouldn't have known how. This is probably why they never went to the school as well. They probably knew they would be asked questions which they wouldn't know how to respond to, so instead they just avoided it" (ibid., 129). Morton Inger (1992) suggests that many schools have unconsciously erected barriers for parents, even through the correspondence that they send home with the children. In some cases, parents cannot comprehend a letter that their children have brought home because of the level of the language used. Educators make the mistake of assuming that everyone reads at their level.

I asked my mother one day if she had ever attended a parent-teacher interview, and she told me, "I did once with your aunty, and the teacher kept asking me questions and telling me things about you guys that I didn't understand, so I didn't go again." She told me that she was not smart enough to attend these interviews and concluded, "You and Ronnie didn't need me there. You were smart enough" (personal communication with Nancy Steinhauer, 22 March 2006, Saddle Lake Cree Nation). How many other Native parents feel that they are not smart enough and conclude that they have no role to play in the school? Barbara Kavanagh (2002) and Jim Silver and colleagues (2002) suggest that there are endless numbers. Like our parents, we have turned the racism inward, and we continue to perpetuate the belief that Native parents do not care about their children's education. This is unfortunate because "our children will inherit the future we teach" (Calliou 1995, 71).

Negative Schooling Experiences and Parental Involvement

Parents who had stressful schooling experiences of their own "may be reluctant to interact with their children's school ... For example, some First Nations parents, and Elders in particular, have a negative view of schools and formal education systems as a result of residential schools" (Kavanagh 2002, 13). As can be seen in the quotations below, several of the participants attributed the lack of parental participation to the intergenerational effects of residential schools:

> My mom never stepped into our school. I had talked to her about that, because even when it came time to register, we would have to register ourselves. She wouldn't come to the school to register us, whereas I always went to the school with my son. She said that ... well, back then there was a lot of alcohol abuse and drug abuse and lots of violence going on, so that was one of the reasons. The other reason my mom said was because, with the way she grew up, parents weren't allowed to be involved because of her residential school upbringing. Her parents weren't involved in any of her schooling. They just came to the school for how many minutes they were allowed to visit in a little tiny room at residential school, and that was it. (Interview with Suzanne, 27 October 2005, Saddle Lake Cree Nation)

"Why can't you people just move on with your lives and quit blaming residential schools for their incompetence?" a non-Native person asked me one day. I gasped. Taken off guard by that remark, I did not even know how to respond. Later, as I was reflecting on this question, I thought, I wish it was as easy as this woman suggested. If people grow up with constant pain, with feelings of powerlessness, apathy, sadness, anxiety, and anger, how are they supposed to turn that off, especially when they cannot fully comprehend where the pain comes from? That would be my question to her today: Show us how to do it, and we'll do just that. The problem is that most non-Native educators are ignorant about residential schools, and it is unfortunate, because without knowing our history, teachers will continue to "convey the attitude that under-involved families do not care about education and have little to contribute when they do participate" (Kavanagh 2002, 13).

Most of the discussion on challenges to parental involvement centred on the topic of residential schools, but the parents also recognized that their own schooling experience had had a significant impact on whether they were involved in in-school activities such as volunteering or sitting on parent advisory committees, or even whether they attended parent-teacher interviews. My cousin once told me that he let his wife take care of that because "she is white." I understood what he was saying, especially after hearing his heart-wrenching story. I cried as he told me the story, and I asked him whether I could use it in my work. He gave me permission, but because I have only my notes to rely on, his story is not verbatim. This story might answer why some parents choose not to become involved:

> When I was in Grade 1, my teacher called me a dirty Indian. I didn't know what she meant by that, so in a casual conversation with my mother that evening I said, "Mom, what is a dirty Indian?"
>
> She asked why I wanted to know, and I responded, "My teacher called me that." She started to cry, and next thing I knew, I was in the big metal washtub, and my mom was scrubbing me with soap and a scrub brush.
>
> Tears were streaming down her face, and she kept repeating, "No one is going to call my boy a dirty Indian! No one is going to call my boy a dirty Indian!" She scrubbed and scrubbed, and she continued to cry. She was crying really hard, and I remember I started crying too. I can't remember if I was crying because the brush hurt or because my mom was in pain.
>
> When I look back now, I think I was probably crying for my mom. She appeared to be in so much pain.

Painful memories such as this prevent many parents from becoming involved in the education of their children, at least if it means that they have to go to the school. I was not surprised when I read through the interview transcripts to find that everyone could recall numerous negative experiences that affected how they viewed formal schooling.

Logistical Reasons

An extensive review of the literature reveals that Aboriginal parents are not involved for the reasons mentioned above, but most of the literature overlooks what I refer to as the logistical reasons that hinder parents' participation in their children's schooling – reasons that are connected to financial and other resources that are visibly absent from most Aboriginal communities.

During a discussion with a school counsellor, she revealed that many families struggle financially and that the school understands why many parents do not attend parent-teacher nights at reserve schools: because they are barely surviving. This reality is evident in the following comment:

A lot of kids depend on our hot lunch program here. They eat because they get breakfast and lunch. I know for a fact that when the after-school program happens at the Boys and Girls Club, they go and eat there, because on the weekends, I don't know what they eat ... Oh, yeah, it is just meeting the basic needs of food, shelter, and some don't even have this. Some don't even have shelter. They move from here to there to here. So it is, "Where are you now? Is it safe?" I do my best in helping and in resources, and there are times I leave school [and just] cry. (Interview with Marleen, 23 September 2005, Saddle Lake Cree Nation)

The reasons for low parental involvement in Aboriginal communities are multiple and interconnected, and they are tied in complex ways to the institutions and practices of Canadian society. The reasons identified by participants are only a few of many, but their words are embedded with interconnections that need to be studied further. Yet I keep in my mind the words of a community member who recently said to me, "Learning what can be done to increase parental involvement is even more important than dwelling on why they don't come."

Conclusion

The data presented here reveal that parents have many concerns about their involvement in their children's education. Most parents would like to be more involved in the in-school portion but do not know how to accomplish this, especially when they do not feel welcome in the environment. Not feeling welcome was a common thread throughout the interviews. Comments such as "You know that your presence there is not really needed or wanted," "I went to a couple of PAC meetings ... I did go, but, you know, I felt uncomfortable," "Oh, Mrs. so-and-so is volunteering ... However, you could come and assist us when the children go skating. You can tie skate laces," and "He doesn't listen to me" are good examples of the source of these feelings. As Leona Okakok (2008, 280) states, "Parents will become more involved when they learn that their knowledge ... is valued." None of the parents in this study ever mentioned feeling valued or appreciated; instead, they spoke more about feeling inadequate.

If administrators and educators are going to realize the goal of more Aboriginal parental involvement in schools, then they may need to consider that their perspectives and definitions of parental involvement are not necessarily the same as those held by Aboriginal parents. They must also recognize that difference does not necessarily mean that one perspective is right and the other is wrong. Rather than pinpointing all the things that Aboriginal parents are doing wrong, time might be better spent on building relationships and discussing all the things that everyone is doing right. If this happens, perhaps the common misunderstandings that often interrupt home-school involvement will turn into more fruitful discussions about "missed understandings."

Works Cited

Abele, Frances, Carolyn Dittburner, and Katherine Graham. 2000. "Towards a Shared Understanding in the Policy Discussions about Aboriginal Education." In *Aboriginal Education: Fulfilling the Promise,* edited by Marlene Brant Castellano, Lynne Davis, and Louise Lahache, 3-4. Vancouver: UBC Press.

Ascher, Carol. 1988. *Improving the School-Home Connection for Low-Income Urban Parents.* New York: ERIC Clearinghouse on Urban Education.

Auger, Shawn T. 2006. "Visions of Aboriginal Education." Master's thesis, University of Alberta.

Calliou, Sherilyn. 1995. "Peacekeeping Actions at Home: A Medicine Wheel Model from a Peacekeeping Pedagogy." In *First Nations Education in Canada: The Circle Unfolds,* edited by Marie Battiste and Jean Barman, 47-72. Vancouver: UBC Press.

Castellano, Marlene Brant, Lynne Davis, and Louise Lahache. 2000. "Conclusion: Fulfilling the Promise." In *Aboriginal Education: Fulfilling the Promise,* edited by Marlene Brant Castellano, Lynne Davis, and Louise Lahache, 251-55. Vancouver: UBC Press.

Freire, Paulo. 2001. *Pedagogy of the Oppressed: 30th Anniversary Edition.* New York: Continuum International.

Friedel, Tracy. 1999. "The Role of Aboriginal Parents in Public Education: Barriers to Change in an Urban Setting." *Canadian Journal of Native Education* 23, 2: 139-58.

Hampton, Eber. 1995. "Towards a Redefinition of American Indian/Native Alaskan." *Canadian Journal of Native Education* 20, 2: 261-309.

Harding, Robert. 2005. "The Media, Aboriginal People and Common Sense." *Canadian Journal of Native Studies* 25, 1: 311-35.

Inger, Morton. 1992. *Increasing the School Involvement in Home Literacy.* New York: ERIC Clearinghouse on Urban Education.

Kavanagh, Barbara. 2002. "The Role of Parental and Community Involvement in the Success of First Nations Learners: A Review of the Literature." Policy paper presented to the Minister of Indian and Northern Development, Ottawa.

Mackay, Ron, and Lawrence Myles. 1995. "A Major Challenge for the Education System: Aboriginal Retention and Dropout." In *First Nations Education in Canada: The Circle Unfolds,* edited by Marie Battiste and Jean Barman, 157-78. Vancouver: UBC Press.

Makokis, Patricia. 2000. "An Insider's Perspective: The Dropout Challenge for Canada's First Nations." PhD diss., University of San Diego.

Morrisseau, Calvin. 1998. *Into the Daylight: A Wholistic Approach to Healing.* Toronto: University of Toronto Press.

Okakok, Leona. 2008. "Serving the Purpose of Education." In *Indigenous Knowledge and Education: Sites of Struggle, Strength, and Survivance,* edited by M. Villegas, S.R. Neugebauer, and K. Venegas, 268-86. Cambridge, MA: Harvard Education Review.

Ross, Rupert. 2006. *Dancing with a Ghost: Exploring Aboriginal Reality.* Toronto: Penguin Canada, 2006.

Silver, Jim, Kathy Mallett, Janice Greene, and Freeman Simard. 2002. *Aboriginal Education in Winnipeg Inner-City High Schools.* Winnipeg: Canadian Centre for Policy Alternatives.

Steinhauer, Evelyn. 2008. *Parental School Choice in First Nations Communities: Is There Really a Choice?* Saarbrucken, Germany: VDM Verlag.

5
Skilay, Portrait of a Haida Artist and Leader

Carolyn Kenny (Nangx'aadasa'iid)

FIGURE 5.1   Ernie Collison (Skilay), 1948-2001

IF YOU ASKED ERNIE COLLISON (Skilay) what he was, he would probably say "a politician." But it was not that simple. In Old Massett, Haida Gwaii, as in most Native communities, being a politician is complex. Ernie was a Haida first and foremost, but also a father, grandpa (and thus a baby-sitter), community organizer, artist, fisherman, cook, negotiator, administrator, activist, master of ceremonies, carpenter, tailor, singer, drummer, dancer, designer, clown, and anything else the community needed him to be. To me, he was a treasured friend and also my adopted brother.

I met Ernie in 1997. Verna Kirkness had organized a trip to New Zealand for thirty-five First Nations people from Canada. We would visit the Māori people and study their language and other cultural revitalization initiatives. We travelled for three weeks by bus, visiting Māori immersion schools, staying in *mārae* (communal or sacred places), and making new friends. I made several fast friends on that trip. In our traveling group, there were four Haida – Dorothy Bell, Gertie White, Danny Matthews, and Ernie Collison.

One day when we were leaving a mārae in a remote territory, a Māori leader took Ernie and me aside. He invited us to join him on a special tour outside of the planned tour. We spent an entire day with our special guide, Anaru Kira. He took us into one of the Māori forests to show us healing plants, told us many sacred stories about Māori history and protocols, and treated us to a special lunch. At the end of the day, he said, "Do you want to know why I chose you out of the thirty-five people in the tour?" "Of course," we said. "Well, you are the only brother and sister pair on the tour." From that day on, we knew.

When a cohort of Haida and non-Haida who lived on Haida Gwaii graduated with their master's of education degrees from Simon Fraser University, Ernie served as the master of ceremonies and singer for their graduation dinner in Massett. As a professor of First Nations education at Simon Fraser University, I had been the supervisor of this cohort. Ernie worked with me to make a special occasion for these students. And when I decided to create a research project in Massett to study the role of the arts in the revitalization of Haida culture, Ernie was one of the twenty-five people I interviewed in the Old Massett community. He shared a tremendous amount of traditional knowledge with me at that time, as well as telling me a lot about his own life and his own experiences with arts and culture.

Artists, as dreamers, are often pushed to the edge of societies. This is not the case in Haida society. Ernie's experiences show that the Haida place artists in the centre of society. Artists are considered esteemed creators in the preservation and revitalization of culture. Their dreams are essential guides to the way society should function. And, certainly, the arts, along with the Haida language, have played a critical role in the revitalization of Haida culture.

The process of becoming and being an artist was a core discipline in Ernie's own development as a leader and as a reflective man who took on the challenges of life as an opportunity to develop himself and his nation more fully. Ernie emphasized the importance of learning the basics, the foundations of arts expression, practice, and performance. One strives for the perfection demonstrated in the Haida arts. "Once you learn a song, you can then compose new songs. All things are linked together. This creates a cultural stream of consciousness in your life, and it reaches a point where you don't really think about it as culture – you live it," Ernie said. He emphasized the importance of always bringing new things into the culture, often through the youth, but also through integrating elements from Western society. "In order to keep the culture strong, you've got to bring new things into it all the time," he said.

In this chapter, I draw primarily from my discussion with Ernie Collison in January 1999 because his statements paint a comprehensive portrait of his art and leadership.[1] His story reveals the integration of art and leadership at all levels. He also describes the complexity involved in being an artist-leader. There are no silos in the way Ernie functions as an artist-leader. He is an artist here, politician there, and community organizer over there, in some other place. Ernie teaches us about caring in the Haida way. He also teaches us about learning and adaptability and what it means to keep ourselves in accord with our cultural heritage.

Ernie Collison was born in 1948. He lived in Massett until he was thirteen years old, then he was sent off to residential school. When he was sixteen, he moved to Skidegate, British Columbia. After that, he lived in logging camps. He returned to Massett in the 1970s but then moved back to the city (Vancouver). When he returned to Massett in the 1980s, he spent a great deal of time with Haida people who were working on Haida cultural revitalization. During our discussion, he described how the culture had been kept alive over the years: "Our culture was kept alive by the generation in my great-grandmother's time of life. When she was young, they still had a lot of canoes and longhouses around, and they all spoke fluent Haida – the old-fashioned Haida they call it. They did everything the old way. The culture consisted of just about every discipline that you see in most civilizations anywhere in the world. There were rules and doctors and people that had all other sorts of talents, and you found these throughout our society."

Ernie said that his great-grandmother was a lifelong weaver who did things in the old-fashioned way. She didn't use forms. She started all pieces, hats and baskets of spruce wood, on a disk of wood and finished them free-hand. He described his great-grandfather Charlie Thompson as a composer: "He did a song that was interpreted that says, 'My heart's really broken because my aunties are here to dress somebody from my family again.' If you only read that without knowing what the background was, you wouldn't realize that it is a mourning song. When someone's aunties are dressing a family member, it means they are preparing them for a funeral. Someone has passed away, and that's why his heart's been broken." A great deal of Haida art reflects events, and one has to know how to read a song or a totem pole, just like any piece of art. Totem poles, like songs, tell beautifully rendered stories; they describe an entire event from the perspective of the household where the totem pole stands. In our discussion, Ernie associated spirituality with Haida arts and culture:

> I should speak of our culture because it is unique to us. It is ancient and where everything originates. All components of our culture are important, language being the main way that culture is maintained. We speak, sing, paint, carve, draw, and connect to the land, water, and spirituality. All elements are represented in various ways. I don't believe there is a word in our language for art, but it seems to have taken a very long time to evolve into what it is – a very disciplined process comprised of various elements that have to be configured so that they contain and exude "Haida." The art has to be fluid. Very similarly, our songs are fluid.

In fact, Skilay mentioned spirituality quite often: "The arts are Haida arts whether they are visual, songs, oral histories, dances, or anything. They all basically come from our spirituality in which everything is looked at in the links to the land and the sea. Every part of the environment that we live in has a spiritual quality to it."

Haida Gwaii is a special place. When I go there, I feel it. Gentle sea waves lap against a shore strewn with driftwood and broken shells. I walk on a beach beside five or six eagles, who share the territory. Often, there is a cool mist dancing into the neighbourhood from the sea. Rainforests call from within. Spirit abounds. In most houses, members of the community work on arts of some kind – baskets, button blankets, carvings, and jewellery. Being an artist is a way of life on Haida Gwaii. It is a Haida way of being.

Ernie addressed this intimate connection between art and life:

> Excelling at the artwork means that you do things with your personal life, too. Like, you can open up your own perception of the world, and the world opens up to you, too. You get good at it, stay disciplined and stay focused and think about how the world works and how you work within it and how the economy works, and you can find yourself marketing your work very well. You are not marketing just your work. To a degree, you market yourself a bit, too. And in order to do that, you have to know about our history, culture, oral tradition, stories, and some of the facts about the islands and where people live and lived.

So Haida arts are relational. They tell the stories of the nation. They are created for special events. They are made for people. Skilay observed:

> I do things for my relatives and friends – button blanket designs, vest designs, and any kind of two-dimensional design that I can draw on paper. I haven't started painting yet, but I am certainly going to. I made a commitment to the repatriation committee[2] that I'd paint some designs on bentwood boxes that are being made for the burial of human remains being brought home from museums. I don't often think about it consciously. But I know instinctively that art represents a real visual representation, in my case, of my family. We have crests, and then, if I'm doing something for somebody from another family, from another clan, that has a different crest. But I think about them in the same way.

Ernie told me he had created a lot of designs for Lucille Bell's wedding, and, in each case, he considered the qualities of the person when he made the design. One was proud and elegant like a frog. One was young like a little baby eagle. While he imagined his designs, he reflected on the lives of the people he was creating for. He said: "I guess, when you're thinking about those things, it influences the way the pencil moves on the paper."

The last time I saw Ernie, he showed me the design he was drawing for my Haida blanket after Naanii Dorothy had decided to adopt me.[3] He was making a beautiful skate – a fish that moves swiftly through the waters surrounding Haida Gwaii. On that day, he also gave me ten cans of salmon to take home. He had caught the fish, smoked them, and canned them. He also showed me some of the carpentry he had done in his house. These were all things that Ernie did in addition to his job as the administrator for the Council of Haida Nations – a role with many hats. A good leader knows how to work up front and behind the scenes. And Ernie did both ever so well.

As a music therapist, I was particularly taken with Ernie's descriptions of Haida songs and the process of learning them:

When I started learning songs, I was kind of bashful about it at first, but I went out and did stuff in camps, and Guujaaw was there, and he imposed songs into my life around the camp first.[4] He taught me a lot about songs – how to sing, how to breathe, how to use the drum properly, how to find spirituality in the singing and drumming. I also watched videotapes and listened to records and audiotapes. And then what really came to light for me was the sense of strength that you can get from doing songs, especially if you're a group, and even if you're not singing. You feel the strength, and then you get this feeling of reassurance about the constant link between our ancestors and our young people. There's always kids around whenever we're doing songs. It doesn't matter where we are, what time of the day or night it is, there are always kids there. And I always look at the kids, and then I always look at the old people when I'm singing, and then there's a lot of times I can't see my eyes open when we're singing because I started to get emotional. And it's not like I'm just on the verge of crying or anything – but I start getting emotional, and I have to concentrate to be able to keep singing. So, I started learning how to sing because I thought if I started singing I'd be able to learn more about what evokes these emotions in me, to bring me to tears when I hear Haida songs. Songs seem to bring ceremony to a higher plane of consciousness, and it affects me such that it brings out emotions that normally don't appear. I enjoy singing, either by myself or in a group. I feel songs in me that may someday surface as a composition, songs that have a sense of purpose and reality.

Ernie had a lot to say about songs and singing. His words remind me so much of our visit to New Zealand and the Māori. As Tina Ngaroimata Fraser, a Māori scholar, writes in Chapter 7 of this volume,

In Kapa haka, the focus of tutoring and performing is having a greater understanding of Māori historical knowledge and recognizing the need for it to be passed down in order for future generations to survive ... Through performance, people are taught to understand, live, and experience historical knowledge. Motivation to perform haka can be acquired through spiritual connections to the ancestors, the land, and to one another. We call upon them for guidance and protection ... To sing of the past is to remember those that were part of it. When we sing of our mountains, we remember all those who were connected to or associated with them – birds, trees, and ancestors. There is much learning contained within Kapa haka, and learning through Kapa haka extends to the audience as well. A Kapa haka tutor explained to me that when he sings, he tries to sing to people's spirits. He understands that not everyone can speak or understand Māori, but all of them can feel.

Song is such an important aspect of life for the Māori people. So often, the members of our travelling group were moved to tears when sixty or more children at the immersion schools greeted us – all singing in perfect unison. They sang in their own language. And even though we could not understand a word of the Māori language, we felt the spirit and strength of these children. At one point, I asked a Māori Elder why the arts were everywhere in the schools – songs, carvings, sculptures, and paintings hung all over the walls of the classroom, and every aspect of the curriculum was infused with arts production. She responded: "The arts provide the aesthetic and spiritual environment for the raising of healthy children."[5] At that moment, I had a desire to bring my own grandchildren into the Māori schools.

Ernie continued to talk about the songs in our interview:

I've felt songs of mourning, of celebration, of closure, of social commentary, of spirituality, and of good old fun. Songs are important. They bring genera-tions together. They bring us, as a people from other villages, together. Songs give us a common feeling of strength and power. A person can learn a lot about another from sharing a song. Our songs in common vary a lot in tempo and relationships in life. Drums have a life in the songs that generate emo-tions and evoke spirituality and [the] meaning of life that we honour with artworks and prayer. I love songs and doing them. I think everybody has music in them, and when people learn one song in Haida – you get thirsty to learn more.

We found that, as Haida, we had many things in common with the Māori. Our myths and stories were similar. As coastal peoples, our nations had travelled the vast seas for commerce, trade, exploration, and migration. We are both "canoe" cultures, and we share similar cultural protocols. We had to wonder if there had not been significant exchanges between our cultures long ago. Many of our cultural arts and practices were so similar. We visited an arts centre in Rotorua and observed the ancient art of the tattoo. During our discussion, the Big Eagle and I reminisced about this visit to the arts centre because tattooing had also been a Haida art form in the old days. "In the old days, when anyone was going to build a new house, the head of the clan would have a big potlatch, and they would name all the kids that were coming of age and announce all the ones who had already come of age, and they would get tattoos. We had them on the chest, forearms, and thighs. And they were done in the same way (as the Māori), with a little hammer and chisel, and then the pigments were put into the little cut marks."

Ernie mentioned "being young" or "the young people" quite a bit. Indeed, the system of apprenticeship in Haida culture is fully functional in formal and informal ways. Ernie provided an example of how this works: "Carvers open their doors up to young people, and if anybody wants to learn, they can pick up a piece of the same material right beside the artist. And they'll say, 'Okay, try to carve like this.' Then they soon discover that you have to learn the fundamentals of the art form itself first before you can carve. And then, once you learn that, you can learn it as you go."

Whenever I visit Haida Gwaii, I see carvers opening up their doors to young people. Apprentices, the children of the carvers, and other children play in carving areas. I see this as classic intergenerational education. The apprentices have a formal relationship with carvers, but the children are always in the carving area, taking in the experience of carving, smelling the shaved wood, playing with designs, making things out of the shorn fragments, and hearing the carvers' instructions in their peripheral consciousness. These gatherings combine formal and informal processes in the village and prepare the younger ones for their eventual interest in carving. Yvonne McLeod and other contributors in this volume likewise note the importance of the intergenerational transmission of knowledge to building strong communities.

In Haida culture, carving is integrated with other art forms. The carvings are part of the dancing and singing. Ernie stated: "So, the importance of it to young people is a high standard – to have high-quality pieces that people carve, paint, draw, weave, sing, or speak about. I want it to be looked at as a piece made by a guy who was so proud that everything that he made, he made it just like it was going to be the last thing that he made." He continued, emphasizing the importance of the transmission of arts expression to young people:

> So, when we talk about the importance of how it is for our youth – we see a lot of the young people. When we have a death here, the young people come forward and participate in honourable ways and also sing Haida songs. They step forward and take the responsibility of being Haida very seriously at times of celebration and at times of mourning, to ease people through, because there's a lot of comfort in hearing our songs when people are mourning. And it is as equally important then as it is when we're celebrating a birth of a new baby, or somebody graduating, or somebody getting married.

Ernie returned over and over again to the importance of singing. And he was a great singer. I saw him perform on many occasions. Towards the end of our interview, I asked him to say a bit more about singing:

> Again, it goes back to when I was a kid and used to hear my great-grandmother sing to us kids. She did the same thing to all of us as babies, I guess. There's an age when you can pick a kid up and sing a bouncy song to them, and the kid starts dancing. She used to sing Haida songs to us like that. And I saw that with all my younger siblings. She sang a song to me when I was about fourteen, and I asked her about it. It was about when the road was put through between Massett and Port Clements. She said our uncle composed a song to commemorate that event, and the song said: "We're so happy we could go and see our relatives again, but go carefully." And what that meant is "don't take anything for granted about driving a car because there are car accidents, and they knew about that." She sang that song to me, and I never learned it.

I've travelled that road many times myself. Once, I rode with Ernie. Several times, Lucille picked me up at the ferry dock and drove me to Massett on it. I also drove the hour-and-a-half stretch between Massett and Skidegate when I rented cars. But there was one special time when I drove Auntie Gertie's car to a memorial feast. I wrote a story about it. In my story, I describe my road trip with Auntie Gertie and Naanii Dorothy, my mother, and how we returned to Massett at three in the morning, driving along that road. Here's the beginning: "The road to Skidegate is dangerous at the best of times. It looks easy. But it's not, even in the light. It twists and turns and undulates. Pockets of wind push and pull us this way and

FIGURE 5.2   Eagle design by T'aakeit G'aayaa (Corey Bulpitt). Ernie was in the Eagle Clan, and we often called him "Big Eagle" in English.

that. Storms come. Then there's sometimes the flooding to maneuver. Little Brother Ernie flies on that road. But then, of course, he's driven it for many years. He goes along talking a mile a minute while his car soars like the wind itself."[6] Since I wrote that piece in 2002, I have thought about Ernie's comment: "All things are linked together. This creates a cultural stream of consciousness in your life, and it reaches a point where you don't really think about it as culture – you live it."

Notes
1 This chapter is written using the research method called portraiture, a qualitative research method articulated by Sara Lawrence Lightfoot and Jessica Hoffmann Davis in *The Art and Science of Portraiture* (San Francisco: Jossey-Bass Publishers, 1997). They write:

> Portraiture is a method of qualitative research that blurs the boundaries of aesthetics and empiricism in an effort to capture the complexity, dynamics, and subtlety of human experience and organizational life. Portraitists seek to record and interpret the perspectives and experiences of the people they are studying, documenting their voices and their visions – their authority, knowledge, and wisdom. The drawing of the portrait is placed in social and cultural context and shaped through dialogue between the portraitist and the subject, each one

negotiating the discourse and shaping the evolving image. The relationship between the two is rich with meaning and resonance and becomes the arena for navigating the empirical, aesthetic, and ethical dimensions of authentic and compelling narrative.

2 Since 1994, the Haida have worked tirelessly to recover ancestral remains and Haida arts that have dwelled in museums around the world for many years. They place the ancestral remains in beautifully carved bentwood boxes and bury them with honour in their home in Haida Gwaii. Over the last eight years, the Haida Repatriation Committee has formalized the process of reclaiming Haida ancestral remains and valuable art objects. For further information see: http://www.virtualmuseum.ca/ Exhibitions/Inuit_Haida/haida/english/repatriation/index.html.

3 Naanii subsequently designed the blanket herself and created a design with two hummingbirds facing each other. The hummingbird is our family crest. Vincent Collison and Lucille Bell then began making my blanket under Naanii's strict supervision. "Two hummingbirds," she insisted. "Two hummingbirds facing each other like this," she motioned.

4 Guujaaw has been the president of the Haida Nation for the last ten years. But long before that he was involved in extraordinary initiatives to revitalize Haida traditions. Like Skilay, Guujaaw is another example of stunning Haida leadership in action and with a focus on the arts. To hear Guujaaw sing and play his drum is to feel the presence of hundreds of years of Haida ancestors flow through your blood and into every bone in your body. He is often called the "Heartbeat of the Haida Nation."

5 See Carolyn Kenny, "The Sense of Art: A First Nations View," *Canadian Journal of Native Education* 22, 1 (1998): 77-85.

6 See Carolyn Bereznak Kenny (Nang Jaada Sa-ĕts), "Blue Wolf Says Goodbye for the Last Time," *American Behavioral Scientist* 45, 8 (2002): 1214.

PART 2

Collaboration Is the Key

6

Indigenous Grandmas
and the Social Justice Movement

Raquel D. Gutiérrez

As I WAS TAUGHT to do, I begin by telling my story. My interest in the cultural transformation of social justice leadership is grounded in my own life experience as a third-generation social justice worker. Having come from a family that emphasizes knowing your history, knowing on whose shoulders you are standing, I recognize the importance of learning how to make meaning out of one's own actions in the present so that they will hold value for those who follow. This is classic seventh-generation thinking.[1] This foundation for forming self-knowledge is a key factor in my ability to understand my role and place in history and in relationship to the discourse of leadership and social justice work.

My parents gave my sisters and me a beautiful gift by creating a solid cultural foundation that cultivated a sense of knowing who we are. This foundation has allowed me to explore different ways of understanding the world without feeling as if I will be compromised as a cultural being. More importantly, this gift has allowed me to see the commonalities and differences in our human experience without judgment and with a more open heart. Like my ancestors, I experience the world through multiple paradigms that require me to shift seamlessly between the gifts of leadership passed on from generation to generation. These gifts include an eagle eye, the ability to move from a micro to macro perspective with ease; seventh-generation thinking, a multigenerational framework for making decisions; and a Pachamama heart, the know-how to consider the physical and metaphorical ecosystem when making choices and determining action. This awareness allows me to recognize that my life experience fundamentally shapes the questions I ask as a scholar, my interpretation of the answers, and what I deem valuable for the field of leadership studies and those working for inclusive and sustainable social justice.

Personal Motivation: Born into Activism

If you look into your hand, you will see the lines of the legacy from which you came. When cupped, my hand is marked with deep crevices that mimic the Cañón del Cobre in Mexico, the place where my Tarahumara great-grandfather was born. The Tarahumara are a tribe of runners that I resemble, not in my plump legs but in my resilient spirit. The softer, subtler lines on my hand look like the tributaries that run into this great canyon. They are endless and melt into my skin the same way my Spanish great-grandmother melted into the life of my great-grandfather. My great-grandparents' opposing cultures symbolically represent the tension between the story of leadership I was born into and the story of leadership I am trying to create.

The story of my vocation begins before I was born, with my parents' choice to be leaders who work for a belief, not people who work for a job. They held the belief that everyone has a right to dignity, respect, and equality with those in power, regardless of race, socioeconomic standing, country of origin, or legal status. This belief was so strong it pervaded every aspect of their lives and the lives of those who extend from them.

The story of my vocation also exists in a context that extends beyond me, my family, or one group of people. My passion for strengthening the lifetime efforts of leaders working for inclusive and sustainable social justice is grounded in the Chicano movement, which emerged during a time in history when the fear to speak publicly and to live as a cultural being was challenged. It was an era when speaking up as a cultural being defied those in power and challenged them to see our humanity and the inequities in our relationship with them. Three values came to the forefront as necessary requirements to transform fear into courage: knowledge of self, self-sacrifice, and nonviolence. My belief is that these values are still present in activist culture and, out of dire need, are in the process of being reinterpreted. This reinterpretation will maintain their essence while transforming them into different forms of individual and organizational practice than exist at present. My understanding, vision, and experience of leadership do not reside solely in these three values, but they certainly shaped my contribution to the field of leadership and change, and they have been a driving force in my interest in the transformation of the culture of social justice work.

As the fourth and final child of Raquel and Gustavo Gutiérrez (see Figure 6.1), I was born at the onset of the United Farm Workers movement, when the southerner Fannie Lou Hammer's cry of "I am sick and tired

FIGURE 6.1   Raquel and Gustavo Gutiérrez in 1972 at the state capital in Phoenix, Arizona. *The Gutiérrez family collection.*

of being sick and tired" echoed the feelings of those women and men across the nation who were involved, either directly or indirectly, in upholding the human rights of documented and undocumented migrant farm labourers. My mother was the main breadwinner in our home. She had a successful career as a registered nurse, maintained a house with four children, supported my grandmother in tending to my ailing grandfather, and managed to find time to pursue her own interests, such as gardening, herbal medicine, sewing, crocheting, and reading. Her conscious effort to pursue knowledge and activities outside of direct activism is what makes her opinions (and she has many) valuable and insightful contributions to emerging social justice leaders. My mother intrinsically understands that creating a better and more just society – one with healthy, resilient families who can cultivate their gifts for the world – cannot happen through activism alone. To create this society, we will need to negotiate the complexities of living right every day.

My father's contributions to social justice work would not have been possible without the support of my mother. To this day, she provides him and other social justice workers with a perspective grounded in the right action of placing family first. She understands that this worldview-in-action demonstrates what social justice work strives to accomplish. Her ability to move between her insider and outsider view of movement work has had a tremendous impact on how I approach my work as a practitioner and a scholar. Her contribution to social justice work continues to be supporting her husband and her daughters in their varied approaches to social transformation by reminding us what the work is really about.

In 1965, my father, a Grade 6 graduate and veteran of the Korean War, initiated our family into the growing social justice movement. He left his job as a cook at a hospital at the Tohono O'odham Nation and began working for the Migrant Opportunity Program, an initiative to organize migrant farm workers. One year later, my family met César Chávez, cofounder of the United Farm Workers (UFW),[2] opening up a relationship that, in 1968, would result in my father's resignation from the Migrant Opportunity Program and in his becoming the central leader of the Arizona branch of the UFW, the Arizona Farm Workers Organizing Committee (Rosales 1997).

The Arizona Farm Workers Organizing Committee formed in 1968 in the wake of the UFW's success winning basic human rights for documented and undocumented workers in California (Rosales 1997). At the national level, decision making and alliances were shaped by a palpable tension among competing grassroots approaches – militant, nationalistic, and pacifist – to organizing. Chávez was influenced by Gandhi's writings on leadership based in the values of nonviolence and self-sacrifice (Ferriss and Sandoval 1997). The ideas of nonviolent action and self-sacrifice helped lay the foundation for Chávez's leadership of the United Farm Workers movement and are a large part of his leadership legacy in activist culture. Chavez's beliefs have influenced the wider activist culture, giving legitimacy to a number of different issues. My father, influenced by Chavez's interpretation of Gandhi's values and other readings on leadership, social justice, politics, and education (e.g., John Gardner, Paulo Freire, and John Steinbeck) incorporated these ideas into his own leadership approach to *la causa* (the cause).

In 2006, my parents celebrated their fiftieth wedding anniversary, a rare accomplishment for any couple, let alone one that has managed five decades of social justice activism. My parents served as role models of the ideals of a movement that generated creative tension between the values of nonviolence and self-sacrifice and attention to familial responsibilities. They helped shape how I developed my leadership philosophy as a professional and an academic.

The Professional Implications of My Personal Experience

Over the last twenty-five years, my work has evolved into a vocation, into a commitment to strengthening the lifetime efforts of leaders working for inclusive and sustainable social change. My choice to move in this direction was deeply rooted in the personal. As a third-generation activist, I have been surrounded my whole life by people working for social justice. They fostered a culture that leads to behaviours, attitudes, and systems that impose physical, mental, spiritual, and emotional costs on activists and those around them. I know activist colleagues who suffer from posttraumatic stress disorder, clinical depression, suicidal tendencies, and other health issues related to the demands of the model of social justice work to which they are committed. In some cases, their exhaustion had been the downfall of their organizations; in others, it has severely diminished their organizational capacity (Kofodimos 1993; Hormann 2007). The negative toll on the people who surround these leaders inspired me and others to transform the culture and practices of social justice work.

In order to transform one's own way of being, let alone that of an organization or a whole social movement culture, one must have clear leadership intentions, intentions that strengthen and sustain their commitment. The death of two people, one who I knew personally and one who I met only twice, was a turning point for me and many of my colleagues in the social justice network. Like so many others, the work of these two leaders had been shaped by the historical discourse of social justice work, by a history rich in detail about the sacrifices necessary to foster progress in human and civil rights. The highly acclaimed documentary *Eyes on the Prize* (1999), for instance, details how, during the civil rights movement, people of all ages demonstrated their commitment to the movement by jeopardizing their livelihoods, education, and physical well-being (Hampton 1999). Stories about collective songs, prayers, marches, sit-downs, and other nonviolent actions ending in mass arrests were popular forms of motivation.

The new generation of activists openly discusses the negative effects of high levels of stress placed on individuals, families, and whole communities engaged in social justice work. People now understand that many aspects of social justice work, as defined in the past, are no longer sufficient and do not contribute to sustainable or shared leadership. These intentional conversations are reversing the tendency to romanticize social justice work and reflect a deeper commitment to understanding the role of spirituality in sustainable leadership practices. These conversations are transforming how emerging generations of activists are "schooled" in realizing social justice.

The Next Step in My Journey: The Thirteen Grandmothers

In December 2009, my mother, father, and I travelled over a dusty washboard road on our way to see the International Council of Thirteen Indigenous Grandmothers.[3] My father had been asked to speak about the Peace and Dignity Journeys to the gathering.[4] As we made our way slowly down the road, the red rocks of Sedona reached into the clear blue sky of an Arizona winter day. Fine red powder from the road floated in the air like prayer smoke.

It was nice to be with my mom and dad without other people around. My best memories of my parents are of being with them by myself, and we have to be fully attentive to one other. In many ways, it is the same person-to-person connection that I imagine people hope for when they come to see the grandmothers, that moment when they are gifted with the experience of being completely present with a grandmother across from them. Being completely present with another person while surrounded my hundreds of people milling around and wanting your attention is something the grandmothers are masterful at doing. When they talk to you, *they really talk to you.* You are called to be deeply and fully present with them. I grew up around people who are able to create moments of connection that have a lasting impact on others. I have learned

FIGURE 6.2 The council members at Mago Retreat Center, December 2009. *Courtesy of Linda Rettinger.*

to recognize the privilege and sacredness of witnessing or being a part of that "connection" in the instant it happens.

The International Council of Thirteen Indigenous Grandmothers is a circle of women who came together in October 2004 in Phoenicia, New York, to realize a prophecy that exists in many Indigenous communities around the world. The host for the event was a woman named Jyoti who had learned that she and other women had had a series of visions of grandmothers from different parts of the world coming together to pray (Schaefer 2006). The grandmothers who were invited did not know one another. They travelled with the inner knowledge that something profound, beautiful, and predestined was going to happen. During the first gathering, several events confirmed that the prophecy was being fulfilled. Yupik grandmother Rita Pitka Blumenstein's eyes filled with tears as she introduced herself on the first day of the gathering. She handed out thirteen stones and thirteen eagle feathers to each of the grandmothers.

Her great-grandmother had bestowed the sacred objects on her at the age of nine and instructed her to hold on to them until she could give them to the women of the council (ibid.). Sharing these sacred items is an excellent demonstration of aesthetic leadership, a style of leadership concerned with sensory knowledge and the felt meanings associated with leadership phenomena (Hansen, Ropo, and Sauer 2007).

Since the first gathering, a large community of supporters has formed into a nonprofit organization to support the work of the council and the projects of each grandmother. As stated on their website, the organization's mission is as follows:

> We, the International Council of Thirteen Indigenous Grandmothers, represent a global alliance of prayer, education, and healing for our mother earth, all her inhabitants, all the children, and for the next seven generations to come. We are deeply concerned with the unprecedented destruction of our mother earth and the destruction of Indigenous ways of life. We believe the teachings of our ancestors will light our way through an uncertain future. We look to further our vision through the realization of projects that protect our diverse cultures: lands, medicines, language, and ceremonial ways of prayer and through projects that educate and nurture our children.

The Council's Purpose and the Indigenous Research Agenda

It is difficult to describe the full purpose of the council. In an interview in January 2010, one of the grandmothers, Mona Polacca, stated that "Our No. 1 priority is promoting peace and good relationships with everyone in the world" (Rico 2010, 63). Their official statement reads as follows:

> We are thirteen Indigenous Grandmothers who came together for the first time from October 11 through October 17, 2004, in Phoenicia, New York. We gathered from the four directions in the land of the people of the Iroquois Confederacy. We come here from the Amazon rainforest, the Alaskan Tundra of North America, the great forest of the American northwest, the vast plains of North America, the highlands of central America, the Black Hills of South Dakota, the mountains of Oaxaca, the desert of the American southwest, the mountains of Tibet and from the rainforest of Central Africa.
>
> Affirming our relations with traditional medicine peoples and communities throughout the world, we have been brought together by a common vision to form a new global alliance. We are the International Council of Thirteen

Indigenous Grandmothers. We have united as one. Ours is an alliance of prayer, education, and healing for our Mother Earth, all Her inhabitants, all the children, and for the next seven generations to come.

We, the International Council of Thirteen Indigenous Grandmothers, believe that our ancestral ways of prayer, peacemaking, and healing are vitally needed today. We come together to nurture, educate, and train our children. We come together to uphold the practice of our ceremonies and affirm the right to use our plant medicines free of legal restriction. We come together to protect the lands where our peoples live and upon which our cultures depend, to safeguard the collective heritage of traditional medicines, and to defend the earth Herself. We believe that the teachings of our ancestors will light our way through an uncertain future.

We join with all those who honor the Creator, and with all who work and pray for our children, for world peace, and for the healing of our Mother Earth. For all our relations.

The self-efficacy that the grandmothers demonstrate in defining their purpose as an organized group, and abiding by it, is a tremendous example of self-determination, the core concept that forms the Indigenous research agenda. In the seminal work *Decolonizing Methodologies: Research and Indigenous Peoples* (1999), scholar and activist Linda Tuhiwai Smith argues that when Indigenous communities create their own research agendas, they determine what needs to be known by those outside their communities. They declare the meaning and value of their lives and culture rather than allowing others to define them. Through their active participation, Indigenous scholars are encouraging communities to inquire into and interpret their own lives in a way that will influence decision-making by external power holders. In addition, Tuhiwai Smith notes the difference between Western research terminology, which strives to present the appearance of neutrality and objectivity, and the Indigenous research agenda, which uses social science research methodologies that reflect and purposefully carry social and political implications. This historical discourse is evoked through the words *healing, decolonization, transformation,* and *mobilization* and the meanings they have for Indigenous peoples. This approach to the social sciences can lead to what Native scholar Alannah Young Leon calls reanimation (see Chapter 3). To animate is to bring somebody or something to life or to arouse someone or something into action or motion. Reanimation is an incredibly powerful concept when it is applied to leadership development and social transformation. It encapsulates resiliency and self-efficacy, the story of Indigenous peoples, and the essence of the grandmothers' council.

The council and the respective actions of each grandmother have the power to effect the resolution of social justice issues because they have the capacity to influence power holders and leverage resources and knowledge. They make a concerted effort at each council to highlight a social justice issue in addition to the council's core message of healing Mother Earth and her inhabitants. For example, at the gathering in Sedona, the grandmothers shared information about water issues around the globe. Presenters offered detailed information about cultural sustainability and social justice issues associated with water rights in the American Southwest. The grandmothers' poignant stories about the significance of water to their spiritual and traditional Indigenous cultures raised the level of consciousness among the participants about the role and use of water in their own lives.

The grandmothers clearly understand that elevating one's consciousness means little if it is not followed by action. Through stories of their own life experiences, the grandmothers inspired participants to consider how they might change their own behaviour and educate others to bring about more socially just uses for water. More importantly, as a participant, I did not feel like I had been preached to or coerced into changing my way of thinking about the subject. What I did feel was time pausing as the grandmothers told their stories, the rise of consciousness among those who sat around me, and a deeper awareness about my own relationship to water. The grandmothers demonstrated transformational leadership in action. They engaged with their followers in such a way that both their followers and themselves, the leaders, moved to a higher level of motivation and morality (Burns 1978).

In 2009, the story of the grandmothers, their founding, and their gatherings became the subject of a widely distributed feature-length documentary directed by Carole Hart (Hart 2009).[5] The film explains why the grandmothers share their Indigenous wisdom with the masses, Indigenous and non-Indigenous alike: "The time is now ... thirteen indigenous grandmothers from all four directions heard these works in prophecy and came together. They were told their Mother was in agony and that they must come forward now to help us to heal her ... and all her inhabitants. They were told nothing will change, unless we change all of us." In *Grandmothers Counsel the World* (Schaefer 2006, 206), Lakota grandmother Rita Long

Visitor Holy Dance interprets the signs in a different way: "One night when there was no moon and just the stars ... I prayed to see the Creator, and when I saw Him, he wasn't Lakota, He was universal."

When I was at the council's gathering in Sedona, I was surprised to be in the company of so many non-Indigenous people. Honestly, I felt disappointed. On some level, I am skeptical about non-Indigenous people participating in such powerful ceremonies. In my lifetime, I have observed non-Indigenous people using their experience of Indigenous ceremony as evidence to prove that they are qualified to create a similar space and experience for others, often under the guise of spiritual and leadership development. The most infamous example is that of international self-help leadership guru James Arthur Ray, who in 2009 conducted a sweat lodge ceremony in which several people died (Ellerby 2009). In 2011, he was sentenced to two years in prison for three counts of negligent homicide. He embodies, at the extreme end, what can happen when misappropriated knowledge of Indigenous ceremonies is coupled with an overflowing ego, an attitude of superiority, and an entitlement ethos. The deaths in this case reveal the desperation of people to be healed in mind, body, and spirit.

On another level, because I was raised to understand that seeking out spiritual fulfilment is part of the human condition, I believe it is important to offer compassion to those seekers whose familial spiritual practices are no longer easily accessible. My family intimately understands that all peoples are connected through the cosmos and our Mother Earth. My parents, grandparents, and extended family taught me that the human experience transcends race, culture, and age. I was taught that we are bound together profoundly through spiritual experiences. Growing up, I was exposed to many types of spiritual traditions. I have rarely felt uncomfortable around spiritual traditions that are not my own. On the contrary, I thrive on recognizing the commonalities that exist between these traditions and my own. When I see, hear, or feel an intersection between spiritual traditions, a small, knowing smile comes to my face, and I feel as if I have been privy to a heavenly secret, something experienced by many but not the masses. Consequently, on some other level, the overwhelming attendance of non-Indigenous people at the council's Sedona gathering made perfect sense. It was not important because all of us have the potential to heal our Mother Earth, and, if people's actions are guided by a wisdom that comes from a tradition different from their own, then so be it.

This is why the question about who should or should not practise Indigenous spiritual practices (the question that lies at the heart of the issue of cultural misappropriation) quickly gets complicated for me. I am an individual who practises spiritual traditions that differ from those I followed when I was growing up. I feel completely all right in doing so because I know that I do not own or try to teach these traditions. I strive to continuously acknowledge and learn about the people and cultures from which these practices came. As a Mexican American brought up with an understanding of being an Indigenous woman, I also realize that, on some level, it would have been impossible for my parents to raise me solely according to Indigenous spirituality because colonization and the conversion to Christianity of Native people in the Americas are part of the legacy from which I come. I also feel compassion for people who were not given the right to practise or did not have access to their cultural and spiritual traditions. And finally, who am I to pass judgment on fellow seekers of spiritual development? I see that these conflicting thoughts can be reconciled by a higher knowing. When I feel myself resisting the idea that anyone can practise Indigenous spiritual traditions, that feeling is a cue to step back, breathe, centre myself, move into equanimity, and have faith that I will proceed with the right actions. This realization lies at the heart of my effort to transform the culture of social justice leadership.

A New Generation of Social Justice Leaders

My research and work as a practitioner in the field is informed by my passion for strengthening the lifetime efforts of leaders cultivating inclusive and sustainable social justice. My doctoral research explores the experiences of spiritual activists from around the United States who are at the forefront of transforming the culture of social justice leadership (Gutiérrez 2008). My work as a practitioner in the field of leadership development involves creating and facilitating spaces for people to share their lived wisdom with others to enrich their work. In 2005, years before I met the International Council of Thirteen Indigenous Grandmothers, I co-designed and co-facilitated a gathering of spiritual activists from across North America. Much like the gathering in Sedona, social justice leaders came together to share their spiritual practices and their insights as leaders. The gathering, titled "Spiritual Activism: Claiming the Power and Ideology of a Liberation Spirituality," was held during a typical muggy June in Garrison, New York. For three days, participants met on the grounds of an incredible Capuchin monastery now used for nonsectarian gatherings.

During this period, I was coming to a precipice in my lived experience, to a major transitional moment in my development as a woman and a leader. As an Indigenous being, I recognize that all moments are connected together and influence how we show up in the world. This interconnectedness naturally influences how we see, hear, and feel the moments that reveal our self-truths and capacity for growing, and it offers insight into how we can be in the future. The gathering was grounded in the four-directions model – an approach that connected and clarified the tensions between the local, regional, and global agendas of the spiritual activists in attendance while simultaneously determining the condition and state of being of their work.

More specifically, the purpose of the convention was to

gather for a weekend of practice, creative reflection, dialogue, and strategy ... to codify the principles, beliefs, and strategies behind our work. We are aware that our perspectives, practices, constituencies, and methodologies differ widely and that this diversity is the root of our strength. We seek a more profound understanding of our commonalities and our differences, and we are curious about what may be recognized as a collective ideology and vision. Is there a wisdom we can claim and share, a naming of the truths that we sometimes keep nameless? (Claudia Horwitz, personal communication to author, January 2005)

Claudia Horwitz and Jesse Maceo Vega-Frey, co-conveners of the gathering, discuss its purpose and results further in *Spiritual Activism and Liberation Spirituality: Pathways to Collective Liberation:*

The fruits of this gathering made clear that our work in spiritual activism and liberation spirituality is developing in maturity and sophistication as time goes on. While the field is varied and vast, we are beginning to *see* each other, and as a result, we are beginning to understand what we share: a commitment to spiritual life and practice; a framework of applied liberation; an orientation towards movement building; and a desire for fundamental change in the world based on equity and justice. (Horwitz and Maceo Vega-Frey 2006, 1)

We are moving towards a doing that grows more deliberately out of being; an understanding that freedom from external systems of oppression is dynamically related to liberation from our internal mechanisms of suffering. It provides us with a way to release the construct of "us versus them" and live into the web of relationship that links all. Instead of being limited by the reactions of fight or flight, we encounter a path that finds fullness in presence. The humility of not-knowing allows truth to appear where fear once trapped us. We recognize the pervasive beauty of paradox, the dynamic tension between two simultaneous truths that seem contradictory. We enlarge our capacity to hold contradictions and to be informed by them. And our movements for change are transformed as a result. (Ibid.)

On a personal level, I have come to realize that my state of being during the gathering was a mere microcosm of the higher work taking place. I learned to accept my own personal struggle with spirituality and how it affected my work. This acceptance has been liberating – my feelings of sadness and guilt about what I had brought into that moment and what I could have contributed had I been in a different state of being have now slowly evaporated away.

Since the gathering at Garrison, other researchers have been inspired to document the stories and knowledge of spiritual activists working for social justice. *Out of the Spiritual Closet: Organizers Transforming the Practice of Social Justice* (2010) by Kristen Zimmerman, Neelam Pathikonda, Brenda Salgado, and Taj James reflects the diversity of spiritual activists and their spiritual practices and documents the effects spiritual practices are having in social justice work. *The Activist's Ally: Contemplative Tools for Social Change* (2007), produced by the Center for Contemplative Minds in Society, comes with a CD that includes music and practice instructions. This book is an excellent resource for those activists who intrinsically feel that "something more" is needed to sustain their work but who are not quite sure where to start. Although it appeared before the Garrison gathering, a foundational piece for this type of inquiry is *The Spiritual Activists: Practices to Transform Your Life, Your Work, and Your World* (2002) by Claudia Horwitz. Horwitz's basic premise is that connecting to one's deepest truths is vital to the way spiritual activists approach, carry out, and sustain their work. Horwitz understands that the spiritual development of activists is necessary if spiritual activism as an approach to social change work is to mature. The stories in her work show us that we are like seasons: if we commit to enduring practices, we will be able to experience the subtleties of birth, growth, death, and rebirth and the suffering, joy, and grace that accompanies them. This delicious insight into the human experience ultimately connects us all.

These books have two important characteristics in common that are important to the field of leadership development and social justice activism. First, these works are accessible in tone, presentation, and phrasing. Although they offer tremendous value to those who study leadership development or social justice history, they also notify those who want to practise, and remind those who already do, that they will not be alone in their struggles. Second, each of these works, and others like them, is written by and for practitioners, for people who are not necessarily trained scholars, although some of them are. When I point out to my spiritual activist colleagues that they are already using social science methodologies in the way they contemplate and approach their work, they often respond with "Really?" or "What's that?" or "Why is that even important?" As a practitioner-scholar, I think it is essential that spiritual activists strengthen their capacity to tell their stories effectively. Framing their work within a formal method of inquiry provides a sense of legitimacy, which is demanded by many power brokers. Learning formal inquiry methods will help spiritual activists communicate the importance of the social transformations they hope to bring about. When these methods are used in formal inquiries and documented, they enhance knowledge about social justice work by presenting the perspectives of practitioners in the field. This work not only builds bridges between scholars and practitioners, it also contributes to the transformation of social science research methodologies in general.

Conclusion

This chapter tells the story of how the historical interpretation of social justice work is undergoing radical renovation, allowing a new paradigm for social change leadership to emerge. I show how this transformation has worked in my own life and work. The new approach seeks to create a resilient and just society through the cultivation of individual spiritual practice and insight, the intentional pursuit of self-transformation, and collective action. The International Council of Thirteen Indigenous Grandmothers is part of this transformational movement. The messages they bring to a diverse audience are rooted in healing our Mother Earth. They create spaces for people to learn about pressing social justice issues and inspire people to act from a higher level of consciousness. To other spiritual activists, the grandmothers are practitioners, not simply advocates of spiritual practices. They embody the essential relationship between spiritual concepts, spiritual practice, and personal and collective action for social justice.

As a practitioner-scholar, I am enthusiastic about seeing the grandmothers' council recognized as a vital player in the larger network of spiritual activism. The work of the grandmothers, like that of other spiritual activists, demonstrates that they are their own scholars. In this sense, they are mending the gap between practitioners and scholars and challenging old ways of thinking that devalue the practitioner experience. I hope that practitioners and scholars will increasingly work together to realize a just society.

Notes

1 Seventh-generation thinking, which comes from the Haudenosaunee, the people of the Iroquois Six Nations Confederacy. In its most basic form, seventh-generation thinking is a way of thinking and acting in the world that takes into consideration the effects on the future (see Clarkson, Morissette, and Régallet 1992).

2 Dolores C. Huerta is the other co-founder and first vice-president emerita of the United Farm Workers of America, AFL-CIO.

3 Because of commitments at the local level and health-related issues, it is not always possible for all the grandmothers to attend their biannual gatherings, as was the case in Sedona in 2009.

4 Peace and Dignity Journeys have been held since 1992. The spiritual run takes place every four years and is dedicated to a specific theme. The 2010 run, for instance, was dedicated to water. Runners begin in Alaska, United States, and Tierra del Fuego, Argentina, and meet in the umbilical cord of the Americas, Panama.

5 Previews of the film are available on the film's official website (http://www.forthenext7 generations.com/) and at YouTube (http://www.youtube.com/carolehart). The film is also available for purchase to share the wisdom of the grandmothers.

Works Cited

Burns, James McGregor. 2003. *Transforming Leadership*. New York: Harper and Row.

Center for Contemplative Mind in Society. 2007. *The Activist's Ally: Contemplative Tools for Social Change*. Northampton, MA: Center for Contemplative Mind in Society.

Clarkson, Linda, Vern Morissette, and Gabriel Régallet. 1992. *Our Responsibility to the Seventh Generation: Indigenous Peoples and Sustainable Development*. Winnipeg, MB: International Institute for Sustainable Development.

Ellerby, Jonathan. 2009. "Are Sweat Lodges Risky?" *Huffington Post*, 15 September. http://www.huffingtonpost.com/jonathan-ellerby/are-sweat-lodges-risky_b_322833. html#.

Ferriss, Susan, and Ricardo Sandoval. 1997. *The Fight in the Fields: César Chávez and the Farm Workers Movement*. Orlando, FL: Harcourt-Brace.

Gutiérrez, Raquel Dolores. 2008. "Life-Affirming Leadership: An Inquiry into the Culture of Social Justice." PhD diss., Antioch University.

Hampton, Henry, producer. 1999. *Eyes on the Prize: America's Civil Rights Years, 1954-1964.* VHS series. Blackside, Inc.

Hansen, Hans, Arja Ropo, and Erika Sauer. 2007. "Aesthetic Leadership." *Leadership Quarterly* 18, 6: 544-60.

Hart, Carole, director. 2009. *For the Next 7 Generations.* New York: Laughing Willow Company.

Hormann, Shana. 2007. "Organizational Trauma: A Phenomenological Study of Leaders in Traumatized Organizations." PhD diss., Antioch University.

Horwitz, Claudia. 2002. *The Spiritual Activist: Practices to Transform Your Life, Your Work, and Your World.* New York: Penguin.

Horwitz, Claudia, and Jesse Maceo Vega-Frey. 2006. *Spiritual Activism and Liberation Spirituality: Pathways to Collective Liberation.* Mebane, NC: Stone Circles.

Kofodimos, Joan. 1993. *Balancing Act: How Successful Managers Can Integrate Successful Careers and Fulfilling Personal Lives.* San Francisco, CA: Jossey-Bass Publishers.

Rico, Diana. 2010. "Grannies with a Mission." *Ode Magazine* 8, 1: 63.

Rosales, Arturo. 1997. *Chicano! The History of the Mexican American Civil Rights Movement.* 2nd ed. Houston, TX: Arte Público Press.

Schaefer, Carol. 2006. *Grandmothers Counsel the World: Women Elders Offer Their Vision for Our Planet.* Boston, MA: Shambhala Publications.

Smith, Linda Tuhiwai. 1999. *Decolonizing Methodologies: Research and Indigenous Peoples.* New York: St. Martin's Press.

Zimmerman, Kristen, Neelam Pathikonda, Brenda Salgado, and Taj James. 2010. *Out of the Spiritual Closet: Organizers Transforming.* Oakland, CA: Movement Strategy Center.

7

The Legacy of Leadership

From Grandmothers' Stories to Kapa Haka

Tina Ngaroimata Fraser

THE TŪHOE GRANDMOTHERS and great-grandmothers in Figure 7.1 shaped my leadership practices. They were the community leaders who played a significant role in shaping my ways of knowing and being. They were the ones who taught the language, traditional values and practices, and customs and ceremonies. They were responsible for teaching young girls to weave, to gather traditional plants, and to understand the significance of the prayer that goes with each plant. I spent a great deal of time playing around the grandmothers, watching, learning, and listening to their stories, their songs, and their famous *waiata tawhito* (ancient songs). They moved so graciously and used facial expressions so effectively as they performed their songs and dances. I am the proud descendant of these *kaukuia* (female Elders), and I weave the knowledge they left behind into my daily life.

It was a pleasure growing up with them. Perhaps some consider them distant memories, but to me, the grandmothers are the receptacles of traditional knowledge. They, like me, were the product of their mothers' and grandmothers' knowledge. My memories of them include corncob pipes filled with a brand of Pocket Edition tobacco, streams of smoke floating in the air, and sweet conversations in Te reo Māori (the Māori language). In my memories, the grandmothers and great-grandmothers are stern but together. They hold centuries of tribal knowledge and leadership. They teach from the land, and they carefully cut, prepare, and weave flax, which is abundant. They work against a backdrop of ancient trees, the umbilical cords of the world, and they tolerate the sweltering heat while wearing their black clothing. Although the winters are long, damp, and cold, their bent, arthritic fingers continue to weave mats, knead bread, cook over open fires, wash clothes in shallow creeks, haul water, and care for children. I embody the lived experience of witnessing

FIGURE 7.1 Faces of Tūhoe women. Painted by Harry Sangl. From *The Blue Privilege: The Last Tatooed Maori Women – Te Kuia Moko* (Auckland: Richards Publishing/W. Collins, 1980).

the grandmothers' tireless efforts to build strong communities. Their visions and collective leadership contributed greatly towards who I am today, and sharing my stories of these heroes, role models, and teachers will help shape the leaders of tomorrow.

I was born into Tūhoe, a Mataatua tribe located in the Eastern Bay of Plenty, in Aōtearoa, New Zealand. The term *Mataatua* refers to one of the many great canoes that helped people migrate to Aōtearoa. The main landmass of the Tūhoe is known as Te Urewera, a rugged, forested region. The inhabitants, who are often referred to as "the children of the mist," share myths and legends shaped by the environment. They are surrounded by a variety of native trees, prolific bird life, rolling hills, raging rivers, and flowing streams, both hot and cold. When I walk through the mist and listen with my heart, I often hear the chants and the evocative lyrical call of the ancestors. The Tūhoe people are fiercely proud of their language, dialect, protocols, proverbs, customs, and traditions. All members are related to one another by blood descent, and a record of the common thread is preserved in family genealogies. I heard these oral narratives and ancient genealogies frequently during my upbringing.

My grandmothers were the women who played a significant role in traditional child-rearing. They taught me the fundamental principles of life, cultural survival, retention, and sustainability. I am a product of my ancestors. I am my grandmothers' legacy. At times, my grandmothers brought forth their knowledge of old into the present, things they had learned from their mothers and grandmothers and wanted to share with me. They often took me back into their past, affording me a glimpse of their childhood, the times of their grandmothers. Sometimes, they intentionally took me back in time by pointing out various places of significance and sacredness and relaying to me the events that had occurred in those places. Other times, the journey was unintentional. I entered the world of old each time they stared beyond the horizon when certain ancestors' names or events were mentioned. When a storm hit or when death claimed the life of a loved one, their eyes moved, and I could literally see them scouring their minds for an explanation, one justified through the values and beliefs that they had been raised in. When these women wailed with their heads lowered, their cries echoed in the valley. As I contemplated the many lessons my grandmothers were trying to teach me, I often recalled my first smell of Pocket Edition tobacco and visualized the smoke drifting like a slow-moving cloud and blending into the mist.

Mainstream discussions of leadership likewise transport me back through the mists of time, to the traditional education of my childhood. The classroom that I was taught in was a *mārae* (sacred gathering place), and the school was the vast Tūhoe territories of Waiohau (windy waters) and Ruatoki (two axes). These were the landscapes where I skipped and played knuckle bones. These landscapes had also served as the setting for historical events that helped shape the Tūhoe people. In my memories, my grandmothers sit on *harakeke* (flax) mats dressed in black clothing. They work on mats for the marae, *piupiu* (grass skirts), and *kete* (baskets) to hold potatoes, *kūmara* (sweet potato), traditional plants, and many other foods. I fetch water as required and help to pick or carry *harakeke*, which is also used to build shelters and in traditional medicine.

These women held natural power derived from their lived experience and shared knowledge. They would sit and talk about the health and well-being of the community or others, and they cared for them by using traditional plants. I always felt safe and carefree around them. They did not speak a word of English but made many attempts to engage with non-Māori through gestures, facial expressions, and body language. Their wrinkled but fine features and their *moko* (tattoos) on their chins were a sure sign of their leadership skills. The aging of their skin impressed upon me the many things they must have witnessed in their lifetime. The moko showed their strength, for I knew the pain they must have endured during the ceremonies. Their gnarled hands likewise reminded me that they were not afraid of hard work.

These stern women, born in the late nineteenth century and early twentieth centuries, never complained. They occasionally growled at the children but never without cause. As we children played, they taught us the old ways of sustaining Tūhoe culture. They spoke to us and told us stories in Te reo Māori. As we gathered and prepared the flax, we repeated an ancient chant that the grandmothers taught us and asked us to think about. Some days, we accompanied them to the bush to gather herbs and important healing plants, just as they had accompanied their own grandmothers when they were little girls.

Many of my grandmothers were community leaders. They maintained harmony in communities, particularly in *whānau* (families), *hapū* (sub-tribes), and *iwi* (main tribes). They were often responsible for tribal teachings and learning, and in most cases, this process started in the family. To Māori people, whānau goes beyond the immediate family: it extends to include close friends, distant relatives, in-laws, and unknown tribal members.

According to Māori mythology, the earliest example of whānau was Ranginui (Sky Father) and Papatūānuku (Mother Earth) and their many children, including Tāne Māhuta (god of the forest), Tangaroa (god of the sea), and Tāwhirimātea (god of the winds). The legends of this family display the dynamics of whānau and *hui* (meeting, as in a gathering). As the story goes, Ranginui and Papatūānuku were clasped in an eternal embrace, their children situated between them. This embrace was so tight that no light could enter between the parents' entangled bodies. The brothers, tired of being enshrouded by darkness, longed to see the light and called a hui. Some of the brothers (including Tāne Māhuta) agreed to the separation; others (including Tāwhirimātea) were against it. The brothers engaged in heated debates until Tāne Māhuta successfully tore his parents apart, allowing light to enter the world. Such stories gave us young girls an opportunity to learn about working together, much like our grandmothers served as a concrete example of people working together to produce food and utensils for the sake of the community.

I recall that the evenings appeared quickly after an eventful day. The grandmothers tucked us into bed and then began their debriefing. Their incantations often brought me from a deep sleep. They often said, "The best time to call upon the ancestors is in the early morning hours because the physical body has become quiet and still, allowing the mind and spirit to open." The early morning in the mārae always seemed brisk, cool, and damp. I heard the lyrical sounds of ancient chants in the morning and during prayers. Peripheral learning happened on a daily basis, not only as we ran around having fun but also as we slept.

In a sense, living close to my grandmothers increased my learning capabilities. In particular, it allowed me to learn the ancient customs and protocols for women, which helped build my self-esteem and taught me to know who I was, no matter where I was in the world. Knowing who I was assisted me in setting goals and a vision for my life.

My mother, grandmothers, and great-grandmothers had their own visions for me. It has only been in the last decade that I have been able to reflect on and attempt to understand how and why these visions are important today. My mother always made sure that I was dressed nicely and appropriately for each cultural occasion. To my grandmothers, however, the most important thing was not so much my attire but my presence. The fact that I existed must have been quite an achievement for women who had experienced the firm hand of colonization and multiple deaths during the time of the black plague (the 1918 influenza pandemic), which claimed the lives of my grandmother's mother and younger sister. My grandmother told me that when she was a child, her family tried to escape the plague by travelling by horse and cart to Ruatoki. Just outside their destination, my great-grandmother was still suckling my grandmother's younger sister. By the time they reached Ruatoki, my great-grandmother and the baby had passed away.

Schooling was important to my parents. I needed to be educated if I was ever going to survive in a white world. The views of my mother and grandmother differed somewhat. My mother expected me to attend school every day. All my grandmothers expected of me was to be present when they chanted during their weaving sessions or when they sat and chatted with other grandmothers. While my mother focused on preparing me for my future, my grandmothers focused on preparing me for the past. My mother wanted me to build a future for myself. My grandmothers wanted me to build that future on the foundations of a rich Māori past. My mother tended to my physical needs, while my grandmothers tended to my spiritual needs. The grandmothers encouraged me to learn the ways of old, to have an understanding of the values and beliefs of my people.

Although my mother and grandmothers had visions for me, bringing them to fruition required the input of the family, extended family, sub-tribal members, and tribal members. Having been raised in these forums themselves, they would have understood this. White law required me to attend school, and I did so eagerly. I loved the interaction with other children, and my grandmothers had already taught me that it was fun to learn.

The bell rang at 9:00 a.m. sharp. It meant it was time to gather for assembly line. The day always began with "God Save the Queen." I found it odd that we had to sing about an old white woman whom none of us had met. We then marched into our classroom, where we continued the day with yet another lesson on how to read, write, and comprehend mathematical skills. The teachings were very different from how my grandmothers taught, and I struggled to find the needed balance between the two contradicting worldviews. Even though there were challenges and differences in the two educational approaches, one thing was consistent – my desire for learning, in or out of the classroom setting.

Among my fondest memories are the nature walks we took with our social studies teacher. He took us up and down the gorge to explore the river and bush environment. He instructed us to gather samples of plants and rocks, take them back to the classroom, and then share our observations or findings with the whole class. Some days, our class travelled to the ocean, where we walked along the beach and collected driftwood that resembled faces or other shapes. We gathered up seashells and held them to our ears in order to listen to the sound of the waves. These were hands-on activities that I could relate to, and the teacher's manner of instruction influenced my own practices in education.

I always took home what I learned each day, and I was always anxious to see my grandmothers. They too had an interest in what I was being taught in school and wanted to see if I had learned anything new. They always expected me to share my newly gained knowledge. Sometimes, they rolled their eyes; sometimes, they giggled; and sometimes, they simply nodded.

At first the separation from my grandmothers bothered me, but they kept encouraging me, as the youngest child at the time, to enjoy learning. Although we were rich in land and from hunting, gathering, fishing, and planting, we were farmers who couldn't afford shoes. We were fortunate if my grandparents didn't need the horse and cart to use in the fields. It meant that those in the family who didn't have shoes could catch a ride to school. Winter days were the worst, cold and damp. We walked to school and ran through fresh cow dung to keep our feet warm. Once we arrived, we took a few minutes to wash our feet and prepare ourselves for school.

Reflecting back on my schoolgirl days, I would have to say that the best lessons were learned at the hem of my grandmothers' black skirts. They told stories about when they were little girls who learned by watching their older siblings and mimicking their mothers and grandmothers. My great-grandmother told us stories similar to "Cinderella" and "The Three Bears," but they were Māori versions and much more serious in theme than classroom storybooks, and they always had a moral. I continue to hold on to these lessons. They have influenced my thinking during my own lived experiences, and I have passed them down to my children and my grandchildren.

My grandmothers encouraged me to attend community gatherings, to collect and share knowledge with other grandmothers and tribal members. My grandmothers were not only leaders in their communities, they were also leaders in other communities. I remember accompanying my grand-mothers to larger communities, or sometimes cities, for their medical appointments or grocery shopping. Often, they would pack our lunch, and we would wait for an old green and yellow Cave's bus to pick us up. The bus driver happened to be my grandmother's brother. He was a polite man who had great respect for my grandmother and the work she did with other women in our community. The roads back then were narrow and gravelled, and some areas had thin trails for carts and horses. Back in those days, it was a big step for Māori Elders to leave their communities. When they travelled into town, they were on a mission. They got what they needed, attended their appointments, and then anxiously awaited the bus to return to their communities.

My great-grandmother, who was also a social activist and an active Elder in her community, was viewed as a woman who meant business. For example, she would ask if I was interested in attending a Māori Women's Welfare League (a support group for Māori women) meeting, one of her many passions. I would happily go for the walk just to play with other children. I was learning about social justice, education, and decision making without realizing it. She was involved with the Tūhoe School Trust Board for many years, and her input into Māori education was valued. She encouraged everyone to attend and to stay in school. She also promoted the idea that my aunts should attend prestigious Māori schools. She believed in children, families, and communities.

The greatest memories I have of my grandmothers are of their ability to lead naturally as tribal women. I still remember my grandmother telling me about one of our feisty great-grandmothers who had been arrested for following the surveyors and pulling out their land markers. She taunted the surveyors by performing a *haka* (war dance). Eventually, she was arrested and taken away. She raised her skirt to the men of the tribe to indicate to them that they were cowards for not attempting to stop the surveyors. My grandmothers would say, "That *kuia* (Te Raiwhara) was a woman who knew how to scare the *pākeha* [European people] while performing a *pukana*" (facial expression, enlarging of the eyes). It was her way of showing resistance to those who were illegally confiscating our lands.

Much of the grandmothers' strengths developed out of a desire to protect their land and language. These corncob-piped women with their moko and their stern, wrinkled faces discussed community politics, crop sharing, occupation of the land, and upcoming mārae affairs such as deaths and births. Their communal leadership was based on respect, collectivism, tribal preservation, and sustainability. For Māori people, and most Indigenous peoples, identity emanates from the land. The land is the place where self-awareness, *mana* (prestige), and importance originate (Bennett 1979, 74-79). Their wisdom and input were often sought after, particularly when it came to weaving, maternal health, chanting incantations, and traditional child-rearing. Within the chants lay the stories of old, stories about how the deities help guide us and, in many cases, protect us against danger. Most of these stories exist to ensure the survival of the tribe, the land, and the language.

As a child, I often thought about the carved figures that adorned our mārae and what they might represent symbolically. My grandmothers explained that they represented our deities or ancestors and were there to protect us. Some of the carvings had three fingers. According to Māori mythology (and, of course, my grandmothers), the three fingers represent *Te Kore* (the world of nothingness, void, or emptiness), *Te Pō* (the world of darkness), and *Te Ao Mārama* (the world of light). These beliefs, as explained to me, stem from the notion of how Māori people came into being. These deities hold the values and philosophies of *māoritanga* (Māoriness), which is demonstrated in Māori art.

In traditional Māori performing arts, most of the visions of a single family, sub-tribe, or tribal group rest within the forty people who make up a single *Kapa haka* (performing group). They weave the stories of our ancestors, histories of our tribes, and plights of Māori nations into song and dance. They tell and aggressively display the abhorrent treatment of Māori by the Crown through *haka* (war dances). Loved ones long since passed are remembered through a display of hand gestures and lulling harmonies. The performers imitate birds and explain the roles of women by using the poi, a plaited handle with a ball at the end. (The instrument was invented by the men to exercise the wrist, but it was later given to the women to use in the dance.)

Māori traditional performing arts lie at the core of Māori development and are inextricably linked to language, culture, and community. The mārae and Kapa haka are the most suitable places for teaching and learning. Māori culture gave our mothers, grandmothers, and great-grandmothers the opportunity to prepare their daughters, granddaughters, and great-granddaughters for life on the mārae, including preparing them for their roles as women. Kapa haka allows the group to come together to learn historical knowledge in a familiar and controlled environment while under the disciplines of haka (Fraser 2009). Tutors are expected to weave our stories and histories into song and dance, keeping the struggles of our ancestors alive while informing new generations. These oral narratives can be attained only from our ancestors, our grandparents.

When I was child, the grandfathers were present during practices, but it was the grandmothers who guided the haka groups, sometimes subtly, most times not. It was important to them that we got our stories right. We had to learn to be expressive, to smile through happy songs, to cry through sad songs, and to stand rigid during haka. We had to tell and relive stories through our entire body. By the end of a performance, I felt drained but had a sense of achievement.

In Kapa haka, the focus of tutoring and performing is having a greater understanding of Māori historical knowledge and recognizing the need for it to be passed down in order for future generations to survive. Writing about historical knowledge is only half the task. Through performance, people are taught to understand, live, and experience historical knowledge. Motivation to perform haka can be acquired through spiritual connections to the ancestors, the land, and to one another. We call upon them for guidance and protection. In Chapter 5 of this volume, Carolyn Kenny shares a similar story about the interconnectedness she experienced when she visited New Zealand with Ernie Collison, a Haida artist, and was told they were related. The phrase *all my relations*, which is often used by Aboriginal people in Canada, comes to mind. This powerful phrase is used to connect to knowledge, much like Māori use songs in Kapa haka. To sing of the past is to remember those that were part of it. When we sing of our mountains, we remember all those who were connected to or associated with them – birds, trees, and ancestors. There is much learning contained within Kapa haka, and learning through Kapa haka extends to the audience as well. A Kapa haka tutor explained to me that when he sings, he tries to sing to people's spirits. He understands that not everyone can speak or understand Māori, but all of them can feel.

Before festivals made haka competitive, all performances took place on the marae when the gatherings were held. The marae was a good place for learning and teaching because there was no pressure. Performances were done to entertain guests and the home crowd. I recall that I felt the presence of my ancestors, and this helped me to express emotions and traits such as love, caring, trust, passion, ownership, resistance, a sense of security, and empathy. Although the Tūhoe's haka gathering is now competitive, it still provides a platform for marae learning to take place. Young girls are taught to *karanga* (to make the traditional call of welcome at the marae), to take leadership roles, to be responsible for one another, and to call words of encouragement to one another during a performance. Young boys are taught to deliver speeches and to train as warriors.

When I was a child, Kapa haka was not restricted to the marae or to the stage, it was also taught in school, which helped me to connect with other Māori children. Kapa haka tutors helped me building a strong foundation for my future. My tutors were great leaders, but they had to be, because a performing group is only as good as its tutor, and the group can only perform as well as its leaders. The quality of a group's performance is attributed to the tutors, because during Kapa haka practices, the tutors are the ones with the vision. It is their job to ensure that the group understands this vision and the tutor's intent. Once a group takes the stage, the leaders take the tutor's role and thus become responsible for ensuring that the group portrays that vision well to the audience. If you watch a haka and feel your body tense in response to the sound and actions of the group, you understand its intent. To weep during a group's performance of a song of an ancestor that has passed is to fulfill the tutor's vision. Once the audience has connected with the group, a bond of unity, self-healing, and spiritual connection has been created among the ancestors, the performers, the audience, and the environment.

The performing arts are one of many tools that Māori women use to identify and connect with who they are as tribal women. They are not about one person or one family, nor are they centred on one principle; rather, they are a combination of everything and everyone. The performing arts have no set boundaries for us as mothers and grandmothers. We perform every day. We talk to our babies while they are still in our womb. We teach them how to stand upright and take their first steps. We rub their wounds when they stumble and fall. We sing them to sleep at the end of a long day. But we keep the best stories for our grandchildren.

Works Cited

Bennett, Manuhuia. 1979. "Te Kupu Whakamutunga: The Last Word." In *He Mātāpuna: A Source – Some Maori Perspectives,* edited by New Zealand Planning Council, 74-79. Wellington: New Zealand Planning Council.

Fraser, Tina Ngaroimata. 2009. "Maori-Tūhoe Epistemology: Stages of Sustaining Tribal Identity through Tūhoe Performing Arts." PhD diss., University of British Columbia.

8

The Four R's of Leadership in Indigenous Language Revitalization

Stelómethet Ethel B. Gardner

GRASSROOTS LEADERSHIP IN Indigenous language revitalization comprises individuals who have taken the lead in mobilizing action towards keeping Indigenous languages alive. Their leadership approaches are rooted in Indigenous spiritual values and belief in the sacredness of Indigenous languages; they recognize that language, land, identity, culture, and spirit are interconnected and intertwined. Blending ancient Indigenous ways with modern Western ways often presents challenges that require innovative interventions. In a world where the majority of Indigenous languages are slated for extinction, these grassroots leaders are adamant that we can keep our languages alive and bring them to full functional use once again.

I raise my hands in thanks and respect to the Creator for all who engage in the work of revitalizing our Indigenous languages. This chapter examines the language revitalization work associated with two research projects in Grand Council Treaty 3 and Stó:lō territory.[1] In particular, it focuses on remarkable people at the grassroots level whose leadership approaches are rooted in Indigenous spiritual values and belief in the sacredness of Indigenous languages. We, in our work together, are Indigenous language revivalists, and I use the concepts of respect, relevance, responsibility, and reciprocity to frame our sacred work.

How does one become a language revivalist? I credit my dad, the late Francis Gardner, for instilling this passion in me. He was proud to be Xwélmexw, to be First Nations, and proud of the few words he could speak in our Stó:lō language, Halq'eméylem. At the dinner table, he would say "Ewéta seplil" to my mom, which means "There is no bread." Mom, born Bertha Prest, was also Stó:lō and understood what Dad was saying. He called us "re-e-e-al Xwélmexw," which he said meant "re-e-e-al Indian." The lengthening of a word in that way transfers to English how some words are structured in Halq'eméylem. Hearing the few phrases my dad was able to say intrigued me; it made me want to know more about this language which was associated with who I was as a Stó:lō person. Being raised in northern Québec, where I learned to speak French fluently, also fuelled my interest in the intricacies and cultural meanings embedded in different languages, especially Halq'eméylem.

I eventually moved back to southern British Columbia, to my home territory, where I maintained my interest in Halq'eméylem throughout my university studies and my professional and academic career. Soon after I arrived, I discovered that Halq'eméylem was nearing extinction, and this saddened me very much. Living and working in BC enabled me to connect in meaningful ways with Halq'eméylem and with the work that was being done to revitalize it (Gardner 2000). Indigenous language work, my passion, grew out of my love for Halq'eméylem and learning what it means to be Stó:lō.

The Stó:lō live in the Upper Fraser River region in southern BC. *Stó:lō* in our language means "river," and we are referred to as "People of the River." Our language, Halq'eméylem, is close to extinction. Only one fully fluent Halq'eméylem speaker, Siyàmiyatéliyot Elizabeth Phillips, remains in the world, and she is currently the main mentor-Elder working with us to revitalize our language. Stó:lō Nation, the political organization that represented the twenty-four Stó:lō First Nations, put out a call to the community in 1994 for individuals to step forward who would be willing to learn Halq'eméylem in order to teach it. About twenty or so people, mostly women, answered the call to, in effect, become leaders in Halq'eméylem revitalization. In 1995, the Stó:lō Shxwelí Halq'eméylem Language Program was established to support these individuals. It offered Halq'eméylem learning opportunities that were part of a course of study that eventually led to teacher certification. *Shxwelí* is Halq'eméylem for "spirit or life force" (Carlson 1997, 55).

In 1998, when I began my doctoral dissertation on what Halq'eméylem means in the everyday lives of our Stó:lō people, I enrolled in a Halq'eméylem linguistics class in the Stó:lō Shxwelí Language Program. The new Halq'eméylem leaders were at that time honing their language skills (Gardner 2008). In March, upon learning of my interests, one of my classmates, Tl'ówkomot, approached me and said, "If you want to examine the meaning of something, you should look at the term *S'ólh Téméxw.*" As she wrote the Halq'eméylem words on a piece of paper, she proceeded to explain that the term *S'ólh* means "our," "respectful," or "sacred" and that *Téméxw* means "country," "land," or "world." "Us, the people, are included in our term for the land," she said, "and this links us to all of our ancestors." She continued, "See the *méxw* in *Téméxw*? That part of the word refers to us, the people, like in *Xwélmexw*, the word for 'First Nations,' the word we use for ourselves." With this brief story, I began to understand what the Elders mean when they say things such as the following:

- Language is culture; culture is language.
- Language is central to cultural identity.
- Language enhances self-esteem and pride.
- Language expresses the worldview of its speakers.
- Without our language, we will cease to exist as a unique people.

It was like an epiphany for me to discover the meanings embedded in these words.

Tl'ówkomot and others in the linguistics class became participants in my research project at Simon Fraser University titled "An e-Master-Apprentice Pedagogy (eMAP) for Critically Endangered Languages." The research aimed to determine how computer and World Wide Web technologies can serve as effective pedagogical tools for developing highly fluent speakers and how the role of Elders in language revitalization can be expanded using these technologies. In effect, we wanted to discover what happens when an ancient Indigenous language interfaces with new media technologies. A dozen Stó:lō women and three Elders – Ts'áts'elexwót (Elizabeth Herrling), Siyàmiyatéliyot (Elizabeth Phillips), and Xwiyólemot (Tillie Gutiérrez) – served as co-researchers in the project. They were charged with working together in a master-apprentice relationship that involved computer and internet communications. Sadly, we lost Ts'áts'elexwót, and Xwiyólemot, who was less fluent in the language, was able to participate only minimally.

In 2006, I left my home territory to work at Lakehead University among the Anishinaabe. They welcomed me to their land and invited me to join them in the work of revitalizing Anishinaabemowin, the spoken Anishinaabe language. "We have been doing language work for thirty years and have not produced one new fluent Anishinaabe speaker," said Debbie Lipscombe, policy analyst for Grand Council Treaty 3. "We want to know what we are doing wrong, what we could do differently, and what we could do that we are not doing." Debbie and her fellow Treaty 3 members, Alannah Cooke and Denise Bluebird, wanted answers to these questions. They had summed it up succinctly. They saw an opportunity to engage in research with scholars at Lakehead University, located in Thunder Bay, Ontario. I had just taken up a position as chair of the university's newly established Department of Aboriginal Education and had been invited to meet with Treaty 3 representatives by the chair of graduate studies, John O'Meara, who had already been in discussions with representatives of Treaty 3 regarding a possible project. Our meeting spawned a partnership to develop a research project titled "Language Planning for Anishinaabemowin Revitalization in Grand Council Treaty #3." The territory includes twenty-eight First Nations in southwestern Ontario and straddles the Manitoba border.

When the Anishinaabemowin project began, we established a steering committee of representatives from the four regions of Treaty 3 and from the overarching Grand Council Treaty 3 political body. The project initially called for three community researchers and three graduate assistants; however, the Steering Committee decided that we needed four community researchers, one from each region – north, east, south, and west. Thus, we reduced the number of graduate assistants from three to two. The Steering Committee selected who would be the community researchers from each region. I thought they might recommend some up-and-coming Anishinaabe scholars from their territory, but to my surprise and delight they instead chose three grandmothers and a grandfather. The grandfather, however, withdrew early in the project, and another grandmother was selected to replace him. The decision made sense, since Elders are considered the keepers of the culture and are highly respected for their expertise. The project aimed to answer the following questions: What needs to change in Grand Council Treaty 3 communities to produce Anishinaabemowin speakers? What does the Grand Council Treaty 3 leadership need to know to make effective policy decisions for language revitalization?

The Four *R*'s and Grassroots Leadership Experience

How do we talk about grassroots leadership approaches and language revitalization? I found the framework of the four *R*'s –respect, relevance, responsibility, and reciprocity – conceptualized by Verna Kirkness and Ray Barnhardt (1991) to be most useful in examining the grassroots leadership experience of the two groups of language revivalists. Others have found the four R's a particularly useful concept for describing how First Nations worldviews and identities fit alongside and within Western society. For example, in Chapter 3 of this volume, Alannah Young Leon uses the four R's and adds two additional R's – relationships and reverence – to describe transformative leadership informed by collective values and outcomes that move towards equality and social change. In Chapter 9, Michelle Pidgeon also makes reference to Kirkness and Barnhardt's work, particularly relating to "the responsibilities we have to the collective 'we' rather than the 'I.'" It seems that the concept of the four R's is broad enough that it can have particular and specific applications. In my analysis, the four R's are particular to the concept of leadership and specific to the grassroots leadership of language revivalists.

Respect

Respect – respect for the language, respect for the ancestors, and respect for one another – is the basic philosophical value that dictates how we act and how we interact with other humans and with all things. If the interconnectedness of all things is taken into consideration, then it is possible to see that anything that one does, says, or thinks will affect all things. Actions, words, and thoughts must therefore be carried out carefully and respectfully.

When we began the eMAP project in early 1995, we held meetings at Simon Fraser University in the Mac laboratory and in various Stó:lō community venues. During one of the early meetings, we met in the home of a participant who lived on Skwah Band territory on the outskirts of Chilliwack. We were to begin shooting footage for the participants' iMovie projects. Siyàmiyatéliyot attended. My colleague Laura Buker and I arrived and witnessed a flurry of activity. Someone was making a fruit salad with various kinds of berries, someone was getting fish ready to bake in the oven, and someone was making soup. "Oh my," I said, "is someone making a movie about cooking traditional foods?" "No." came the reply, "We are preparing this food for you and Laura." Of course, the food was for everyone, but it was their way of honouring the expertise and skills we were sharing with them, expertise that would contribute to their work in Halq'eméylem revitalization. Laura and I were really touched by the gesture, and we convinced a couple of the participants to make a movie project of them preparing a traditional feast. Laura was the education technology expert for our project.

It was quite the sight to see what was going on in that home that day. The house contained several looms for weaving blankets, and the participants made a movie with Siyàmiyatéliyot, who talked about Halq'eméylem words for weaving. It was inspiring to see how they were using technology to document an important cultural tradition, Salish blanket weaving. The participants shot footage of Siyàmiyatéliyot wearing a woven blanket. They had all helped weave the blanket to honour the Halq'eméylem expertise they were gaining from their Elder-mentor. These ways – honouring and respecting others – came naturally to the participants, and, in effect, they were also bringing honour and respect to themselves. We witnessed many examples of the participants showing respect throughout the three years of the project.

The Anishinaabe participants in Treaty 3 territory were no strangers to the concept of respect. The committee's insistence on four community researchers meant that the four regions – north, south, east, and west – were represented. Inviting grandmothers and Elders to participate acknowledged the expertise of the people in each region. We acknowledged that they would know how best to approach the language work in their region. We opened our first meeting, held on 1-3 April 2008, with prayers and speeches in Anishinaabemowin and with a smudge. These traditions helped guide us to do things in "a good way." We also shared Anishinaabe traditional foods such as wild rice, moose meat, and berries.

Nancy Jones, an Elder, said, "In the work we are doing with Anishinaabemowin, we need to recognize that our language is sacred and that the work we are doing is sacred." In the beginning, there was a great deal of concern about doing things in a way that respected the culture and traditions of the territory. "We need ceremony," Nancy continued. "We need guidance and acknowledgment from our ceremony that we are doing things in a good way for the language." A ceremony did take place, and word came back that the ancestors' spirits were smiling on us. We could continue with this knowledge. We had been reminded to include Anishinaabe traditions and the drum in the work we were about to do. Out of cultural respect, the nature of the ceremony is not described here. We were reminded to always keep respect for traditions, ceremony, and prayer in the forefront of our work in Anishinaabemowin.

Relevance

If our work was to be relevant, it had to show respect not only for traditions, ceremony, and prayer but also for the environment, the land, and the resources of each territory. Each group of language revivalists, Stó:lō and Anishinaabe, insisted that we meet them on their territories as much as possible and that we rotate the locations of each meeting to cover different regions in each territory. The premise "The land is our culture" required us to be on the land. Our languages are expressions of our environments. People are identified by association with their environments. Each project therefore aimed to respect each community on their territory.

The Stó:lō Halq'eméylem revivalists insisted on creating digital stories that reflected their individual community identities, stories about their activities, language, and their landscape. For example, one student created an iMovie about smoking salmon, another focused on fishing for salmon, another explored picking berries, and another created a community weather report on the land. Their riverworld, a worldview grounded in life on the river, was reflected in their digitally created worlds. How did they gain the language for these unique digital stories? It came from the ancestors who lived on the land, in deep interconnectedness with the land; from those who have kept Halq'eméylem alive throughout the years; and from Siyàmiyatéliyot, the sole fluent Halq'eméylem speaker today. Thanks to the innovative software of Apple computers, Siyàmiyatéliyot could connect with the co-researchers face to face in real time via iChat and with up to three other persons at one time. The digital world was seen as a perfect way to capture the colour, sound, movement, and textual representations of the Stó:lō and their riverworld. The Stó:lō Halq'eméylem revivalists took to this technology naturally. They knew what they wanted to capture, what was important.

The Anishinaabe emphasized the importance of representing the traditions of their territories and honouring all of the people in each community in their territory. If we met on a particular territory, we were to honour the protocol in that territory. We made offerings of tobacco, invited the locals to drum, and acknowledged local leaders. We also invited local people to provide traditional foods or entertainment.

The Treaty 3 project included a conference designed by the community researchers. They honoured the protocol. Diane Kelly, *ogichidaakwe* (grand chief) of Grand Council Treaty 3, gave a welcome and spoke to the participants about the importance of the language and the language work being done and about the importance of drawing on the expertise, skill, and knowledge of the people of Treaty 3. The community researchers understood the importance of the ogichidaakwe's words and had done just that in developing the program and protocol for the conference. The conference was relevant to the people, by the people, and for the people. The community researchers felt it was important to include all the people, youth, adults, and Elders. They selected a youth to be one of the keynote speakers. There were workshops for teachers on important aspects of the language and on incorporating culture in the learning process. There was an evening when all of the Elders in attendance were invited to speak to the youth about the importance of learning their language and practising their culture. There were workshops for youth on traditional games, dance, and drumming; traditional regalia; and traditional roles for men and women. Everyone was invited to workshops on name-giving and the meaning of the names of particular clans in Treaty 3 territory. The conference began with the drum and a prayer from the local people whose traditional territory we were on and respected, and it ended with the drum and prayer. The community researchers made sure everything was done "in a good way." In their evaluations of the conference, many of the people stated that it was the best conference they had ever attended.

Language revivalists do what they do naturally. It is second nature to them. Ernie Collison, a Haida artist discussed in Chapter 5 of this volume, describes the second-nature aspect of this process: "All things are linked together. This creates a cultural stream of consciousness in your life, and it reaches a point where you don't really think about it as culture – you live it." Language revivalists live it by enacting the cultural ways in relation to their language work.

Responsibility

In both the Stó:lō and Anishinaabe cases, the participants felt a huge responsibility to keep Halq'eméylem and Anishinaabemowin alive. The Stó:lō co-researchers knew they would be responsible for transmitting the language to others, even though they themselves were not fully competent in the language. At one time they had had many Elders upon whom to depend, but within a short period of time they witnessed Elders fluent in Halq'eméylem pass away one by one. Today, they depend on Siyàmiyatéliyot alone. They do, however, have those who worked hard to "put it away," to document the language on audio and videotape, people who work with linguists Brent Galloway, Strang Burton, and others to create a writing system, grammar, and a variety of language resources. The Stó:lō Halq'eméylem revivalists have undertaken many initiatives to learn the language, to learn the linguistics of the language, and to learn to become teachers and curriculum developers. They undertook this tall order with a full understanding of the importance of incorporating Stó:lō culture and the Stó:lō worldview into the learning process. This burden of responsibility required great sacrifices, such as time spent away from family and home, and it required enormous amounts of energy to continuously learn new things in an environment where Halq'eméylem use is minimal. Recreating a community of language speakers is no small task. In Stó:lō territory, a Halq'eméylem language teacher might be the only person doing language work in his or her community, school, or program. It is often a lonely task.

The Anishinaabe co-researchers also felt a tremendous burden of responsibility to create a language plan for all people within Grand Council Treaty 3, a territory that includes twenty-eight communities and approximately eight thousand people. They hoped to ensure that everyone who wanted a voice regarding their language would be heard. They felt a responsibility to include all sectors of their communities, youth, adults, and Elders. They wanted their interaction with the people to be respectful and done according to each community's protocol. Their project work included doing a survey, organizing conferences and other gatherings, making presentations to the Grand Council Treaty 3 leadership, organizing youth workshops, and making sure that each voice was heard "in a good way."

The Treaty 3 project includes pilot projects such as an initiative to promote digital storytelling among youth. The co-researchers decided that it would be good to have a workshop in each of the four territories and to invite youth from each of the communities in each region to participate. By doing so, the workshops will include digital stories from each community. Elders will be on hand to work with the youth to develop the language they need to tell their stories. The storytelling workshops will lead to the creation of books, which will be shared with all Treaty 3 communities. The hope is that the digital workshop for youth will reveal the language needs of youth. Language revivalists carry a burden of responsibility to ensure that the needs of youth will be met for the next seven generations.

Reciprocity

Reciprocity in language revitalization work means we cannot keep our languages alive alone. We know that our work must respect the legacy of traditions left to us by our ancestors and that it must be relevant to the communities in question and acknowledge their interconnectedness with the land. We know that we are responsible for reversing language loss and bringing our languages to functional use in ways that are relevant to each community's needs. Reciprocity means that we do not live on an island: we want to share our rich Indigenous cultural heritage and languages with everyone and, in turn, we want the broader Canadian society to support our efforts. Our own communities are aware of our needs. In Stó:lō territory, participants in the eMAP project are now bringing their language, teachings, and newfound technology skills to bear in preschools, daycares, and Head Start programs; public and Catholic schools; community schools and programs; and college and university programs. They now bear the fruits of their labour as leaders in Halq'eméylem language revitalization. It is good, yet so much more needs to be done. The participants need continuing professional development and opportunities to hone their Halq'eméylem language skills. They cannot continue to be solely responsible for every aspect of teaching and learning Halq'eméylem. They need an organization that represents their interests as Halq'eméylem teachers and workers and as Indigenous language workers in British Columbia. The creation of a national Indigenous language teachers' organization would make them feel less isolated in their work and would look after their interests.

In Treaty 3 territory, the Anishinaabe language is strong, yet there are many challenges. Although the culture and cultural practices are strong, the language is being taken for granted because there is a stronghold of speakers. As each Elder fluent in Anishinaabemowin passes, however, language use diminishes. The challenge is to develop a movement to keep Anishinaabemowin alive, to not let it slide as Stó:lō Halq'eméylem did. People with the language need to be inspired to share it with others. Community researchers have raised awareness about the importance of preserving Anishinaabemowin and brought to the forefront the concerns of the people in Treaty 3. Governments and institutions with resources in the broader community need to reciprocate – to partner with them, hear them, and respond to them to determine how to support the language revitalization process. Those entities need to find a way not only to think "outside the box" when it comes to Anishinaabemowin maintenance and revitalization but also to think "inside the circle." By doing so, they will recognize the intelligence and expertise of the Anishinaabe people and bring Anishinaabe thought into Western institutions, such as schools, colleges, and universities. There needs to be a reciprocal exchange of worldviews, a two-way exchange of ideas that honours both Western and Indigenous knowledge and lifeways.

Conclusion

The grassroots leaders in both the Stó:lō and Anishinaabe language revitalization projects shared a common concern to do things "in a good way." The Anishinaabe people are driven by the philosophy of *bimaadiziwin*, which means "living in a good way," achieving harmony within the self and the wider world, living a life in balance (MacLeod et al. 2010). The Stó:lō people are driven by the teachings of Xá:ls (the Transformer), a deity sent to the world "to put things right," and the *sxwōxwiyám* (stories) that teach us how to act as Stó:lō people and to recognize how *smestíyexw* expresses the Stó:lō's spiritual relationship with the land, which is based on harmony and respect (Gardner 2008). As Indigenous language revivalists, our leadership is defined by who we are, by the traditions and teachings passed down to us by our ancestors. These teaching are alive and strong today. The concept of the four *R*'s offers a useful framework for the work of Indigenous language revivalists, illustrating how our language, culture, land, spirit, and identity are intertwined and interconnected in grassroots leadership.

Note

1   Both research projects received funding from the Social Sciences and Humanities Research Council (SSHRC) of Canada, a federal agency that promotes and supports university-based research and training in the humanities and social sciences.

Works Cited

Carlson, Keith Thor, ed. 1997. *You Are Called to Witness: The Stó:lō in Canada's Pacific Coast History.* Chilliwack: Stó:lō Heritage Trust.

Gardner, Stelómethet Ethel B. 2000. "Where There Are Always Wild Strawberries." *Canadian Journal of Native Education* 24, 1: 7-13.

–. 2008. *Tset Hikwstexw Te Skwélteltset, We Hold Our Language High: The Meaning of Halq'eméylem Language Renewal in the Everyday Lives of Stó:lō People.* Saarbrüken: VDM Verlag Dr Müller.

Kirkness, Verna J., and Ray Barnhardt. 1991. "First Nations and Higher Education: The Four *R*s – Respect, Relevance, Reciprocity, Responsibility." *Journal of American Indian Education* 30, 3: 1-15.

MacLeod, Kathy, Renee Southwind, Helen Cromarty, and Esther Van Gennip. 2010. "Bimaadiziwin: A Menoyawin Program for Building Cross-Cultural Competency and Client Safety." http://www.slmhc.on.ca/traditional_support_program/bimaadiziwin.

9
Transformation and Indigenous Interconnections
Indigeneity, Leadership, and Higher Education
Michelle Pidgeon

INDIGENOUS COMMUNITIES EXIST in many different contexts, from remote rural locations to the heart of Canada's urban centres. Our communities are not only defined by geographical boundaries but are also built inherently on the relationships within these spaces. University and community college campuses are recent sites of community for Indigenous peoples. Postsecondary institutions are communities unto themselves in relation to the cities and towns with which they coexist. Aboriginal peoples have generally not had a positive experience with educational institutions in Canada. Over the last sixty years, however, Indigenous scholars, administrators, and staff, along with their allies, have been tirelessly transforming our universities and colleges into places of community for Indigenous peoples. This chapter explores the key role Indigenous leadership continues to play in the development and implementation of institutional changes to improve the postsecondary experiences of Aboriginal peoples. This leadership is evident in a wide variety of academic disciplines where programs have been changed to include a First Nations specialization or focus. It is also evident in the inclusion of Indigenous content and more inclusive pedagogical approaches. These systemic changes to policies and practices directly affect Aboriginal student engagement and success.

As an assistant professor, I am honoured to add my voice to this conversation on Indigenous leadership. My use of the first person suggests that I speak from a position of some understanding. I recognize that in this stage of my career and my life I am still learning, but I also take seriously my responsibility to share what I have witnessed in my research and my lived experiences. In this chapter, I present the lessons I learned as I researched and explored higher education's responsibilities to Aboriginal peoples within an Indigenous framework. This research involved over two hundred people (Aboriginal Elders, students, faculty, staff, and administrators and non-Aboriginal faculty, staff, and administrators) from three universities and one college in British Columbia, Canada. I have permission to tell their stories, but I protect their identity out of respect and at their request. Although not all two hundred stories can be presented individually, I present their shared connections and teachings on leadership with honour and respect. I raise my hands in thanks to the mentors, colleagues, and others who continue to provide amazing guidance and leadership.

In discussing Indigenous leadership in higher education, I think it is important to first provide an overview and brief outline of how indigeneity exists and resists dominant hegemonies within mainstream universities and colleges. I set out to define Indigenous leadership within higher education by drawing on my own research, the literature on Indigenous leadership, and the literature on educational leadership. Specific examples, such as SAGE (Supporting Aboriginal Graduate Enhancement), an interdisciplinary and cross-institutional peer-mentoring program in British Columbia, show how Indigenous leadership is heading transformative change within mainstream institutions, and I make specific recommendations to improve the mentoring of Indigenous leaders and for institutional transformation

Indigeneity in Mainstream Postsecondary Institutions

Indigeneity both embodies and is expressed through Indigenous knowledge (see Chapter 13, this volume). Indigeneity occurs within mainstream institutions of higher education to varying degrees, depending on the Indigenous peoples present and the institution's willingness to respect Indigenous ways of knowing, being, and living (Kuokkanen 2007; Montes 2007; Pidgeon 2008).

As Figure 9.1 illustrates, Indigenous ways of knowing reflect the interconnectedness of the physical, emotional, intellectual, and cultural realms, and they are interwoven with the interconnected relationships of the individual, family, community, and nation. Indigenous knowledge is therefore inherently tied to place, connected to and embedded in the land, sea, and air (Pidgeon 2008). These same principles guide and shape our understandings of Indigenous leadership, as Yvonne McLeod (see Chapter 2, this volume) demonstrates using the framework of the medicine wheel.

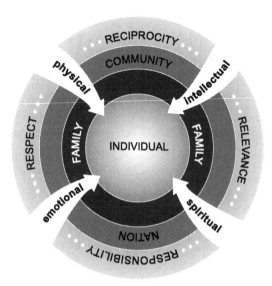

FIGURE 9.1   Holistic indigenous framework

In some sense, Indigenous peoples' presence in mainstream post-secondary institutions in Canada is a new phenomenon, given the university's long history in this country. Although some Aboriginal students attended college and university during the late nineteenth century, they did not become a noticeable presence on campuses until the 1960s and 1970s, when relevant programs and courses (e.g., Native teacher education, First Nations studies, and Aboriginal law) and Aboriginal student services were offered (Montes 2007; Pidgeon 2008). Indigeneity continues to evolve in the curriculums of academic programs that choose to focus on Indigenous issues (e.g., forestry, math, the sciences, education, and fisheries). As a result, there has been a marked increase in academic program choices for Aboriginal youth as communities and institutions recognize the need for diverse educational pathways and career expectations and that postsecondary education plays a critical role in the broader goals of Aboriginal community economic development, sustainability, and self-determination (Human Capital Strategies 2005; Royal Commission on Aboriginal Peoples 1996).

Indigeneity is also present on campuses through the presence of Aboriginal faculty, staff, administrators and, of course, students (Pidgeon 2008). There are growing numbers of Aboriginal faculty, although the numbers do not yet reflect our presence in the population. The same can be said for Aboriginal students. Although we have more Aboriginal students enrolled in postsecondary education now than in the 1960s, there are still many Aboriginal people not participating. For example, research indicates that 20 percent of non-Aboriginal Canadians have some form of postsecondary education, compared to just 8 percent of Aboriginal people (Human Capital Strategies 2005; Mendelson 2006; Statistics Canada 2008). Increasing participation rates in postsecondary education are largely due to increased high school graduation rates for Aboriginal youth, which allows direct entry into postsecondary education, and federal government funding for Aboriginal participation in postsecondary education. The funding formula does, however, have its problems, for example, limited access and capped amounts since 1996 (Mendelson 2006).

Indigenous Leadership within Higher Education

Discussions of leadership within the contemporary indigenous world are filled with either pity and pathos or mystique and romanticism; that is, such discussions are often focused on the social ills of poverty, not on current efforts of indigenous peoples to reclaim legitimate rights of self-determination and full participation in the democratic process.

— *Maenette Benham and Elizabeth Murakami-Ramalho, "Engaging in Educational Leadership"*

In the above quote, Maenette Benham and Elizabeth Murakami-Ramalho (2010) refer to Westerners' incorrect interpretations of Indigenous leadership. Whether overt or covert, these representations of Indigenous peoples' failures are problematic. They romanticize and, more often, ghettoize Aboriginal peoples by implying that they are less than able to lead their peoples. Indigenous leadership is dynamic and resilient, and we need to focus on the strengths and unique contributions that Indigenous leaders bring to our people throughout multiple spaces.

It is evident in my research and in stories from our communities that contemporary Indigenous leadership thrives within communities working towards self-determination, empowerment, and participation. Evidence of this resiliency also exists in our educational systems, in this instance, postsecondary institutions. The growth of Indigenous participation and knowledge, discussed in the previous section, is the result of Aboriginal peoples and allies working for years within and outside of institutions to make strategic changes and create spaces within mainstream institutions for indigeneity. These changes included the following initiatives: developing specific admissions and recruitment policies for Aboriginal students; on-campus housing for individual Aboriginal students or families; financial awards; strategic and institution-wide plans to guide policy and program development for Indigenous education; and creating positions for Aboriginal candidates in senior administration (Pidgeon 2008). Aboriginal student services clearly represent indigeneity in postsecondary education for they provide holistic and culturally relevant support to Indigenous students across Canada (Pidgeon and Hardy Cox 2005). First Nations centres not only support student success as their main mandate, they also work to build bridges and relationships with other student affairs and services units and with academic departments and the broader administration (Pidgeon 2008).

Many colleges and universities have Aboriginal advisory committees that typically represent local Aboriginal communities, Elders, students, and faculty (see Chapter 3 of this volume for further discussion of the important role of Elders in Indigenous leadership). These committees assist in guiding the institution (Pidgeon 2008); however, they are often only advisory committees with no formal voting power on the Board of Governors, in the Senate, or in Education Councils. To bring about systemic change, it is important that Aboriginal peoples be able to take up positions as elected members (with formal voting power) in such governing bodies.

Day (2008) reminds us that leadership is earned: it is not bestowed on anyone. Many Aboriginal faculty, staff, and students find themselves being asked to be leaders, or are presumed to be leaders, simply because they are the only Aboriginal people in the room (Pidgeon 2008). Yet one also has to recognize that, within these formal and informal leadership roles, Aboriginal people are making substantive changes within their institutions and to curriculums, pedagogies, and policies. Indigenous leadership in mainstream institutions falls into two categories: leaders as relations and leaders as warriors. These categories are not linear or independent – they are strongly interconnected.

Leaders as Relations

Indigenous leadership is not confined to individual actions or traits. Being a leader means having meaningful and respectful relationships with others. In their articulation of Indigenous community leadership from the Native

Hawaiian perspective, Maenette Benham and Elizabeth Murakami-Ramalho (2010) describe four key elements of educational leadership. The first is the concept of *ha*, the breath of life that connects us to all living things, past and present. It reminds us that we are not alone as we lead. The second is the concept of place, the inherent connections we have as Indigenous peoples to our micro and macro systems. The third element is the sacredness of relations, and the fourth is the idea of individual generosity and collective action.

Relationships are based on the principles of respect and responsibility (Kirkness and Barnhardt 1991). Relationships extend beyond "who we know" – they remind us of who we are related to and the responsibilities we have to the collective "we" rather than the individual "I." Elders play a pivotal role in teaching, mentoring, and leading younger generations in many of our communities (however you define community) (see Chapter 3, this volume). The intergenerational component of Indigenous leadership is critical. Some postsecondary institutions are exploring how Elders can help support the success of Aboriginal students by informally inviting Elders to be guest speakers or visitors to the campus. Other institutions have created opportunities for more formal leadership in terms of program development and research as it relates to Aboriginal communities by establishing First Nations advisory committees that involve Elders and other community members, along with those from within the college or university. Others institutions are in fact moving to create permanent and meaningful relationships with Elders to ensure that their programs, services, and campuses continue to be relevant to Indigenous students (Pidgeon 2008). Institutions can further support the participation of Elders through Elders-in-residence programs or mentoring programs (in First Nations centres or Aboriginal student services centres), Elder-taught courses (e.g., language), Aboriginal advisory committees (with representatives and Elders from the campus and surrounding Aboriginal communities), and representation at the Board of Governors level.

In my work, Aboriginal staff, faculty, and Elders are seen as important role models of traditional leadership and as successful representatives of indigeneity within the academy (Pidgeon 2008). Throughout British Columbia, institutional leaders are implementing changes and creating spaces for Aboriginal voices at the table; however, it is also clear that an Aboriginal presence is still limited at the higher administrative levels (Pidgeon 2008). The most reoccurring example of this trend is lone

Aboriginal representatives on committees being silenced or hindered by those who are unsupportive (either intentionally or inadvertently) of the Aboriginal agenda. Institutional transformation requires incorporating Indigenous ways of knowing throughout the institution. As one of the people I interviewed stated: "It is important that people see themselves in the administration and that on some levels they see themselves being successful in a particular faculty ... and that is dealing with specific issues and negotiating with particular student services" (personal communication with author, 2006).

Leaders as Warriors

Warrior is a powerful role within many Aboriginal communities. Indigenous notions of the warrior imply much more than the war cries and physical battle skills portrayed in Hollywood movies. Donald Day (2008, 6) uses the term *warrior* to speak of remarkable Indian educators: "[They lead] for a larger purpose, the welfare of humanity. These people are protectors of the people around them, the society they serve, the environment, and their loved ones. The Anishinaabeg call these protectors 'ogichidaag,' or warriors ... They are great role models and they all make a significant difference in the lives of people they touch." Mohawk scholar Taiaiake Alfred (1999, xxiii) uses the term *warrior* to describe contemporary Indigenous peoples' empowerment, and he argues for a return to "leadership based on traditional values." The warrior spirit is also alluded to in the work of Maenette Benham and Elizabeth Murakami-Ramalho (2010), who employ the notion of spirit to describe Indigenous leadership. Each case they discuss is "grounded in the concepts of *ha*, place, relations, and collective action" (ibid., 83). The authors use the metaphors of wave, light, and sound to describe the various elements embodied in the practice of each case of Indigenous leadership.

Institutional transformation or change often begins as grassroots initiatives by Aboriginal peoples and allies working within their specific units, departments, or faculties (Pidgeon 2008). Claudine Montes (2007, 4) argues that "leadership in Native American higher education is more important than ever. There are too few scholars in general and even fewer leaders. Of those leaders there are even fewer who are community-minded rather than 'privatized.' Native communities need leaders who are willing to take a risk and do the difficult work for the greater good of the people. And our leaders, in turn, need to know just what that 'greater good' is so that they can focus their efforts accordingly." Continuing with the notion of collectivity, community, and responsibility, Elgin Badwound and William Tierney (1998, para. 21) describe the leader of a tribal colleges as one who acts as "a facilitator and promoter of group values and interests ... Participants follow the leader not because of rules and regulations, but because the leader has demonstrated appropriate leadership qualities."

Indigenous understandings of leadership extend beyond descriptions of one's location within the hierarchy of an organization or the power held within one's title. Some universities and colleges are changing their governance structures to include Indigenous people in strategic senior management positions. For example, the University of British Columbia created two positions: associate dean of Indigenous education, Faculty of Education; and senior adviser to the president on Aboriginal affairs, also the director of the First Nations House of Learning. Simon Fraser University created the position of director of the Office of Aboriginal Peoples, who reports to the Office of the Vice-President, Academic. The University of Victoria, Thompson Rivers University, and the University of Northern British Columbia, like UBC and SFU, have written or are currently articulating specific mission statements or strategic-planning policy documents pertaining to Aboriginal education. (This list of institutions is not exhaustive and is not meant to be exclusionary in any way. The author wishes to acknowledge the many others institutions working to become better places for Aboriginal peoples.) There are also Indigenous public institutions in British Columbia, such as the Nicola Valley Institute of Technology, which model relational leadership and leaders as warriors in all aspects of their institutions' existence, from their mission statements and policies to day-to-day interactions with students. For example, institutions such as the Nicola Valley Institute of Technology are governed by Elders and communities. Their academic programs are responsive and relevant to local Aboriginal communities.

The directors of Aboriginal student services and their staff are the unsung heroes of many Canadian campuses: they are often the key leaders of institutional change on campus. First Nations centres (also known as Aboriginal student services or Native student services) have been fostering relationships with Aboriginal students, their communities, and their host and other institutions for years; they have been transforming policy and practices of their campuses to make them better places for Aboriginal students (Pidgeon 2008; Pidgeon and Hardy Cox 2005).

Just as the presence of Aboriginal peoples and places on campuses creates opportunities for change, the lack of Aboriginal people in leadership positions can have detrimental consequences, for example, when institutional support for Aboriginal initiatives is tied to an individual and not to an institution, initiative, or the program itself. In my research, I found several examples of programs or initiatives that disappeared into the institutional bureaucracy when a particular advocate left. In other cases, programs had their funding cut or eliminated, and initiatives were removed from the formal approval process (Pidgeon 2008). In all of these cases, Aboriginal peoples and their allies have to be watchdogs. They have to constantly keep an eye on what is happening on their campuses and speak out, resist, and fight against obvious attempts to undermine Indigenous leadership and an Indigenous presence on campus.

I have used the four *R*'s – respect, relevance, reciprocity, and responsibility – to draw on examples of Indigenous leadership. Indigenous leadership reflects the interconnected nature of relationships and focuses on the whole, not the parts. For example, Indigenous leadership not only focuses on the intellectual needs of the group but also addresses their physical, emotional, and cultural needs. Indigenous leadership therefore means that one person alone cannot meet all of these needs: intergenerational relationships are the key to ensuring holistic leadership, to acknowledging that everyone has something to contribute to the circle and to the communities within which we live and work. To explore the institutional changes that still need to occur on campus, I focus on a program called Supporting Aboriginal Graduate Enhancement (SAGE) as an example of how to engage in mentoring and supporting future Indigenous warrior leaders.

Mentoring Indigenous Leaders: SAGE

For many of us to become leaders, we will need to make changes in ourselves. The time to make these changes is now. We must put our ideals into practice. We need to start walking the talk. We must take responsibility for ourselves and all the things we do and don't do.

– Donald Day, "Reflecting upon Indigenous Leadership"

Intergenerational leadership has the power to transform Aboriginal peoples' postsecondary experiences and institutions. As Donald Day suggests, we need to start talking the talk and walking the walk within our institutions. The Supporting Aboriginal Graduate Enhancement (SAGE) initiative offers one path to doing so. SAGE is modelled on New Zealand's Maori and Indigenous Graduate Program (MAI). It began in British Columbia in 2005 under the guidance of Graham Smith and Jo-ann Archibald. Graham Smith is a leading Māori scholar and leader in Māori education. At the time of writing, he was also CEO of the Te Whare Wānanga o Awanuiarangi, a Māori postsecondary institution that focuses on graduate education and community-relevant programs in New Zealand. Jo-ann Archibald, Stó:lō Nation, is currently the associate dean of Indigenous education in the Faculty of Education at the University of British Columbia and a past recipient of the Aboriginal Peoples Award for her leadership and contributions to Aboriginal education. SAGE is a peer-mentoring program that extends beyond institutional and disciplinary boundaries through its four regional groups (in Vancouver, the Okanagan, Prince George, and Victoria). Each group is called a SAGE pod. The name refers to the whale pods seen off Canada's west coast and honours the importance of family, kinship, and relationships. SAGE pods are organized by Aboriginal graduate students, with the support of faculty members, and coordinated by a provincial coordinator, who is also an Aboriginal graduate student. Ontario also has a SAGE group under the guidance of Jean-Paul Restoule of the Ontario Institute for Studies in Education, University of Toronto. The group refers to its pods as nests to reflect the importance of birds to the Anishinaabe peoples of the region. Indigenous faculty members serve as mentors and offer guidance to SAGE; however, the important leaders of the initiative are the graduate students themselves.

In describing the program, Jo-ann Archibald and Lee Brown (2008, 22) state: "the students essentially support and advise each other and reflect the Native saying that *there is always more wisdom in the circle than there is in one individual*. SAGE is culturally supportive and provides an Indigenous knowledge orientation to student support and mentorship." The SAGE program, therefore, is not only culturally relevant to Aboriginal graduate students, it also welcomes into the circle those allies who are non-Aboriginal, such as graduate students or faculty who are working with Aboriginal communities. The key is that SAGE is founded on and grounded in Indigenous understandings of the four *R*'s. The program provides a culturally relevant environment for Aboriginal students to come together and speak about their experiences, concerns, and successes in negotiating the various phases of graduate school. The meetings balance social gathering and information and resources sharing with cultural protocols. In such an environment, students can feel safe to not only talk about their experiences but also help each other negotiate challenges and celebrate their successes. The SAGE program is interdisciplinary and interinstitutional. It focuses on what is important – Aboriginal graduate students.

From 2008 to 2010, Jo-ann Archibald, Colleen Hawkey, and I were involved in a provincial research project titled "Aboriginal Transitions: Undergraduate to Graduate Studies" (see the project's website for research reports and resources). As part of this project, we evaluated SAGE to examine developing a similar province-wide initiative to help Aboriginal undergraduates make the transition to graduate school (Archibald, Pidgeon, and Hawkey 2009). The SAGE program provided invaluable insight into the everyday experiences of Aboriginal graduate students at five BC universities. The program became a model for SAGEU (SAGE-Undergraduate). SAGE-Undergraduate's goal was to develop and provide resources to support Aboriginal undergraduate students in their transition to graduate school – from the time they first consider applying to the successful completion of their first year. Being a co-investigator of the "Aboriginal Transitions" research project and attending the SAGEU gatherings was inspiring. I saw not only the power and potential of our up-and-coming undergraduate students but also the leadership enacted by research assistants who were also undergraduate and graduate Aboriginal students. Through this project, I witnessed indigeneity, leadership, and institutional transformation in action.

The SAGE programs provide us with insight into the ways in which many Aboriginal students are becoming leaders in their fields academically and also on their campuses. As peer-mentors, they are sharing their knowledge, understanding, cultural and emotional support, and sense of belonging and relationships with one another. Relationships played a key role in the mentorship process, whether at the graduate or undergraduate level. Understanding the system, being able to know where to get resources, and knowing who in the institution one could rely on for information empowered individual students. These outcomes of the program also furthered the process of institutional change as staff and faculty became more aware of Aboriginal students' specific needs, and this awareness translated into culturally relevant graduate advising and support.

Conclusion

Indigenous leadership is conceptualized in this chapter as the embodiment of Indigenous ways of knowing. It connects the physical, emotional, cultural, and spiritual with the four *R*'s – respect, relevance, reciprocity, and responsibility. Indigenous leadership is shaped by Indigenous peoples' cultural knowledge, experiences, connection to place, contexts, and relationships. Theories of leadership have evolved from considering only individual traits and values to recognizing the complexity of leadership, that it is contingent on context, politics, and power, on situations, motivations, relationships (e.g., servant or transformational leadership), cultures, and gender, along with other factors (Northouse 2006). The qualities or traits of Indigenous leadership presented by Donald Day (2008) (e.g., vision, passion, character, thoughtfulness) are transferable to broader understandings of effective leadership. The qualities outlined by Day match those identified in my own research and discussions with Aboriginal educational leaders. In addition, Indigenous leadership implicitly suggests that Indigenous leaders take strength from their cultural teachings and integrate the lessons learned from their families, Elders, and communities (see Wihak et al. 2010 for information regarding Indigenous youth leadership and alliance-building). What is often missing from mainstream conversations about leadership is an acknowledgment of the inherent philosophical, epistemological, and cultural differences in *how relationships work* within Indigenous leadership. It is critical for Indigenous peoples to be part of these conversations because Aboriginal leadership involves another way of thinking about leadership (see Calliou 2006 for an extensive online bibliography on Indigenous leadership).

I have observed that Indigenous initiatives in higher education rarely originate from positions of power or formal leadership roles. Indigenous leadership is exemplified by those who work within the organization to build relationships with allies (whether Aboriginal or non-Aboriginal) to support an initiative. They continually engage in respectful and reciprocal practices that build trust, and they are committed to having relevant programs and services for Aboriginal communities. Aboriginal leadership is articulated through the concepts of reciprocity and relevance and through our cultural connections to place, in our sacred relationships with not only other beings but also the land, sea, and sky. Leadership, from an Indigenous community perspective, is, in fact, a communal activity embedded within a particular context.

Elgin Badwound and William Tierney (1988) note that Aboriginal programs in higher education are based on Western rationality, whereas Indigenous programs are based on holism. Within the Western paradigm, they argue, "leadership assumes that the central figure is authoritarian;

the leader has the confidence of organizational participants to make decisions and to lead the organization" (ibid., para. 16). By contrast, within Indigenous worldviews, "Central to the qualities possessed by the leader is the notion of spirituality, a condition that is neither learned nor certified, but is attained through the workings of a higher power or being. Indeed, it is wise individuals who sustain Indian culture and whose vision enables Indian societies to endure" (ibid.); see also Benham and Murakami-Ramalho 2010; Day 2008; and Montes 2007). Spirituality does not refer to a religious affiliation but rather to the essence of a being and to the higher order of the interconnectedness of all things. Shaping our future leaders means empowering them to connect to their warrior spirit, to engage in meaningful and respectful relationships, to honour the cultural integrity of each person, and to be responsible to one's community.

In my day-to-day work and research, I have found evidence that systemic change is not only possible but also sustainable. Indigenous peoples continue to forge and reinforce spaces within mainstream institutions for indigeneity. They are the true warriors and leaders of transformation as they work towards making university and college campuses more successful places for Aboriginal peoples.

Works Cited

Alfred, Taiaiake. 1999. *Peace, Power, Righteousness.* Oxford: Oxford University Press.

Archibald, Jo-ann, and Lee Brown. 2008. "Indigenous Transformational Higher Education at the University of British Columbia, Canada." Paper presented at the "Asia-Pacific Symposium and Workshop of Higher Education of Indigenous People and Nationalities," Nankai University, Tianjin, China, 28 February–2 March 2008 .

Archibald, Jo-ann, Michelle Pidgeon, and Colleen Hawkey. 2009. "Aboriginal Transitions: Undergraduate to Graduate Studies." AT:U2G Phase I final report, University of British Columbia, Vancouver.

Badwound, Elgin, and William G. Tierney. 1988. "Leadership and American Indian Values: The Tribal College Dilemma." *Journal of American Indian Education* 28, 1. http://jaie.asu.edu/v28/V28S1lea.htm.

Benham, Maenette, and Elizabeth Murakami-Ramalho. 2010. "Engaging in Educational Leadership: The Generosity of Spirit." *International Journal of Leadership in Education* 13, 1: 77-91.

Day, Donald R. 2008. "Reflecting upon Indigenous Leadership." *Bemaadizing: An Interdisciplinary Journal of Indigenous Life.* http://www.bemaadizing.org/.

Calliou, Brian. 2006. "Indigenous Leadership Bibliography." http://www.banffcentre. ca/departments/leadership/aboriginal/library/pdf/indigenous_leadership_ bibliography-brian_calliou.pdf.

Human Capital Strategies. 2005. "Review of Aboriginal Post-Secondary Education Programs, Services, and Strategies/Best Practices and Aboriginal Special Projects

Funding (ASPF) Program." Report for Ministry of Advanced Education, Province of British Columbia, 30 June. http://www.aved.gov.bc.ca/aboriginal/educator-resources.htm.

Kirkness, Verna J., and Ray Barnhardt. 1991. "First Nations and Higher Education: The Four R's – Respect, Relevance, Reciprocity, Responsibility." *Journal of American Indian Education* 30, 3. http://jaie.asu.edu/v30/V30S3fir.htm.

Kuokkanen, Rauna. 2007. *Reshaping the University: Responsibility, Indigenous Epistemes, and the Logic of the Gift.* Vancouver: UBC Press.

Mendelson, Michael. 2006. "Aboriginal Peoples and Postsecondary Education in Canada." Report for Caledon Insitute of Social Policy, July. http://www.caledoninst.org/Publications/PDF/595ENG.pdf.

Montes, Claudine. 2007. "Leadership in Native American Higher Education: A Call for a Collective Vision and Contemporary Warriors." *BC Educational Leadership Research EJournal* 8. http://slc.educ.ubc.ca/eJournal/Issue8/Leadership_journal_article_Claudine_Montes.pdf (accessed December 2011).

Northouse, Peter G. 2006. *Leadership: Theory and Practice.* 4th ed. Thousand Oaks, CA: Sage.

Pidgeon, Michelle. 2008. "It Takes More than Good Intentions: Institutional Accountability and Responsibility to Indigenous Higher Education." PhD diss., University of British Columbia.

Pidgeon, Michelle, and Donna Hardy Cox. 2005. "Perspectives of Aboriginal Student Services Professionals: Aboriginal Student Services in Canadian Universities." *Journal of Austrailian and New Zealand Student Services* 25: 3-30.

Royal Commission on Aboriginal Peoples. 1996. *Report of the Royal Commission on Aboriginal Peoples.* Vol. 3, *Gathering of Strength.* Ottawa: Minister of Supply and Services.

Statistics Canada. 2008. *Educational Portrait of Canada, 2006 Census.* Ministry of Industry. http://www12.statcan.ca/census-recensement/2006/as-sa/97-560/pdf/97-560-XIE2006001.pdf.

Wihak, Christine, Lynne Hatley, Sydney Allicock, and Michael Lickers. 2010. "Eagle and the Condor: Indigenous Alliances in Leadership Development." *Diaspora, Indigenous, and Minority Education* 1, 2: 135-48.

10

Translating and Living Native Values in Current Business, Global, and Indigenous Contexts

Gail Cheney

GRANDFATHER TOMMY LIKED to say, "We walk with one foot in the Western ways and one foot in our traditional ways. You need to take the best of both."[1] My grandparents are always with me. Their wisdom helps me to translate our shared Native values every day of my life. This chapter reveals both the values that are the foundation of our collective culture and the process that I follow to practise these values. In addition, I recognize that there are practices or definitions that surround values that we must change as a people, traditions that no longer support a healthy and balanced future. These traditions must be transformed to support, rather than weaken, our communities.

Since graduating from college in 1988, I have worked in a predominantly Western context, and I have learned that there are many similarities among people. What follows is an auto-ethnographic depiction of my personal process of translating traditional values in today's world, from the community to the corporation to the global context. As with many Indigenous people around the world, many of the dilemmas I encounter are ongoing, and my understanding of the world continues to change as I experience life and learn from others.

I move slowly to answer the phone. It is a call from the village. A collection effort is under way to gather money to support one of the families – Clara has been diagnosed with cancer. The money will be used to help pay for fuel to keep Clara warm and to help her family travel with her to see the doctor out of town. After the short call, I agree to send a money order to Ben for the family. I

Dedicated to the memory of Carol Jorgensen, mentor, *mama shaan*, and leader.

am smiling as I hang up on Ben, as I think about how he is always taking on this role, the role of organizing collective resources for other families. He puts himself in the awkward position of being refused so that the family does not have to ask for help when they are hurting and worried, so there are no hard feelings if someone can't contribute or chooses not to give.

I recall many years ago, when family members collected money to help me visit home for important events. I was in college, and my parents couldn't quite swing the bill. I feel melancholy as I remember those who encouraged me to continue in college, the beloved Elders and relatives that have since passed on. These recollections evoke worry about the decline of my hometown, a small Tlingit village in southeastern Alaska.

My memories of the village of my youth are rosy and safe, cradled in the arms of the community and Native traditions. I remember doing cultural dances while wearing a paper headdress. I remember reading the whole Nancy Drew series at the library. I remember the memorial parties in which Tlingit names and gifts were given to the appropriate family. It was safe for me to roam. The combination of Western and Indigenous values simply seemed right, the way of the world. Looking back with eyes that are less innocent and perhaps more wise, if not more cynical, the synergies and conflicts between the two worldviews are evident. The researcher in me strives to understand the framework that contains both worldviews in one house. The amalgamation of colonization, assimilation, acculturation and, finally, self-determination together form that house. Yet this house can hold ceremony, community, the earth, and individualism in harmony for the future. It is a house that holds all and has, at its foundation, traditional values. The translation of those values today, however, would look foreign to my Tlingit and Haida ancestors.

I wander about my rented home in suburban Seattle, feeling as though there are so many things unfinished. There is a Chilkat weaving of the ghost face sitting unfinished and forlorn in the corner, a Raven's Tail belt that has been partially complete for almost ten years, Tlingit language CD's that have been listened to off and on since college, and many unfinished Native clothing projects that strive to cross the boundaries between work and life in contemporary times, on the one hand, and community, family, and my personal worldview, on the other. Sighing, I sit down at my computer and try to summon the energy to work on the school-work I am delinquent on. The PhD program's learning requirements, which are only partially done, whisper my name like a guilty conscience.

The PhD assignments are like a shadow picture of the unfinished crafts. There is a bit of paper here and ideas for another learning requirement there. More things seem unfinished than complete. To top it off, there is more to do if I add my job into the mix of my obligations, a job with a successful regional Native corporation. I am currently part of the successful development of a for-profit subsidiary. All of my studies over the last four years have focused on one main question: How do we translate appropriate Native values into contemporary life? In particular, how can we shape our corporations and institutions to reflect our values? We are taught to consider a corporation a person, and it is important that the "person" we create is one who we would want to be part of our community, a leader who has a say in the future for us all.

I remember the main events that pushed me to pursue a PhD in leadership and change. First, of course, are my maternal grandparents. Grandfather, a devout Salvation Army church officer, took the time to understand how his faith and his Tlingit spirituality were aligned. He spent time trying to understand when there were conflicts between the two and resolve them. In the end, he was confident in his own soul and identity as a mix of both beliefs.

Second, I remember my time working for my village for-profit corporation. I witnessed the clear-cutting of 30,000 acres (12,141 hectares) of trees between 1971 and 1997. When there were 5,000 acres (2,023 hectares) left, I worked for my village as a planner and tried to diversify the economic base. Although I, along with others, tried to develop new businesses, the village embraced none of the proposed options, in part, I think, because the businesses would not pay as well as logging or fishing, in part because the type of work was not in line with the spirit of the community at the time, and in part because of a general unwillingness to face that the trees would soon be gone and life would change drastically for the worse. As part of that experience, I came to understand the harm that a family-centric or clan-centric culture can do within a corporate structure, much the same way that the lack of a collective vision for a business resource can restrict innovative initiatives or solutions. Another harmful idea, however, is the idea that the individual is more important than the health and success of future generations. Within the corporation, it is not the individual or the family that we must consider but the community. The act of logging without planning for the future of the resource was out of alignment with our traditional values, and our actions hurt our collective spirit as a community.

Our decision to log the land was based partially on traditional values, the desire to maintain our active lifestyle and work with natural resources. Grandfather used to say that one of the reasons we went into the logging business was so that our people would not become a welfare society, so they could work every day and feel good about working to support their families. Now, as I look at my village, I see a place where all the trees have been harvested, a place where youth no longer live because there are no jobs. This situation encourages me to scrutinize our values and adapt them to suit contemporary circumstances. In this case, I believe we should have balanced our desire to work with our need to protect resources for future generations, with our responsibility as stewards of the environment. For example, we could have chosen to build a sustainable logging industry.

If we had balanced all of our values, we would not be on the path we are now on. This is not a case of hindsight being twenty-twenty but a commitment to learning from previous mistakes as I move forward. In my studies, I read the work of Ronald L. Trosper, who describes the system that Northwest tribes developed to ensure the sustainable use of resources. With some adaptation, perhaps we could apply these traditional methods to avoid our present situation in the future. We would need to look at the whole system, including the values that underpinned it, in order to determine what actions, processes, and institutions would be needed to create a modern system that is accountable to the community, environment, and future generations. Trosper's description of the traditional system resonated with me:

> First, rights of access and use of valuable lands and fishing sites were recognized as property, meaning that individuals or groups could exclude others. Second, proprietorship was contingent on proper

management of the property. Third, a system of ethics defined proper use; the ethical beliefs defined abuse of land in terms of reduction of its productivity for future generations. Fourth, systems of reciprocity defined economic exchange relationships among people, both individually and in groups. Reciprocity provided incentives that supported proper use of lands both by providing insurance against misfortune and by reducing the incentive to harvest too much. Fifth, enforcement of reciprocity rules was totally public. Sixth and finally, rules about the behavior of chiefs provided a system of governance that could maintain the other five elements and allow modifications as needed. (Trosper 2002, 332-33)

Trosper's statement and understanding that things can be different offer a vision of people lifting one another up and remaining true to themselves, their values, and their community. I understood the real power that people have to shape their present and future from his example. Reminded of my motivations for my work, I return to a reading I am doing for a paper on global change.

As I complete the reading, I take notes on items that touch me because they are relevant and those that seem distasteful. One distasteful subject is colonization. Some authors take on the tone of a victim and blame all hurts in Native communities on this process. Some take on the tone of a militant and demand that all that has been done historically be remedied. The pieces that hold my interest discuss colonization dispassionately, as a piece of history. They make me think about colonization as a process that shaped the national and institutional frameworks in which Native Americans now live. Articles that help Native people value their own ways of understanding the world and move together towards action intrigue me. A quote in Linda Tuhiwai Smith's *Decolonizing Methodologies: Research and Indigenous Peoples* gains my attention: "In a decolonizing framework, deconstruction is part of a much larger intent. Taking apart the story, revealing underlying texts, and giving voice to things that are often known intuitively does not help people to improve their current conditions. It provides words, perhaps, an insight that explains certain experiences – but it does not prevent someone from dying" (Smith 1999, 3). Smith's book teaches me that research with Indigenous peoples must be more respectful, ethical, sympathetic, and useful.

Smith helps me see the imbedded framework that exists and to think about how we, as a collective, might reshape that framework to better address our hopes for the future. I read, however, Robert Innes's criticism that her guidelines are too vague, and I see where he is coming from but don't entirely agree (Innes 2004, 2). Smith's work is too vague for someone who is not a part of the community, but it provides perfect advice for those of us who understand that Native communities are fluid and that there is no one way to move forward on research. Each community is different. I understand that being flexible and inclusive is the only way to deal with a collective identity or entity and move forward.

I turn next to Calvin Helin's book *Dances with Dependency*. Helin helps me understand the reality, or facts, of doing research in the current Native American landscape. He raises the question of whether and how specific tools, methods, or institutions reflect colonialism. Helin indicates that welfare, whether it is negotiated or required by treaty, is a tool of colonialism when it is provided to an individual and not used to help the group become self-sufficient. He writes that welfare to individuals is "the quickest way to kill a man." I am happy to read, though, that there are new opportunities for Native peoples and that Native American groups are understanding and using their power to create the change they want to see. The following passage stands out:

> To exploit these opportunities will require a change in the dependency mindset of Aboriginal people. For lasting solutions, decisions have to come from Aboriginal people themselves. Aboriginals have to consciously choose a more beneficial path than the dependency course they are currently on ... Aboriginal citizens must take ownership of these problems and assert control over their own destinies. (Helin 2006, 39)

I find myself gravitating towards my dissertation topic rather than my global studies project, and I force myself to consider Linda Tuhiwai Smith within a global perspective. I focus on a question that is more relevant to the learning objective: Which Native practices or processes are scalable at a global level? I am surprised when Native ways of being are translated effectively in new contexts, including global contexts. I remember when, about two years ago, I participated in a transnational convention on Indigenous peoples and the environment. Fifty delegates from Canada, Mexico, and the United States came together in Mexico, in an area sacred to the Mayans. In that gorgeous, sacred, and historical place, we came together to agree on how to focus our various environmental actions for the best collective international impact.

The meetings stand out clearly in my mind because they followed the traditional circle formation, and we honoured each voice and perspective to arrive at consensus. Anyone who wished to speak was given equal time to tell the story of his or her own struggle. Before I arrived, I had worked to get materials ready that represented, in part, the efforts of Indigenous people in the United States to rebuild healthy environments. As I gathered the information, I realized how broad and diverse the issues were in the United States. Many people were fighting to overcome the adverse health impacts of mining resources such as uranium; others were focused on land claims; still others were concentrating on managing their own resources. These last two concerns were considered environmental issues because Indigenous people's relationship to place and environment cannot, typically, be separated from day-to-day life. I remember thinking that the broadness of the topic was due mainly to the holistic interdependence that Indigenous peoples see in all issues. I remember that when I talked to my mentor prior to the event, I even stated that the process would not work. How could a group of 150 Native leaders come to a consensus in five days? The lack of relationships, the lack of trust, and the complexity of the issues seemed to me to be barriers to success.

The meetings melded new technologies and contemporary facilitative processes with the traditional values of consultation. The delegates spoke many different languages. To overcome this barrier to true communication, all participants were issued headsets so they could listen to translations of the speeches. A team of experts – translators, policy writers, activists, and lawyers – listened to the participants and pulled themes and text from their discussions. The writing team listened and then translated our respective values, environmental issues, stories of struggle, understandings of protocol and process and, most importantly, visions into a collective call to action, which it presented to us as a written document. On the last two days, the larger group broke down into several smaller groups that shared an affinity for particular sections in the document. The smaller groups discussed the sections, expressed concerns, addressed gaps, and reached at least a partial consensus. Each group had several of the writing team present, and these individuals left the meeting and incorporated our comments into the document. After this revision, a larger group of leaders, along with the writing group, did one last edit and presented the revised document to the group. To my surprise, consensus had been reached; all members of the convention adopted the document.

I recall that I was forced to rethink my own framework. Where had I learned that consensus could only be achieved within a small group of five people or fewer or with a substantial time commitment? The answer was stunning. I had adopted Western ideas about facilitation and discounted the knowledge of my own people. What other Native processes would be effective in a contemporary setting? What elements of this process were fundamental, and what would they look like in other contexts?

I considered the elements that had made this convention a success. First, all people had shared their stories, and everyone had listened and heard. These stories established two things quickly and thoroughly: we had similar struggles, concerns, and visions for the future, and despite distance, different languages, and appearance, we were a community. Without a long relationship or long discussions, we saw the truth in the stories, and we trusted one another and our transient group. We saw in one another the same understanding of community: community is determined by what we contribute for the betterment of the whole, not what each individual receives. I also realized that a contextual model of consultation had been created and used to develop the final document. The first draft came from our stories. The second draft included revisions, which stemmed from deep discussion. The final draft was based on the leaders' and experts' efforts to tie it all together. Finally, we had agreed on a protocol that, although not specific to one tribe, followed a general pattern recognizable to all participants. This protocol helped us to hold one another and the group accountable for the outcome of the convention.

As in all processes, I remember thinking that there were some areas that could have been improved. For a group that honours community and relationships, it seemed a shame that we did not do more to protect the ties we had made. There were several young people in attendance (I consider myself part of this group, although I was thirty-eight at the time) who felt that we should develop a website or an email list to keep in touch, to support one another, and to continue our work. I remember being told that this next step was up to the Elders of the group. I remember thinking, why would the Elders and leaders of this group initiate a website or email list when it was not a tool that they used very much? Musing continued in this vein. What is the disconnect between the Elders and youth and the way we practise our values?

I was reminded of a story about an Indigenous girl who learned to make baskets. I had heard the story at one of Roger Fernandez's performances. In the story, the girl goes into the wilderness, where she learns from the tree, the snake, and the mountain how to make a good basket. She brings her knowledge with her back to the village and teaches her people. The story gave me hope because it reminded me of people like myself, people who, on the urging of their family, go away to school and then want to return and give that knowledge back. Why do so many Indigenous people struggle to earn a Western education and then return home only to be considered outsiders? Why does the knowledge we have been sent out to receive, make us strangers? I wonder if the answer to both questions is that Elders and youth, those educated at the knees of their Elders and those educated in Western colleges, must travel though a process together first, a process that helps each group see that their values are the same, even though the outer trappings and the ways those values are honoured may look different.

As I sit, lost in philosophical thoughts motivated and buffeted by my academic readings, I realize that the conference had expanded my interest in an adjacent idea: how to adapt Native processes and Western processes to come up with a new approach, one that incorporates Native values yet produces results within a time frame that meets modern-day standards. In my research, I began to look for other researchers or tribes who were exploring similar questions. I found two examples. I found the first while I was doing the research for the paper on global change I am now working on. It is the Indigenous Leaders Interactive System (ILIS), a structured dialogue system. The process has been used in international, regional, and community contexts with proven success. I found this description in an article by Laura Harris and Jacqueline Wasilewski:

> ILIS™ enables contemporary Indigenous groups to engage in systems thinking. ILIS™ recaptures traditional values of Indigenous people, for instance, sharing and respecting diverse perspectives in order to come to consensual decisions, the power of collective wisdom, and honoring each person's right to be heard. ILIS™ has helped bring Indigenous ancestral knowledge, in terms of systems thinking, back into our current consciousness. ILIS™ incorporates ancient tribal wisdom into our everyday, modern life. (Harris and Wasilewski 2004, 507)

I find a second example as I read about governance among the Sliammon First Nation of British Columbia. This First Nation melds traditional values and structures (such as family groups) with their governance systems, suggesting that traditional strengths can be harnessed anew to move the tribe forward. The author of the article, Siemthlut Michelle Washington, describes a system in which one family member is appointed to speak for the entire family. This person or an alternate then attends monthly meetings to hear from the community. The meetings are held in an open space so that members can work with others who are concerned about the same issues (Washington 2004, 602). What is wonderful to me about this system is that it allows individuals to be active and accountable as they work towards progress in the areas of their concern. These concerns are also codified and presented to those on council, who are also held accountable for progress against those priorities.

I am reminded that it behooves us to also look at those Western processes that we have adopted but do not fully adhere to our Native values. The use of Robert's Rules of Order by the Alaska Native Brotherhood and the Alaska Native Sisterhood comes to mind. I can understand why these rules were adopted when the goal of these organizations was to facilitate success in a Western context. Now, however, when their mandates also include preservation of culture, the rules do not seem in line with the collective good or consensus-based decision-making. Indeed, is this another example of Native people adopting a process that calls to a part of our values, our love for protocol, yet does not meet our need for collective discussion and generation of consensus? Perhaps it is simply my fear of this protocol that shades my thinking. In my experience, though, the rules feel like a barrier to good decisions rather than an invitation to move the group forward with one mind.

These flitting thoughts pull me to another insight I gained at the conference when two wonderful women from the Inuvialuit Regional Corporation described what they had learned from watching Native peoples' struggles to work within the constraints of the Alaska Native Claims Act. The act created direct breaks in governance by separating tribal and corporate jurisdiction and wealth. Their community, they told me, had been afraid to set up a corporation. They wanted their business and regional corporation to be accountable, directly accountable, to the villages. Their corporation included village corporations whose job it was to ensure that communities remained healthy and sustainable. The community elects members to direct the regional corporation, which, in turn, manages the businesses according to the community's wishes. I have only the two women's perspective on this issue, yet I appreciate that the infrastructure that they created allows the people to collectively generate a vision for the future and that they have the authority to ensure compliance. Although Alaska Native Corporations, such as the one I work for, do not adhere to this structure and in fact may not need to, I do believe that these corporate entities need a common vision of our future. This vision will ensure that the "corporate" members of our community also understand and support our vision. That day at the conference, I realized that we can find a way of generating consensus and a common vision for the future by using both Native and Western processes in Alaska Native Corporations.

The short stories and exploration of my values in practice reflect the constant engagement between my traditional values, my various contexts, and those researchers who have explored this territory before me. I hope that these scattered and yet connected sets of ideas clearly illustrate the ongoing process I follow to make sense of my traditional values and practise them in all contexts, the process I follow to translate and remain true to those values in a changing Western and Indigenous world. I leave you with a final metaphor to explain the embedded process through which I translate my values.

I think of a three-day celebration of Tlingit, Haida, and Tsimshian culture that I recently attended. I saw the transformation of culture happen right before my eyes. One dance group fell more on the traditional side of the spectrum. Their regalia was made from contemporary materials, but the cloth was mainly wool, and the designs were traditional. The songs that they sung came from our ancestors and were the property of the community. At the other end of the spectrum, I saw a small group that likewise blended beautiful traditional art with contemporary, sheer regalia, but they only sang new songs, songs that connect us to the past and yet move us towards the future. We need both to succeed collectively. As Grandfather says, "We need to take the best of both worlds."

Note

1 Thomas L. Jackson Sr. was my grandfather, and this was one of his favourite quotes. It is an anchor for me as I try to make sense of Native values in any non-Native context. Grandfather shared the quote with me when I was young, during the years between 1974 and 1981.

Works Cited

Harris, Laura, and Jacqueline Wasilewski. 2004. "Indigenous Wisdom of the People Forum: Strategies for Expanding a Web of Transnational Indigenous Interactions." *Systems Research and Behavioral Science* 21: 505-14.

Helin, Calvin. 2006. *Dances with Dependency: Out of Poverty through Self-Reliance.* Woodland Hills, CA: Ravencrest Publishing.

Innes, Robert Alexander. 2004. "American Indian Studies Research Is Ethical Research: A Discussion of Linda Smith and James Waldram's Approach to Aboriginal Research." *Native Studies Review* 15, 2: 131-38.

Smith, Linda Tuhiwai. 1999. *Decolonizing Methodologies: Research and Indigenous Peoples.* New York: Zed Books.

Trosper, Ronald L. 2002. "Northwest Coast Indigenous Institutions That Supported Resilience and Sustainability." *Ecological Economics* 41: 329-44.

Washington, Siemthlut Michelle. 2004. "Bringing Traditional Teachings to Leadership." *American Indian Quarterly* 28, 3-4: 583-603.

11

Approaching Leadership through Culture, Story, and Relationships

Michelle Archuleta

IMAGINE BEING ABLE TO live in a community steeped in Native history and culture. Tó Naneesdizí (Tuba City, Arizona) is a small Navajo community located on the western side of the Navajo Nation. The landscape is full of landmarks that tell you where you are by looking into the distance. To the east are the Hopi Mesa Lands; to the south, the majestic San Francisco Peaks; to the west, the northern rim of the Grand Canyon; and to the north, the tall sandstone cliffs that lead to Page, Arizona, and Lake Powell.

When I arrived in Indian country, I had no idea what was in store for me. I remember my first day as if it were yesterday. I was filled with excitement and the realization that this would be a turning point in my life. During the ten years I worked in Tuba City, I made profound friendships with a core group of women who were not only professional colleagues but also guides who courageously and compassionately showed me the way of working and leading at the community level. This group of dedicated women became instrumental in shaping my understanding of leadership from a cultural perspective, a perspective I did not have coming in. I learned from them by participating with them, which is the best way of learning. Marie Nelson and Shirley Nelson helped me understand the nuances of culture, traditions, and stories, and they continue to work in the field of health promotion and disease prevention (HPDP) on the Navajo Nation. Marie Nelson is the Navajo area HPDP consultant for the Indian Health Service, and Shirley Nelson is the HPDP coordinator for the Fort Defiance Indian Hospital, Fort Defiance Service Unit. I discussed the role of culture, particularly narrative and story, in the leadership learning process with these women at Antioch University in August 2010. These women's stories, when shared within the context of historical developments and differing perspectives on leadership (both Native and non-Native), stand as real examples of how Native people lead through culture, story, and relationships.

Leadership Theories: What They Tell Us

Leadership is in the midst of change. The current leadership model, which emerged in step with the industrial age, is mostly outdated. Mainstream leadership theories are generally leader-centric. They reflect the bureaucratic, hierarchical organizational paradigms of industrial structures (Uhl-Bien, Marion, and McKelvey 2007). The practices of rationalization and control were the benchmarks of this industrial framework, and they influenced the traditional assumptions that underpin theories of leadership (ibid.).

Leadership theories also tend to focus on how leaders engage with followers. This focus is apparent in the theory of leadership as emergent social structuring (see, e.g., Schwandt 2008) and in theories of distributed leadership (see, e.g., Gronn 2002) and shared leadership (see, e.g., Pearce and Conger 2003). According to Gary Yukl (1999, 292-93), "distributed leadership does not require an individual who can perform all of the essential leadership functions, only a set of people who can collectively perform them. Some leadership functions (e.g., making important decisions) may be shared by several members of a group, some leadership functions may be allocated to individual members, and a particular leadership function may be performed by different people at different times. The leadership actions of any individual leader are much less important than the collective leadership provided by members of the organization." Other scholars focus on situational leadership. Situational leaders, they argue, amend their style of leadership to match the competence and commitment of their employees; by doing so, they engage in the process of accommodation (see, e.g., Northouse 2007).

Joseph Rost (1993) argues that although we have a robust inquiry into the field of leaders and leadership, the scholarship still lacks a clear understanding of what, exactly, leadership is. In an attempt to define the essence and nature of leadership, I assess my own beliefs about leadership for appropriateness and authenticity – in other words, I examine my own ability to serve Native families and Native communities. Leadership is not unchanging or one-dimensional. As James Youngblood Henderson states, "To see things as permanent is to be confused about everything"

(Kenny 2004, 265). Leadership is therefore the ability to balance traditional culture with strategies to navigate the uncertainty and complexity of our times, bringing forth the resilient nature of all of us.

Culture and Leadership

While writing this chapter I realized the impact of culture on my leadership practice. I recognized that my own leadership story had been shaped by the friendships I made during my time on the Navajo Nation and with my Hopi friends. From a phenomenological perspective, the lived experiences of Marie and Shirley Nelson reveal how their Navajo culture influenced their attitudes and beliefs and, more importantly, how culture provided guidance for their leadership actions.

WHAT IS THE VALUE OF UNDERSTANDING LEADERSHIP IN A
LIFE-STORY CONTEXT?

Marie: This means, to me, having respect and going beyond leadership.
   The context is working with people, colleagues, and other leaders,
   but in terms of respect, and going beyond it means understanding
   one's life within one's culture and being connected to living things.
   For example, recently, I just learned about a governance decision on
   Navajo that sets in motion a divergence of our fundamental laws of
   culture ... shifting the way Navajo people approach guidance to that
   of a Western "leadership" approach. The impact is a replacing of our
   cultural aspect and ways of thinking when making decisions and
   right actions.

Shirley: Some people are naturally born to be leaders ... and some are
   called upon to be led. My upbringing definitely influenced my view
   and understanding of leadership. I grew up in Klagetoh, a small
   community on the south-central area of the Navajo Reservation.
   There was not much in the way of modern development or impact.
   During my childhood, the majority of homes in the community lacked
   modern conveniences, like electricity or indoor plumbing, et cetera.
   I was given certain responsibilities – to care for my siblings, livestock,
   daily tasks, and care for myself. We were encouraged to go to school.
   I was often told, "Experience the challenges of your responsibilities
   and master those skills. They are important and useful." Living in
   harsh conditions forced me to adapt and survive. I was told the
   experiences I learned early in life would be important lessons as
   I got older. I was taught to rise early and train your mind, body, and

spirit, to "learn to be resilient, overcome challenges and adapt to changes and be strong." My Elders cautioned me that my enemies were laziness, poverty, and other self-defeating behaviours that were waiting to defeat me if I did not get up at dawn to prepare for my day with prayer, positive thoughts, and develop physical endurance. They told me, "One day you will be called to lead, make decisions, and you must be ready to lead your people. If you do not prepare now, you will not be able to lead."

These teachings formed the foundation and view of leadership for me. I've developed the skills learned from my childhood, am applying it to my place in Western society, education, and work. Foresight, responsibility, and accountability are highly valued in leaders in my Native culture.

What is challenging is the range of formal leadership "styles" found in corporate culture. The competitive approach in Western culture is another challenge for me. Native (specifically Navajo) cultures emphasize cooperation and collaboration with everyone in a group for the good of the community or nation. True leadership is not what you gain but what you can provide and/or offer for the greater good and for all. Western traditions promote competitiveness for individual gain. This is in opposition to the traditions of my beliefs. My grandparents often stressed the importance and ability of having to learn, think, and speak two languages and the ability to live in two worlds, that of Western society and our Native ways. Native leaders have to meet this challenge daily, leading in a duel system or setting.

WHAT WAS YOUR MOST MEANINGFUL LEARNING EXPERIENCE AS IT RELATES TO LEADERSHIP?

Marie: My most meaningful experience was having the opportunity of being a part of an organization that incorporated Navajo culture into a Western [hospital] culture setting – specifically, the incorporation of the traditional healer. I would say that our leadership saw the value of integrating holistic care practices (alternative medicine), and because of this, it left an impression on me with my own practices with the field of health promotion and my personal wellness. I also appreciated the level of awareness that our leadership had with spirituality, especially with our wellness conferences. This opened me to seeing another way of wellness complementing my own culture.

Shirley: I recollect two significant occurrences that had great impact on me regarding leadership – the first being the influence of my grandfather 'Anihwii'aahii (his Navajo name to mean "the judge") Sam Chee Yazzie and Annie Wauneka, the first Navajo woman to serve on the Navajo Nation Council. I've spent a lot of time in their company as they had their conversations over politics and community issues. As I listened to their conversation, I observed how carefully they said things (words), what they did (action), what they believed in, and their courage to exhibit their leadership.

While life may have been a lot simpler then, major issues today impact our lives with grazing rights, to land and water. Elders were careful about their leadership decisions because they knew it would impact the lives of future generations. When our local Elders discussed issues, they were careful if an issue was left unresolved. It could get out of hand and result in conflict and violence. Leadership requires risk, striving to maintain balance for the best outcome for the people you lead. Sometimes that risk may result in or create conflict, but one must focus on the good of all.

My second memory is when I lost my parents about thirty-one years ago. The loss of my parents forced me into taking more responsibility, an unexpected role that came overnight. My sudden role as a family leader and assuming responsibility for my younger siblings required that I relied on grandmother and father's lessons about knowing yourself, values, identity, beliefs, and culture. Their teaching and stories provided guidance and the strength to lead my family through difficult times.

The history and traditions of our people has prepared me for leadership and learning how to endure in hard times and making important decisions for my family. Sometimes, the circumstances of life and events force leadership on you, as was the case with me. From these experiences, I've learned that, in leadership, there is continual change. Adapting to varied situations is a skill that can be applied to directing and guiding others. Leadership is moulded by many experiences and part of the natural life cycle.

HAVING A LEADERSHIP ROLE ON NAVAJO, HOW DO YOU SEE YOURSELF AS A LEADER? WHAT DO YOU NEGOTIATE?

Marie: I see myself as a person who takes time to understand and listen. I take things very seriously and look for consensus. I make every effort to change and improve based on what is needed. I try not to let barriers prevent us from working together, and I try to find solutions to overcome them. I negotiate a lot of things. I look for win-win efforts. I value participatory approaches to creating win-win opportunities.

Shirley: As a Navajo woman, I highly revere my traditional teachings and philosophy of life. These teachings have been handed down for generations and sustained our people to survive to this day. It is from these lessons that I have formed my approach to leadership and interactions with my colleagues. I am not willing to compromise principles taught through the many lessons from my Navajo way of life. These teachings set the standard by which I am to conduct myself as a woman and the role I play to ensure the well-being of my people. The role of a leader is to make sure that a community is healthy, safe, and continues to thrive.

Navajo leaders are expected to be respectful and treat everyone equally, be a strong advocate, talk to the people in a positive healthy way, and, especially, to protect, value, care, and respect our people and communities.

How has your experience on Navajo shaped your leadership?

Marie: I am a Navajo woman. I was raised traditionally, where I herded sheep, planted corn, and spent time with our Elders. To me, leadership is having the understanding of what is the essence or knowing the essentials of leadership.

The foundation goes back to my cultural heritage – where I was taught about leadership, with self as an individual – and knowing my roles and responsibilities to my family, community, and other clans. All of this has prepared me to be in my leadership position as the health promotion area consultant. There is value in the way I was brought up. I believe that because of my family and culture, I was provided a set of elements or components that serves as a plan for leadership. These core elements are respect, resiliency, listening, and having passion, compassion, and sincerity to strive towards your goal or vision. It is a universal approach.

Shirley: There is so much that I have learned at each place at which I have worked and have come to rely on the teachings of my Elders and our philosophy of life. Working at the various places on Navajo held new and different experiences for me. With all of these experiences, I found myself being tested by life on the reservation, unforeseen events, and nature.

After obtaining my formal education, I returned to work on Navajo. I decided that my education would be most beneficial for my people to work in the prevention field and found the best fit in health promotion. It is interesting how this fit in well with my traditional upbringing. I learned that the skills and experience of my childhood were still valid and applicable today. I had a lot in common with my colleagues when I came to work in health promotion. We had similar backgrounds, experience, and vision for healthy Navajo communities. They, too, related to my traditional upbringing and teachings. It was like a revelation and reconnection to our roots.

Out of this recognition we came to realize the importance of integrating the Navajo philosophy of life and health and the cardinal four directions to organize the health promotion programs on Navajo. The Navajo philosophy of life and health defined the teachings for well-being, striving for harmony, and looking forward to live a long and healthy life.

Our formal education served us by providing the tools and means to plan strategies of how we could apply our traditional view of wellness. We looked at the strength and the positive attributes of our communities and focused on harmony, balance, and respect for the environment and life of all forms. We did not focus on the disease processes, which are contrary to our views of health. We recognized the spiritual realm of wellness as a very important component which lies at the core of our view of wellness.

We acknowledged that the principles, teachings, and philosophy of our Navajo Elders are as valid today as it has been through the ages. Our Navajo people survived on their teachings and practices long before Western medicine was available to them. Reaching old age was in the prayers of our Elders for all generations that followed. Old age was revered.

WHAT ARE YOUR HOPES AND DREAMS FOR THE NAVAJO COMMUNITY, AND HOW DO YOU SEE YOURSELF CONTRIBUTING TO THEM?

Marie: That they would be able to embrace change for the better and that they should not hold back. We need to let go of *shah* (what can you do for me?) and take on the approach of how can I do for you? We mistakenly became conditioned by social services, health care, and welfare, where we have forgotten our sense of self and self-sufficiency. For many on Navajo, there is a loss of cultural teachings on the importance of getting up early, running in the morning to greet the sun, and working hard. In my work with health promotion, I try at every opportunity to support and bring forth the value and understanding of the four directions as a way of sustaining the fundamental practices of Navajo teachings. We now have the Navajo Wellness Model, which is tailored to public health and the socio-ecological framework. This includes the individual, family, community, and environmental contributing factors that have influence on an individual's behaviours.

Shirley: I would like to see strong, healthy, and committed leaders for Navajo Nation, like our old warrior "Chief Manulito." We need strong leaders who have a vision for the future of our children, people, community, and our nation, leaders who will advocate for our youth and who have a vision and hope for the future. We must begin to invest in providing leadership opportunities for our youth. My contribution will be to make sure that our cultural experiences and traditions are not excluded and that I share my life stories and experience with our youth.

HOW HAS YOUR LEADERSHIP ROLE CHANGED? WHEN YOU BEGAN, AT THE PRESENT MOMENT, AND INTO THE FUTURE.

Marie: Coming from a SU [service unit] to an area position, it has changed where I have to find ways of working with SU's at each level. They each have their own plans in place, and now, I have to view myself as a consultant, not a supervisor or management. As a consultant, you give advice and recommendation, and this can complicate things at times, given individual goals. There is a lot of give and take on a daily basis. I have to go with where they are at and look to support them. I am their advocate.

Shirley: Based on the Navajo philosophy of life, and the four directions of life, my leadership has evolved in each stage. East (birth to early childhood) the leadership skills that I learned during my childhood, that I alluded to in previous discussion. South (youth) I received my formal education and teachings of the Western world. West (adulthood), where I brought my leadership learned from rich traditional teachings and cultures with my formal education and applied in my adult role. My work in health and wellness brought the opportunity to apply my leadership experience. I am in the west direction, tenets of doing and or performing. I am moving toward the north direction, tenets of assurance and or self-reliance. I am now a matriarch to my nieces, and this is a new period where providing leadership will take the form of mentoring and validating. I have to rely on my life experience and wisdom to lead. This is a whole new level of leadership and/or responsibility for me. The role of matriarch is ahead for me – the duties and expectations of this role as a Navajo woman in my family and our community.

FROM 1999 TO 2009 WE HAD A TEAM OF HPDP COLLEAGUES ON NAVAJO. WHAT IN YOUR OPINION MADE LEADERSHIP WORK?

Marie: We knew each other and valued each other's strengths. We worked together as a team. We were professional in our interactions and had a vision of where we wanted to go. We also had a very good facilitator with Dr. Percy, and he was able to guide us with our work. He really helped simplify the process, in a way, helping create an atmosphere of teamwork.

We all knew each other at the individual level *(Ke')*. Our journey with each other was personal and professional. We all shared equally in the creating of the journey with compassion and respect. Yes, we may have been different, with ideologies, viewpoints, perspectives and upbringings, but we were all on the same team. We valued each other beyond our professional roles.

Shirley: HPDP coordinators of the time period 1999 to 2009 grew up in a generation, an era, of tremendous social change, for example, the civil rights movement, Martin Luther King Jr., John F. Kennedy, American Indian movement, the women's movement, and youth questioning society.

It was a time of major research and advancement in all areas of our society, such as space exploration, computers, and cell phones. There was a lot of creativity with influences of the Beatles, Elvis Presley, Michael Jackson, and Steve Jobs. Coming from this era left a great impression on most of us, and we were to believe in possibilities and a mindset that we can achieve anything we set our minds to.

Naturally, the HPDP coordinators aspired to building a healthy Navajo community by bringing the strength of two worlds. We brought creativity by bringing together our formal education in public health and our basic teaching of our Navajo culture, bringing about innovations to build a solid and strong health promotion program on Navajo.

We were a generation exposed to major social changes and applied those experiences to create positive changes on Navajo. Our HPDP coordinators had a great deal of respect for each other and valued one another's views and capabilities.

We were pioneers, innovators, and visionaries in the field of health promotion on Navajo, perhaps for all Native people in general. What we created in Navajo became a template for others to follow. I am very proud to have been a part of a very passionate group of HPDP coordinators who were courageous to risk and take leadership in a field in which they created a vision and leadership for the future for generations to come.

I am thankful to our Elders, who long ago laid the basic foundation of their teachings that continue to survive in the modern day. Their ways was our medicine before there was Western medicine. It is our Navajo teachings that launched our leadership. Youth will be challenged to overcome the concept of entitlement and expectation for quick success and advancement on the career ladder. The best approach for leadership is to live, experience, invest time, preserve, learn, and use this wisdom for improving conditions for all.

As a Native person and leader, what will the impact on your life story be if your culture is lost?

Marie: I see the impact happening in the area of health promotion and disease prevention, especially with the work that we, as a health promotion team, try to have in our communities, schools, and health care settings. On Navajo, we align our prevention work culturally with the four directions of Navajo philosophy. If this tenet is not supported from the top, then it will impact health at the community level. What may seem as a good decision based on different cultural norms will be a loss at our expense culturally. The younger generation will not know or hear the stories, lessons, and teachings that are now shared in school settings, immersion programs, or Dine College. The value will not be held as high as it is now.

Shirley: I have a hard time picturing this. There is a lot of information, materials, and history recorded about Navajo culture and heritage. If our culture is lost, it is because we have not been vigilant about keeping our traditions and language. We have an opportunity to learn our language and culture. We do not practise patience as our Elders did in the past. We are fast-paced, time-critical in modern society. Learning and experience in the Navajo way requires patience, discipline, and perseverance. In the past, young people began apprenticeship in childhood, learning traditional healing methods and ceremonies from grandparents and Elders. Young apprentices were guided by Elders through life until one is ready to practise without guidance. Today, young people do not want to devote themselves to learning our traditions or language. Doing so would compete for their time. It is not easy for a person to put time in learning the old ways – it would require personal sacrifices.

My leadership challenge will be to give opportunities for our Navajo youth to learn their language, learn about Navajo teachings, ceremonies, and traditions. We need to make time or accommodate ways that traditional Navajo teachings and practices can be taught to our children and youth so they have an opportunity, as I had, to experience life taking the best of both cultures – Navajo and Western.

Marie and Shirley emphasize cultural influences that have shaped their leadership practice. Their narratives reveal the wisdom of their lived experiences, enriched by feelings, thoughts, and actions. Of particular significance is their common understanding of the role of Navajo teachings and philosophy, the use of persuasion, the need for a collective call to action, and the difficulties and tensions that arise when leadership is thrust upon one because of unforeseen circumstances. Both of these women were aware that they were entering a new time that demanded a new type of leadership, among themselves, in their professions, and for their communities. As formal and informal leaders in our own organizations, we have much to learn from narrative processes in the field of leadership.

Narrative and Storytelling

From a cultural viewpoint, it is imperative that the best possible research methodologies be applied to understanding and framing Indigenous peoples' experiences (Kenny 2004). There are numerous ways to affirm lived experiences, but particularly meaningful methodologies approach Indigenous cultures within a holistic framework. Valerie Bentz and Jeremy Shapiro (1998) recommend an approach that complements both the researcher's style and worldview and the setting. Qualitative research is essential (Smith 1999). A qualitative approach makes identities known and, in particular, draws out the meaning of Aboriginal stories (Kenny 2004). Furthermore, when Aboriginal people tell their own stories, the old story of colonization is deconstructed. Power is brought back to the Aboriginal culture (Smith 1999).

Storytelling and narrative bring forth shared experiences. They provide participants with the chance to make sense of past events and to anticipate constructing a new future. Christina Baldwin (2005, 25) states:

Story – the abundance of it, and the lack of it – shapes us.

Story – the abundance of it, and the lack of it – gives us place, lineage, history, a sense of self.

Story – the abundance of it, and the lack of it – breaks us into pieces, shatters our understanding, and gives it back over and over again; the story is different every time.

Story – the abundance of it, and the lack of it – connects us with the world and outlines our relationship with everything.

When the power of story comes into the room, an alchemical reaction occurs that is unique to our kind: love or hate, identification or isolation, war or peace, good or evil can be stirred in us by words alone. The power of story is understood by the powerful, yet the power of story belongs to all of us, especially the least powerful. History is what scholars and conquerors say happened; story is what it was like to live on the ground.

Relationships

Relational theory posits that being in a dyadic relationship – a relationship that consists of two parts, such as the mother-child, friend-to-friend, or colleague-to-colleague dyad – offers a sense of mutuality. The relationship gives participants a budding opportunity to experience a renewed sense of self-worth, increased energy, and a desire for more connections with others (Miller and Stiver 1997). Being in such a relationship is a creative, dynamic process that promotes the growth of new knowledge and understanding through transformative exchanges. From the perspective of Native leadership as told through the stories of Marie and Shirley, relational theory reflects a core principle in Indian country – the principle that all things are related in a natural way, often referred to as the principle of interconnectivity.

Writing about theory is one thing. Placing it in the context of one's own life lends a different perspective. During a conversation with a colleague, Katie Kilty, whom I met during my time on Navajo, I learned with great surprise that much of my own work in Native communities fit well within the leadership construct of relational cultural theory (Katie Kilty, in discussion with the author, January 2011). Relational theory and relational cultural theory posit that relationships do not exist in isolation and that a shared sense of mutuality must be present for growth to occur. Over ten years in the field of health promotion on Navajo, I definitely observed this to be true in the friendships established among the Navajo area health promotion coordinators. This sense of mutuality allowed us to support one another's actions with the assurance that each of us had something to offer and that, through our connections, we were enhancing and making a contribution towards the greatest good.

Linking the Past, Creating the Future

Kimberly Boal and Patrick Schultz (2007, 412) state, "The concept of complex adaptive systems shows that surprising and innovative behaviors can emerge from the interaction of groups of agents, seemingly without the necessity of centralized control. Here again there is the question of, 'what is the role of leadership in such systems?'" Setting a vision for the group is considered a necessary component of leadership in mainstream leadership theories. Proponents of a holistic approach to leadership, however, suggest that collective organizational storytelling would be more effective. By telling stories, principally stories about their organization's or community's past history, leaders and followers can become catalysts for change. My own experience working on the Navajo Nation were influenced by my colleagues' stories and reflections pertaining to their upbringing and cultural influences, by societal paradigms relevant to public health, by health disparities, and by the dissonance between Western and Indigenous leadership norms and practices and ways of knowing.

Conclusion

By acknowledging the importance of culture, story, and relationship in approaches to leadership, we can begin to change the stories that serve as leadership constructs in Native communities (Carolyn Kenny, in discussion with the author, May 2011). Leadership is complex. It cannot completely be defined by theories or particular research methodologies. Leadership begins with stories of leaders and followers that are unique to each context. Our stories serve to animate and inspire us to move beyond imagined barriers because we know who we are and where we come from.

Works Cited

Baldwin, Christina. 2005. *Storycatcher: Making Sense of Our Lives through the Power and Practice of Story.* Novato, CA: New World Library/Green Press Initiative.

Bentz, Valerie Malhotra, and Jeremy J. Shapiro. 1998. *Mindful Inquiry in Social Research.* Thousand Oaks, CA: Sage.

Boal, Kimberly B., and Patrick L. Schultz. 2007. "Storytelling, Time, and Evolution: The Role of Strategic Leadership in Complex Adaptive Systems." *Leadership Quarterly* 18, 4: 411-28.

Gronn, Peter. 2002. "Distributed Leadership as a Unit of Analysis." *Leadership Quarterly* 13, 4: 423-51.

Kenny, Carolyn. 2004. *A Holistic Framework for Aboriginal Policy Research.* Ottawa: Research Directorate, Status of Women Canada.

Miller, Jean Baker, and Irene Pierce Stiver. 1997. *The Healing Connection: How Women Form Relationships in Therapy and in Life.* Boston: Beacon Press.

Northouse, Peter G. 2007. *Leadership Theory and Practice.* Thousand Oaks, CA: Sage.

Pearce, Craig L., and Jay A. Conger, eds. 2003. *Shared Leadership: Reframing the Hows and Whys of Leadership.* Thousand Oaks, CA: Sage.

Rost, Joseph C. 1993. *Leadership for the Twenty-First Century.* Westport, CT: Praeger.

Schwandt, David R. 2008. "Individual and Collective Coevolution: Leadership As Emergent Social Structuring." In *Complexity Leadership.* Part 1, *Conceptual Foundations,* edited by Mary Uhl-Bien and Russ Marion, 101-28. Charlotte, NC: Information Age.

Smith, Linda Tuhiwai. 1999. *Decolonizing Methodologies: Research and Indigenous Peoples.* London/Dunedin: Zed Books/University of Otago Press.

Uhl-Bien, Mary, Russ Marion, and Bill McKelvey. 2007. "Complexity Leadership Theory: Shifting Leadership from the Industrial Age to the Knowledge Era." *Leadership Quarterly* 18, 4: 298-318.

Youngblood Henderson, James (Sákéj). 2000. "*Ayukpachi:* Empowering Aboriginal Thought." In *Reclaiming Indigenous Voice and Vision,* edited by Marie Battiste, 248-78. Vancouver: UBC Press.

Yukl, Gary. 1999. "An Evaluation of Conceptual Weaknesses in Transformational and Charismatic Leadership Theories." *Leadership Quarterly* 10, 2: 285–305.

PART 3

Healing and Perseverance

12

"We Want a Lifelong Commitment, Not Just Sweet Words"

Native Visions for Educational Healing

Michelle M. Jacob

THIS IS A STORY ABOUT healing, about Native people working to reclaim educational institutions that sit on Indigenous homelands. This story expresses the great responsibility that Native people feel – to our cultures, to our ancestors, to all the leaders, students, teachers, and healers of the past, and to the students, teachers, and healers who are yet to come. It is about fulfilling one's potential to carry out the instructions that the Creator has provided. To be a leader is to be a servant.

This is the definition of Native leadership that I was taught growing up on the Yakama Reservation in Washington State. Family members and tribal leaders taught me the importance of rising to one's potential to make the best contribution possible to our people as a collectivity. Yakama cultural lessons teach us that strong, communally oriented individuals make the strongest collectivity. When I was a child, tribal youth who had good attendance or good grades were honoured each year by tribal leaders. The leaders paid for a special field trip to our tribal headquarters. A ceremony and meal honoured our achievements. Family and community members beamed with pride as they helped to honour the next generation of Native leaders. At each of these special occasions, tribal leaders reminded us that our work as students was a reflection on our tribal nation. We had a responsibility to do our best work so that our people would be represented in a good way, to reach our potential as students and, ultimately, to become leaders within our community.

Although they did not use the language of contemporary Indigenous studies theory, I see now that these ceremonies were steeped in a desire to decolonize tribal youth and educational systems. Like the other Native women contributors to this volume, my cultural teachings inform my work. They are my roots, my foundation for everything I do as a professor of

179

ethnic studies within the academy. In my work with Native women from several tribal backgrounds, I see that we have common expectations for Native leaders. We expect them to be community-based, dedicated to honouring our cultures, and working towards decolonization.

Historically, Western educational institutions have been sites of violence and discrimination for Native peoples. Scholars have discussed how mainstream educational institutions marginalize Native peoples and cultures (Deloria and Wildcat 2001; Mihesuah and Wilson 2004; Tierney 1992). An emerging body of scholarship links violence within educational institutions with Native mental health problems; such work calls attention to the need to heal the historical trauma perpetuated within educational systems (Walters and Simoni 2009). Other important work calls attention to the importance of microaggressions – "subtle insults (verbal, nonverbal, and/ or visual) directed towards people of color, often automatically or unconsciously" – as a form of violence that negatively impacts the mental health of people of colour (Solorzano, Ceja, and Yosso 2000, 60; Evans-Campbell 2008). However, we need to better understand how microaggressions within educational settings may be perpetuating historical trauma among Native peoples. This chapter seeks to help fill this gap by reporting findings from a case study of microaggressions experienced by Native peoples on one California college campus.

Historical Trauma, Microaggressions, and the Need for Healing
American Indians have pressing educational needs. The National Indian Education Association (NIEA) (n.d.) reports that "the national [high school] graduation rate for American Indian students was 49.3 percent in the 2003-04 school year, compared to 76.2 percent for white students. Only 44.6 percent of American Indian males and 50 percent of American Indian females graduated with a regular diploma in the 2003-04 school year." Although primarily focused on K-12 education, the NIEA's recommendations hold for higher education as well. In discussing what makes an educational institution successful, it states, "Schools successfully serve Native students when the parents, families, tribes, and the local communities are actively involved and engaged in the school's programs and activities" (NIEA n.d.). Thus, Native students are best served when their communities are full partners with the educational institutions, a point that Michelle Pidgeon (see Chapter 9) also makes in this volume. Shared power and collaboration are important in transforming educational institutions into places that honour and respect Native peoples. The day-to-day

operation of such educational institutions may help Native students heal rather than suffer further forms of violence that perpetuate historical trauma.

The idea that Native peoples and cultures are not welcomed and embraced within educational institutions is not new. Commenting on the troubled history of Native education in the US context, the NIEA (n.d.) states, "From the beginning, the curriculum in Indian schools offered no Indian languages, culture, or history. There was no recognition that culture and land are interrelated – and that removing the people from their land and denying them their culture would take away their very essence and destroy them." What is needed, as one tribal leader stated during a community forum held on 19 April 2007, is "a lifelong commitment by the university, not just *sweet words.*" Focus group participants revealed that campuses need to transform into spaces of healing for our people, while the community forum participants provided instruction on how to make this happen. (All interviews were conducted in confidentiality, and the names of interviewees are withheld by mutual agreement.)

As part of a larger team effort to understand factors related to diversity and campus climate, two focus groups were held with Native students, staff, and faculty at a California university in 2007. As the only full-time Native faculty member on campus, I was asked to participate in both focus groups. Our discussions revealed the pain and shame that Native people experience on campus. At the heart of many of the problems is the manner in which Native peoples are dehumanized in daily campus life. American Indians are commonly invited to campus to perform stereotypical and historical roles. There is evidence that university personnel often consider American Indians as having value only if they are stuck in history. Various participants were, for example, asked to offer a prayer with smoke and feathers at events, to give traditional cultural performances in traditional costume, or to sit and do traditional arts and crafts as a demonstration while university folks passed by.

Contemporary, critical perspectives by Native Americans are not welcomed because they challenge dominant discourses about who American Indians are. Haunani-Kay Trask (1999) found similar "multicultural" views at a university that preferred Indigenous peoples to be stuck silently in history, to offer traditional cultural performances as entertainment instead of participating in university life as active, equal, contributing members. From a critical Indigenous perspective, multiculturalism is not enough because it embraces a surface-level celebration of "difference" that ultimately promotes assimilation into the dominant culture rather than taking Indigenous perspectives and forms of knowledge seriously. In the focus group discussions, participants said they felt that university personnel assume that Native peoples do not have anything to offer outside of historical and stereotypical roles. When Native students, community members, and I attempted to follow up on the focus group findings, university administrators stepped in, conducted the research themselves, and declared the project a victory for diversity. This narrow, inaccurate claim is integral to neocolonial visions of education. Haunani-Kay Trask (ibid., 103) discusses how these assumptions undermine Indigenous people's struggles for freedom: "Part of neocolonialism, of course, is the ideological position that all is well; in other words, that decolonization has occurred."

In my case study, I found that when university administrators assume that "all is well" and that "we are diverse," they fail to recognize the ongoing struggles that American Indians face in gaining access to the university and, if they do manage to get on campus, the hardships they face in dealing with a neocolonial, colour-blind institution that simultaneously celebrates and tokenizes Indigenous peoples and cultures. The university administrators' vision of diversity relies on a consistent denial of community voices, or, as Michelle Pidgeon states elsewhere in this volume (see Chapter 9), such paradigms ultimately result in Indigenous peoples being silenced or hindered.

A Native student articulated the central message of these exclusion processes during the focus group: "It's like they don't even *want* us here" (focus group, March 2007). This student's statement reflects a larger struggle for representation. Although the university had seventy-six American Indian students in its admissions database, only five students participated in the focus group. On average, fewer than five were active in Native student organizations. Although the university had had a multicultural centre for over ten years, it was not until 2007 that the Native American student organization was officially recognized by the university (making it eligible for government funding). The lack of a shared community and respect was obvious to the few students who participated in community-building activities on campus. The seventy-plus so-called box checkers remained a mystery to the active students. They wondered, "Why would someone check a box on an admissions application but not participate in activities that are relevant to the community they are representing?" During the focus group, students talked about these box checkers and suggested that Native American students' identities are so assaulted on campus that they may prefer to "pass" as non-Native (i.e., white or Mexican). "Passing" is evidence of the historical trauma experienced by Native peoples on campus. Native students literally feel that they must hide their Indigenous identities in order to survive and thrive. The unstated message sent to the next generation of Native leaders is that they should not be proud of who they are; they would, in fact, be better off hiding their Indianness. Other students in the focus group described a common strategy employed by students of colour: "keep your head down and your mouth shut for four years." The message being sent to these students is that they have nothing valuable or legitimate to share; rather, they are expected to submit to the status quo, which renders them ignorant and invisible.

The pain that some students experienced during their educational careers was horrifying. One student, from a local reservation, explained that a professor of US history had skipped the first chapter of the textbook, which covered American Indians, and did not talk about Indians at all during the semester-long general education course. The student, stunned but intimidated by an overwhelmingly white classroom and a white professor, said he coped with the assault by talking himself into believing that the professor was right – that American Indians should not be talked about in a US history course. It was only after a couple of years of being able to process what had happened to him that he realized this was wrong (focus group, March 2007). The focus group was the first opportunity the student had had to speak about the shameful experience.

Other examples of historical trauma and microaggressions came to light when an American Indian professor disclosed the many assaults against American Indian identity he had witnessed on campus. In one instance, a liberal, white colleague, a professor of religious studies, held a "cults fair" on campus. The textbook used in the class defined the Native American Church as a cult. The Native American professor, who was from a reservation that honours the Native American Church as an important spiritual institution, was deeply offended that the professor had asked the students to dress up as cult members and put on a display for the campus. A white student whose project focused on the Native American Church dressed up as an "Indian warrior," complete with "relevant props," including a bed sheet teepee that had a George Foreman grill inside of it. The grill, which was supposed to be boiling hot water, represented a sweat lodge. When the American Indian professor took what Michelle Pidgeon (see Chapter 9) calls the watch-dog role and told her colleague that the representation was offensive, the professor of religious studies had difficulty understanding why it would give offence because, she believed, the student's representation was "accurate" (focus group, March 2007).

Although the university touts itself as diverse, it holds a specific vision of diversity, one that caters to white interests and curiosities rather than attempting to honour and include Native peoples and cultures as true partners in institution building. The Native American professor was also told by a white colleague in the Department of Anthropology that they were "probably related" because the anthropologist thought he may have an ancestor from the same region of the country as the professor. Such claims, which clearly demonstrate a desire to "play Indian," are offensive because they attempt to commodify not only culture but also identity (Deloria 1998; Smith 2005). With microaggressions and assaults on identity such as these occurring on campus, it is easy to understand why Native students go into hiding at the university. Dealing with overt and covert forms of racism and daily microaggressions, on a campus that touts itself as diverse, is difficult to bear, especially in a setting that lacks a strong Indigenous presence, as Pidgeon also argues in this volume.

The Forum: Community Voices and Visions of Healing

As part of an effort to respect Native peoples and cultures, the Ethnic Studies faculty collaborated with key university allies to host a forum on American Indian education issues on 19 April 2007. It was the first gathering of its kind at the university. The forum was lively and exciting, due largely to the overwhelming attendance of Native community members. Leaders and educators from the area's reservations and urban populations gathered inside the university's large ballroom. Numerous university faculty, staff, and administrators also attended. Most were excited to be at the event. Several Indian community members commented on how much they appreciated seeing old friends and relatives at the gathering. Hugs and exclamations of joy occurred frequently as community members made their way around a room that held some two hundred people. The highest-ranking university official in attendance, by contrast, sat in the background, at a table with mostly other (white) university people. He refused to engage with community members and played with his Blackberry, a gesture that showed he was more interested in his email than the opportunity to engage with important community leaders and educators. His behaviour signalled a disconnect between his own view of leadership and those held by Native people. Native conceptions of leadership uphold serving the community as "a gift and responsibility," as Alannah Young Leon articulates in Chapter 3 of this volume.

The first part of the luncheon program consisted of a panel of three American Indian education experts who offered brief remarks on community needs and how universities could meet them. The three women kept in mind the title of the forum: "American Indian Educational Issues: Listening to Community Needs." One of the speakers, a local tribal leader, provided perhaps the clearest advice. Responding to the question "What do educational institutions need to do in order to better serve tribal communities?" the tribal leader recounted the many empty promises that Native peoples have heard from Western institutional personnel and leaders. She then paused and shared her advice for the university, "We want a lifelong commitment by the university, not just *sweet words.*" The room buzzed with excitement as Native community members clapped, cheered, and nodded in approval. This strong leader's advice was built solidly on the principles of Native leadership. Native leadership should entail a lifelong dedication to serving the community, or, as Young Leon states in (see Chapter 3 of this volume), Native leadership is about "stepping forward and demonstrating community responsibilities." Communities need policies that have a real and positive impact. All other attempts are simply sweet words that will do nothing to help our people.

The second panel speaker, a professor emerita from a neighbouring university, discussed the importance of having a lasting, top-down commitment to diversity, especially in regard to working with American Indian communities:

When I retired ... I thought that the one thing I could do for my university ... would be to try to help strengthen the bridges that we had already loosely built [over sixteen years]. A lot of what we did in those early years I think was good. We did a lot of outreach to the Indian community through some cultural programming ... if you fast forward ... President — — came to be our president, and one of the first things she did was establish a tribal liaison position. I thought my job was, but I still think it is, to connect the wonderful brain trust in our faculty, our staff, and our students to the tribal communities, many of them in our region, in a meaningful way, a way that was meaningful to tribal communities.

What mattered most to community members was the former professor's demonstrated commitment to the community and her emphasis on a *structural* commitment to diversity. Her leadership was rooted in a lifelong commitment to Native communities, and the applied focus of her work was valued deeply by tribal members. She mentioned that during the sixteen years she had worked for the university, she had "loosely built" bridges with the Indian community, "cultural" programs in particular. Such efforts, usually typified by powwows, performances, and speakers, are important for campuses that promote intellectual and cultural diversity. However, on their own, such efforts fall short of *changing* campus culture or the diversity of the university body itself. Instead, diversity is reduced to a formulaic exercise: (1) the university brings "outsiders" onto campus, (2) the university body appreciates the "other" (exotic) culture put on display, (3) the outsiders leave campus, and (4) the university goes back to business as usual.

The speaker acknowledged the perhaps necessary but not sufficient nature of such work and then moved on to what she felt was different about her university's efforts to promote diversity: a university president who believed that cultural programming was not enough. The president, upon being presented with information about the importance of partnering with tribal communities, had implemented a structural change – she created a position that would assume this responsibility, that of tribal liaison. Rather than merely *stating* the importance of such work (i.e., sweet words) or simply "adding on" to an existing position's responsibilities, the president *showed* how important this work was to the university by dedicating a line item to the position.

Such structural change in a university's effort to promote diversity can lead to multiple outcomes: (1) it sends a clear message to the university community that tribal communities are important partners; (2) it sends a clear message to tribal communities that the university is ready to go beyond the cultural-programming or "sweet words" approach; and (3) it provides the opportunity for lasting change, for an employee's labour is dedicated to the partnership efforts and that employee has the backing of the university's top leadership. Thus, the diversity work will not be done in vain. A long-term commitment is important if institutions are to be accessible and relevant to future generations of tribal peoples. Furthermore, such commitment also shows a demonstrated desire to reverse the trend of institutional racism and historical trauma upon which our educational institutions have been built. Finally, the purposeful shift away from simple programming demonstrates a desire to shift efforts to promote diversity away from a "token" model that allows university personnel to point to dances or food as evidence of an inclusive and diverse environment. It is important to note that the tribal liaison position, as described at the forum, went beyond tokenism because of the top-down commitment implemented at the speaker's university. Such structural commitments are a necessary condition for ensuring that institutional policies will continue to serve Native peoples for *multiple* generations. Alannah Young Leon argues in this volume (see Chapter 3) that thinking intergenerationally is indispensible for Native leadership development.

The third panelist at the "American Indian Educational Issues" luncheon provided further insight into *how* universities should partner with Indian communities. The speaker, an American Indian professor at another university, began her speech by acknowledging the long struggle for diversity at the host university, the years of work that the Ethnic Studies faculty had put forth, and the "hurt" that students of colour had experienced because of the university's ignorance of key issues. She then complimented some of the university's strengths, such as the recent hiring of two faculty of colour and the strong tradition of community-service learning at the university. She went on to say: "That is something that is near and dear to my heart and near and dear to the American Indian community – because we have been doing community-service learning before it got that fancy title. It's called applied research. That is how you get knowledge of the Indian community – working within the community. So fostering those collaborative relationships is one way this campus can continue service. But really *listening* to the Native Americans within this community is first and foremost."

In this speech, the speaker is clear that serving the Indigenous community is of primary importance in any effort to promote diversity. The leader also prioritizes applied work that serves Native communities. The community-based focus of her comments conveys an important aspect of her vision of leadership. She pointedly states that research with and knowledge production about Indians must be done in a way that has relevance for the community. By doing so, she breaks down the university's "ivory tower" image and states that the university should work *within* the community. Meeting the community's needs will require going "off campus" because the community does not embrace the university as its own. The speaker also comments on the need for long-term commitment to the community, for fostering relationships implies promoting diversity in ways that go far beyond the cultural-programming or "sweet words" approaches. Finally, the speaker provides direction by stating that the university needs to assume a greater humility in its efforts to make its campus more diverse. Listening is the number one goal. If the university can demonstrate an ability to humbly and respectfully listen to Indian communities, then a commitment to diversity is possible.

At the forum, university personnel were instructed to listen carefully to hear the community's needs. Even though listening is a basic request, the third speaker expressed doubt that the university had reached even this elementary stage:

> We always have to create a place, a place of learning, a safe place, and a place that our Native students can feel comfortable ... Not only is it important for them to have a Native faculty, they have to have a tribal liaison position ... A tribal liaison person could help in assisting those bridges and those opportunities ... So, I would really encourage the university to do that, and I would really encourage the university to have a government-to-government relationship with the tribes ... Is the president here? *[The audience responds that the university president is absent from the luncheon.]* Well, maybe someone can relay that message to the President's Office.

In this part of the speech, the speaker outlines the importance of efforts to promote diversity, particularly creating a campus where Indigenous people feel safe and welcome. In short, she calls for a major cultural shift in the way that the university conceives of and goes about promoting diversity. Not fooled by the ease with which sweet words can be uttered, the speaker also asks for institutional support for this cultural shift. Such comments are especially important given that future generations of tribal peoples must view the university as safe and welcoming if they are to attend (or even consider attending). She also expresses her vision of *how* this could be accomplished – by creating a tribal liaison position and through a top-down commitment from the university. In calling for a tribal liaison, the speaker recognizes the temptation that university administrators may have to "add on" to an existing employee's responsibilities or to assume that "diversity work" in general will be a blanket that covers Indian communities' needs, along with other marginalized communities.

Finally, she calls for a top-down commitment from university administrators. Recognizing that it is the people in power within the university bureaucracy who will ultimately make the decisions that will encourage or discourage meaningful (and well-funded) partnerships between the university and Indian communities, she asks for government-to-government relationships. This request frames the issue in a way that demands respect. It is not sufficient to utter sweet words or to look upon Indian communities as pity cases, or as "poor minorities" in the missionary tradition with which the religiously affiliated school is perhaps most familiar. Instead, tribal communities are constructed as powerful, important societies that have their own governments, which should be viewed as at least equally important to the administration of the university. Thus, the speaker places the responsibility for efforts to promote diversity squarely in the lap of the university administration. By "calling out" the university president, who failed to attend the luncheon, the speaker demonstrates the lack of a top-down commitment at the university and thus challenges the notion that the university is even ready to engage in meaningful promotion of diversity. Clearly, the speaker suspects that the university is not yet ready to commit to undoing institutional racism, acknowledging the institution's role in perpetuating historical trauma, and making earnest attempts to transform the institution into a space of healing.

Conclusion: Possibilities for Healing

As a Native woman dedicated to decolonization, I see the potential for educational institutions to become sites of healing, but such a goal must be built upon input from Native community members. Along with my colleagues in this volume, I assert that Indigenous peoples themselves must have a voice in remaking educational institutions into spaces of healing. My analysis reveals that microaggressions and the perpetuation of historical trauma continue to exist within the educational system. Oftentimes, educational institutions attempt to address Indian "problems" by embracing multiculturalism. Critical of such efforts, Indigenous scholar Taiaike Alfred (2005, 248) writes that multiculturalism "is in reality nothing more than a surface celebration of folkloric traditions from various immigrant cultures combined with the promotion of deeper assimilation to monocultural societal norms." I found that community members also condemn such "tokenizing" efforts to achieve diversity. The problem, however, extends well beyond the issue of tokenism. The real issue is whether Native people will have access to institutions that welcome our presence and perspectives. Struggles between universities and Native communities are ultimately about offering Native people access to institutions that are places of healing, not sites that perpetuate historical trauma.

In order to transform, educational institutions must honour Indigenous cultures and peoples. Institutions must build respectful relationships with Indigenous communities and include our perspectives in curriculums and day-to-day operations. People who work in educational institutions, students who attend these institutions, and community members who support the institutions must all pause and reflect on the patterns of discrimination and historical trauma that are the foundation of North American educational institutions. It is a time of great possibility, and as Alannah Young Leon states in Chapter 3 of this volume, we should make "transformative antiracism and action strategies a priority" But in order for educational institutions to reach their greatest potential, personnel must begin with humble listening.

All educational institutions that seek to be inclusive and diverse must consider Indigenous views carefully. If Indigenous perspectives and philosophies are not informing policy debates and decisions, then efforts to promote diversity will never meet Indigenous needs. Native peoples and our allies are engaged in an ongoing decolonization project. Mainstream institutional personnel are at a crossroads: they can persist in excluding Indigenous perspectives to uphold the status quo, or they can honour Indigenous perspectives that have the promise of transforming institutions into spaces of healing. All North American educational institutions are located on the homelands of Native peoples. To ignore Native peoples' recommendations to make their campuses more diverse is to create and maintain institutions that will never be at peace with the land or the original peoples of the land on which the institutions reside.

It has long been a tradition within Indigenous communities to struggle for justice. The current generation of Native students, scholars, and allies are committed to engaging in this struggle in order to honour this Indigenous tradition, and they view it as an obligation to push university administrations to do more than simply utter sweet words to Native communities. At a minimum, administrations should either show good faith in honouring the perspectives of the Indian community or be honest about their role in perpetuating historical trauma. To safely wrap themselves in a colour-blind blanket and celebrate the low-stakes multiculturalism represented by smoke and feathers while uttering sweet words is simply not enough.

Works Cited

Alfred, Taiaiake. 2005. *Wasase: Indigenous Pathways of Action and Freedom.* Peterborough, ON: Broadview Press.

Deloria, Philip J. 1998. *Playing Indian.* New Haven, CT: Yale University Press.

Deloria, Vine, and Daniel R. Wildcat. 2001. *Power and Place: Indian Education in America.* Golden, CO: American Indian Graduate Center and Fulcrum Resources.

Evans-Campbell, Tessa. 2008. "Historical Trauma in American Indian/Native Alaska Communities: A Multilevel Framework for Exploring Impacts on Individuals, Families, and Communities." *Journal of Interpersonal Violence* 23, 3: 316-38.

Mihesuah, Devon A., and Angela C. Wilson. 2004. *Indigenizing the Academy: Transforming Scholarship and Empowering Communities.* Lincoln: University of Nebraska Press.

National Indian Education Association. n.d. "Talking Points for Hill Visits." http://www.niea.org/sa/uploads/legislativesummit/33.18.NIEAtalkingpointsforHillVisits.pdf (accessed 26 March 2008).

—. n.d. "History." http://www.niea.org/About/NIEA-History.aspx (accessed 26 March 2008).

Smith, Andrea. 2005. *Conquest.* Boston: South End Press.

Solorzano, Daniel, Miguel Ceja, and Tara Yosso. 2000. "Critical Race Theory, Racial Microaggressions, and Campus Racial Climate: The Experiences of African American College Students." *Journal of Negro Education* 69, 1-2: 60-73.

Tierney, William G. 1992. *Official Encouragement, Institutional Discouragement: Minorities in Academe – The Native American Experience.* Norwood, NJ: Ablex Publishing Corporation.

Trask, Haunani-Kay. 1999. *From a Native Daughter: Colonialism and Sovereignty in Hawai'i.* Honolulu: University of Hawai'i Press.

Walters, Karina L., and Jane M. Simoni. 2009. "Decolonizing Strategies for Mentoring American Indians and Alaska Natives in HIV and Mental Health Research." *American Journal of Public Health* 99, S1: S71-S76.

13

And So I Turn to Rita

Mi'kmaq Women, Community Action, Leadership, and Resilience

Patricia Doyle-Bedwell

I lost my talk
The talk you took away.
When I was a little girl
At Shubenacadie School.

You snatched it away:
I speak like you
I think like you
I create like you
The scrambled ballad, about my word.

Two ways I talk
Both ways I say,
Your way is more powerful.

So gently I offer my hand and ask,
Let me find my talk
So I can teach you about me.

– Rita Joe (1988, 33)

FOLLOWING RITA'S WORDS, I want to share some thoughts on finding our voice, specifically our stories of leadership. This is a story about resilience, strength, hope, and courage.

Mainstream definitions of leadership have hindered Mi'kmaq women from accepting the true nature of their leadership roles. Aboriginal women do not often exercise power over others while adhering to a more practical perspective on leadership based on experience, wisdom, and action. If you ask a Mi'kmaq woman if she sees herself as a leader, she will likely respond in the negative.

To Mi'kmaq women, leadership means doing the work necessary to move the community forward, not to gain accolades or prestige. To achieve our full potential, we need to move away from the male stereotype of warrior. Aboriginal women have taken up the fight for Aboriginal rights through education, activism, art, writing, and other means. Their warrior hearts are fuelled by tradition, culture, and spirituality. By contrast, the male idea of warriorship and leadership has focused upon physical might or power over relationships. The power of the pen, of art, and of traditions, notably oral traditions, has not been as evident as that of the male political forces. I believe that all Mi'kmaq women have the power of the warrior within, that we can find the spiritual connections between mind, body, and soul. According to the Truth and Reconciliation Commission of Canada, spiritual warriors include the leaders and warriors of today.

How do Mi'kmaq women see leadership and warriorship? How do we press for community change? What supports exist for the work Mi'kmaq women do on a daily basis? How do Mi'kmaq women overcome the impact of colonialism and sexism to make sure our voices are heard? Our cultural values demand we work for the whole within a dominant system that focuses only on the individual. How do we negotiate this cultural conflict and develop skills to operate in both worlds? How do our actions move our community forward? Given self-government and Aboriginal and treaty rights, how can we make sure women occupy a secure place in healing and governing our communities?

Inspired by my mom, Harriet Battiste Doyle (1923-2011), and the words of Rita Joe (1932-2007), a Mi'kmaq poet and songwriter, I dug deep within myself and began to feel a connection to my spirit and my Mi'kmaq culture. Rita taught me to go inwards, to find my voice. I searched for my connection, which I felt I had lost forever. Through my mom and Rita, I have discovered a stronger connection that now sustains me. Being Mi'kmaq demands that we face so many issues, and sometimes our own people attack us in the worst way. Who is Mi'kmaq? Who has the right to belong to the nation? Rita inspired me to find my place by writing about my perspectives and experiences. My mom taught me about faith and the values of Mi'kmaq culture.

I have longed to be a writer, and in this story, I explore my journey as a writer. Identity, truth, law, and my upbringing have all shaped my perspectives and experiences as a leader. Through Rita's writings and my mom's oral traditions I learned to walk gently. She taught me what it means to be a Mi'kmaq woman and a writer.

My Journey

I am fifty-three years old. Both my mom and Rita Joe inspired me to find my place. So, with shaking hands, I will tell you how my mom and Rita fundamentally influenced my life. Finding the strength in each of us is the first step to following our heart, to finding our voice and taking the first step towards warriorship within leadership and self-governance. Finding our place means finding the strength within each of us, the spiritual warrior.

I have always wanted to write stories about my experiences. I have struggled to ground my academic work in my own life. Yet, I hesitate to call myself a writer. To attach that label alongside the many labels that society has affixed to me, both positive and negative, feels a bit dishonest. Rita's description of setting pen to paper while raising her children – in a society in which the label "writer" and "poet" did not fit comfortably with that of mother, Mi'kmaq woman, and grandmother – resonated with me. She continued her writing and was amazed at the honours she won because of her simple, powerful poems. She only described her Mi'kmaq life – what it means to be Mi'kmaq, how white society continues to oppress us. She never gave in for very long to the discouragement that she faced both inside and outside her community. She personified the strong Mi'kmaq woman, gentle yet courageous.

I read *Song of Rita Joe: Autobiography of a Mi'kmaq Poet* (1996) at a time when I felt hollow and depressed. I found strength in Rita's words. Rita inspired me to find my place by writing about her own perspectives and experiences. I began to explore the roles of Mi'kmaq women and leadership, sharing my own story of community action. Mi'kmaq women, despite the experience of colonialism, patriarchy, and abuse, have moved beyond negative experiences to implement change and healing in their communities.

I have also been inspired by martial arts. I study Bujinkan Budō Taijutsu. The grandmaster, Dr. Masaaki Hatsumi, oversees a worldwide organization that teaches us nine different schools or *Ryu*. I am a fourth-degree black belt. I do not tell many people. Who would believe that a somewhat overweight, fifty-three-year-old Mi'kmaq woman finds such strength and sustenance in a one-thousand-year-old martial art from Japan? The training has a spiritual element. I feel connected to the earth and to heaven. I experience oneness. Training provides another mirror to my heart, one that has reflected back my fear, overcome by strength. Training in the

Bujinkan also furthered my warrior spirit, but that discovery began prior to training.

I spent many years disconnected from my spiritual being. I had a difficult time finding myself in male-dominated spiritual traditions, which often ignore the contributions of women. Our role in the past has been educating our children, caring for all in the community, and healing others. In so many ways, traditional Aboriginal male healers have forgotten what we did in the past and what we continue to do today. The quest of the woman warrior means living in the now, living in trust and love, and speaking up for those unable to speak for themselves.

Becoming aware of my own warrior spirit began one day in 1990 as I listened to a Mohawk Elder speak his wisdom and tell his story. The Elder started to drift away, and his white hair connected with the white light in the room. I felt like nothing. I felt like everything. Words cannot explain the brightness of the light that animated from this man. I felt caught up in his white light, connected to him. I felt enveloped with love, connectedness, and complete acceptance. I knew without a doubt that my spirit was connected to everyone, that nothing separated us except the illusion of our own minds. I felt connected to a higher power. I felt love throughout my body and soul. The huge room became distant, and all I saw was the white light of God. I sat in this bliss for a long time. I did not try to make it happen, and I did not try to stop it. I felt no fear. I felt only love and connectedness. The spiritual connection I experienced that day led to a healing process that pushed me into discovering my warrior spirit. And I believe that my martial arts training, my personal healing process, and finding my voice has created a oneness within, a core of strength and courage (see Yvonne McLeod's chapter in this volume).

While moving my body through exercise, I also discovered hidden memories of my abuse and the source of my self-loathing. Through movement, my body began to exorcise the demons hidden in my physical self. I sometimes felt a wonderful lightness of being. I felt strong. At other times, shame reared its ugly head and sent me to the depths of despair. I have an image of myself that I can never meet in real life. I still struggle against that perfect image and work on accepting my body as it moves and as it looks. This type of inner work was also a part of my leadership development.

I have also benefitted from talk therapy at various times over the past twenty years. Through talk therapy, I have struggled with the concept of leadership as a power position. But, inspired by Mi'kmaq women, notably Rita Joe and my mom, I discovered that leadership in Mi'kmaq communities remains grounded to the personal. Each Mi'kmaq woman reflects the unique and effective roles of leadership in our community. Mi'kmaq women have always performed leadership roles in the community and nation. Prior to contact with Europeans, Mi'kmaq women taught children, tended the sick, and held strong spiritual positions. With the imposition of colonialism and patriarchy, Mi'kmaq women often faced legal exclusion from their own communities based on the Indian Act. Today, Mi'kmaq women have re-entered the realm of political leadership as elected chiefs and councillors as well as through nongovernmental and advocacy organizations. Mi'kmaq women exercise leadership as spiritual warriors.

In my own leadership journey, I have gained confidence by learning to trust myself, my heart, and my soul. Leadership means trusting the path the Creator has set out for each of us. Much of mainstream society, however, continues to draw upon negative stereotypes of Aboriginal women (Mihuesuah 2003). These negative stereotypes force their way into our hearts. I have a difficult time believing in the goodness of my intentions with these negative images and words surrounding me. I wonder if I am really the child of the Creator. I think about the struggles I have faced because of my Mi'kmaq face and Mi'kmaq body. I have suffered. My body has failed me in the past, and I have raged at my physical limitations. I have suffered physical abuse and emotional abuse; sometimes I have hated myself the most. None of us take this journey alone. Despite my own limitations, my mom influenced me in significant ways.

My Mom

My mom influenced me greatly with her courage and resilience. I grew up in Maine, but my mom is from Chapel Island, Nova Scotia. Born on the reserve, part of a family of eight, my mother and her sisters were removed from their home by the Indian Agent to attend residential school. When we were children, we always travelled by car to the reserve. One summer, my mom said, "Let's stop at my old school." It was 1969, and the government had closed down Shubie School. The building, however, still stood, tall and intimidating, a testament to the pain and horror experienced within. Dark, spooky, and musty, Shubie School enveloped me with fear. The darkness seemed stronger than Nagooset (the sun). I had never seen a school so dismal. I could not imagine attending school there.

My mom had little formal education, but she pushed us to get an education. Despite her struggles, she hoped for a better life for her children. Her perseverance encouraged us to become educated. If I had to describe my mom in one word, it would be *strength*. No matter what life threw at her, she managed to survive and thrive. She convinced me to speak out, stand up, and never take anyone's bull. When I was twelve years old, for instance, I passed a history test but was last in line. Because I was last in line, a nun ripped up my test and told me I was nothing but a stupid Indian. I sat at my desk and cried. I went home that day and told my mom what had happened. My mom got in the old car we had and drove to the school and gave the teacher a piece of her mind. I felt protected. I recognized her strength in standing up to the teacher.

If I had to pick another word to describe my mom, it would be *courage*. She has faced many illnesses and losses, and she has also faced death. A serious car accident fifteen years ago put her in the hospital. The doctors told us we might lose her. But she rallied and survived. My nephew Josh died almost ten years ago. I was certain Josh's loss would kill my mom. But again, she rose up and survived.

If I had to pick another word to describe my mom, it would be *faith*. Her faith in God inspires me. Many times, I have faced racism and discrimination. Her faith sustained me when I did not believe in the Creator. She is the Elder who dresses the statue of St. Anne during our annual gatherings. She told me, in no uncertain terms, that I should never let the bastards get me down. This mantra repeated itself in my mind as I attended law school. During law school, I experienced racism as insidious, powerful stabs. Never had I met people so limited, so conservative, so narrow-minded. My mom's strength sustained me during my legal education.

Dalhousie Law School aims to assimilate and acculturate students into the profession of law. It ignores the cultural foundations of minority and Aboriginal students. I studied law to find justice but I instead found oppression. As Patricia Monture states (1995, 59),

When I enrolled in law school, I honestly believed that Canadian law would assist Aboriginal people in securing just and fair treatment. This is why I agreed to study law. Since then, I have learned that the Aboriginal experience of Canadian law can never be about justness and fairness for Aboriginal peoples. Every oppression that Aboriginal people have survived has been delivered up to us through Canadian law. This is true of the taking of our land and our children. Residential schools were established through law. The same is true for the outlawing of our sacred ceremonies and what is currently done to our people in the criminal courts of this land. What I learned long after my law school graduation was that Canadian law is about the oppression of Aboriginal people. My years in law school were so painful because oppression, even if only in study, is a painful experience.

I experienced how law school strips students of their personal perspectives. Somehow, I had to write papers and exams without showing who I was. The law school reduced me to a number. "Do not write anything that will identify you." I found that quite difficult and oppressive. Yet law school, while painful, also taught me a fundamental truth: I am a Mi'kmaq woman no matter what anyone says. I also discovered that I could write from my own perspective, through research and papers. I found inspiration when I attended the launch of a book titled *Kelisultiek: Original Women's Voices of Atlantic Canada*. I cried when I heard the truth and the feelings of these Mi'kmaq women who wrote with their souls. I cried because they also spoke my truth. I discovered the power of telling our stories, writing our truths, and standing up for our realities. I cried with joy to hear our voices loud and clear. I finally understood the power of our oral traditions, written and spoken aloud, as my mom tried to teach me so long ago. Listening to the writers gave me the courage to speak of my own experiences.

Rita

I met Rita Joe when I was twenty-one. I told her my name and that I was Mi'kmaq from Chapel Island, that my mom was Harriet Doyle. I asked her how I could become a writer. She simply smiled up at me and said, "Write!" The answer could not be that simple. I said thank you but wondered, who would be interested in what I had to say? I still had unspoken dreams that I felt too scared to pursue. Writing must be more complicated than that. Writing meant I had something to say. I did not think that I could speak from my own experiences. Who would care? But since I was a young girl, I found refuge in the blank page of possibilities.

Law school almost ruined the blank page as refuge. My writing no longer created a safe space for me. I lost the power of writing in law school because law school tried to strip me of my words. Healing for me has meant regaining my voice though the written word. I again went back to Rita. I read her book again. I searched for my voice. I knew that I had to explore the process of writing my thesis on residential schools, and find healing. I discovered in detail the pain of my family. I had to grieve for my mom's experience.

I had spoken my truth in my thesis but again felt the sting of disapproval. I felt excluded from discussions about residential school compensation. I learned that some people have no honour, that although the thesis committee dismissed my work, many people benefitted from my family's stories of about the residential school experience. Some academics dismissed my writing but then profited from it, by working with government agencies on compensation while I sat on the sidelines, helping members of my family. I spoke to others about my thesis. Some congratulated me on not following a typical legal format. "You should be proud that you could intertwine your personal experience, Mi'kmaq oral history, and legal analysis." Despite positive comments from other Aboriginal academics, I continued to feel ashamed of my work. The law school told me in no uncertain terms, "You are not good enough to teach here."

Searching for hope, I took comfort in Rita's words. In *Mi'kmaq Anthology*, Rita states, "The image of my people is uppermost in my mind, the beauty told, the thought inspiring another. *Nensite'ten ke'luk weji tu'ap* (remember I found the good). *Jika'winen we'jitutqsip kutoy ninen* (look at us and you will find the good). Being a stranger in your own land is a sad story, the turnaround may be the curriculum content in the schools. Let us have our say or none at all. *Iknmulek na!* (We give! Let us!) (Joe and Choyce 2003, 270).

Let us have our say! I began to heal. Following my spiritual path means writing and speaking my truth. Rita Joe offered her words to all of us. Although the dominant society gave her honours for her writing, I believe she ultimately wrote to heal herself and to find her truth. By sharing her experiences, she gave all Mi'kmaq women permission to explore their lives and truths. Her bravery gave me the courage to reach out to the blank page again, if only to honour her with my words.

Rita also taught the mainstream about Mi'kmaq culture. The values of the Mi'kmaq community have persisted for a long time, as has our need for family, relationships, community, and healing. I began to recognize how the Elders help us to maintain our values, our character, and our strength. They hold us up and embrace us when we feel alone and isolated. Elders have told me that my truth comes from within. Searching for inspiration during a particularly low point in my life, I read Rita Joe's autobiography. I felt her strength flowing from her words. I recognized that I carried the same values and came from the same line of Mi'kmaq women. I finally recognized that the dominant society has always focused its destructive laws and policies on Aboriginal women and children. I began to understand that my ancestors' fight to maintain the Mi'kmaq Nation accounted for us being here today. I realized that Rita Joe had found her inner courage to put pen to paper, to speak her truth, and to empower women to find their own courage and truth and to express it through writing, art, and living the Mi'kmaq values of kindness, sharing, caring, honesty, and spirituality.

Despite my inner awareness of Mi'kmaq oral traditions, as taught to me by mom and my inspiration from Rita, I still hesitate to call myself a writer or a leader. But people have attributed both labels to me. Following Rita Joe's lead, I was inspired to do both. Rita believed that she could educate the mainstream. She believed that her poems could be the link between the Aboriginal and non-Aboriginal worlds. Through books such as *Song of Eskasoni* (1993), *Lnu and Indians We're Called* (1991), and *We Are the Dreamers* (1999), she made her message known: if only the mainstream understood us, racism could disappear.

Ah, the truth. What is our truth? Each person must begin from his or her own personal experience. Rita did just that. Her poetry explores and defines what it means to live as a Mi'kmaq woman in a world that ignores our truth. Speaking the truth about racism, oppression, and the ongoing impact of living with social problems that flow from poverty and discrimination can marginalize the writer further. Yet Rita exposed her truth and her reality of living as a Mi'kmaq woman in the twentieth century in a gentle, non-threatening way that allowed readers to share in her world without feeling attacked. Rita showed us how to speak powerfully and share our stories in a way that leaves readers whole. To me, Rita epitomizes the phrase *speak truth to power*. She did not hide her pain and joy but instead transformed her experiences into literary masterpieces.

Following Rita's lead, and carrying my mom's values, I began to teach law at Dalhousie. I discovered the true nature of oppression. But through teaching, I have also learned to find strength from the past and the present. I have learned that my life does have value. I have learned not to let other people hurt me. I have learned to lean on the strength of being a Mi'kmaq woman. I can achieve my dreams, despite the pain, despite those few people who seek to hurt me. I received tremendous support from Elders in the community. Writing helped me to purge the pain of completing my master's thesis. My thesis committee saw my work as simply something "Patti had to get off her chest." Although true on one level, this assessment did not tell the entire story. In fact, my thesis felt like a medicine song to me. To have many legal academics dismiss it out of hand devastated me. To have the support of my Elders and my mom gave me the strength to continue my journey

My Elder took the time to write me and tell me not to give up on writing, teaching, and my thesis. I began to recognize how the Elders help us to maintain our values, our character, and our strength. They hold us up and embrace us when we feel alone and isolated. I have not given up. I went back and faced the law school again in 2001 as director of the Indigenous Blacks and Mi'kmaq Initiative at Dalhousie. And in doing so, I learned that people listen. People understand, and I learned that giving up is not the answer.

I believe that Mi'kmaq women must put pen to paper to explore their lives and find their courage. I feel the emotional brunt of Mi'kmaq women's stories because they speak my truth. Exploring what it means to be a writer means facing the negatives. I wonder what it will take to completely disengage myself from the opinions of an oppressive society that demands that we maintain the status quo – the one that is not our own. We often put ourselves down because of internalized colonialism, and we often mistrust one another. I have internalized the negativity that leads to depression and lack of motivation. I feel fear when I sit down at the computer to write. I shake inside when non-Native people spout off about our lack of writing skills, or any academic skills at all. I want to remove writing from the list of impossible accomplishments and instead create a safe space for Mi'kmaq people to write their stories, keep their journals, and publish their truths.

Aboriginal women carry our traditions and our strength. I believe that our traditional knowledge and our spiritual power remain hidden, and I had to search hard to find them within myself. The words of Rita Joe helped me to find the unspoken values that I had known while growing up. Even today, many of our spiritual leaders still denigrate women. The dominant society has twisted our spiritual traditions, which recognized the power of women in our societies. Still, Rita spoke the truth, as she knew it, about surviving, about being Mi'kmaq in the modern world, and about the losses she had experienced at residential school. She maintained her spiritual connection to our ancestors, and this connection gave her the courage to speak her truth. My mom did the same.

Moving Forward

Sometimes, I feel I don't fit in either the Mi'kmaq world or the dominant society. I cannot always find the connection to my community because I do not speak Mi'kmaq. At the same time, I am out of sorts with the dominant society because I sometimes feel trapped by stereotypes and oppression. Once again, I find it hard to say that I am a writer. I find it hard to say that I am an academic. I find it hard to say that I am a teacher. I do not know if I have the courage to face the blank page when I feel I have little to contribute to the dialogue of Aboriginal women's rights and community.

I believe in our power. I see clearly that the government tried to divorce us from our communities through the Indian Act, that it imported sexism and patriarchy. I am unsure of my role since I do not fit in either world. My own struggles mirror Rita's, but at the same time, I hesitate to place myself there in her world. Through her words, I learned to honour the strength of my spirit and the strength of the women in my family, the women who worked their fingers to the bone to provide for their children, who struggled to rise above poverty, overt racism, and what the dominant culture thought about them.

Racism is an ugly word. It is difficult to talk about it without people being hurt. Racism does hurt, but until we begin to explore its impact on us, we will never begin to heal. We will never be able to detach ourselves from the dominant society's view of Indians. In traditional times, we had strong communities and worked hard. We still need to work hard to receive an education (an education that at one time would have meant the loss of our identity as Indian people), and I will not allow others to silence me again or doubt my worth as a Mi'kmaq woman. I am trying to purge the negative stereotypes that continue to haunt me. It is up to each one of our Mi'kmaq sisters to reach out and encourage others.

I am still scared sometimes. So, I sit and hope and pray that I have followed the right path. I pray that more Mi'kmaq women will follow our mothers' and Rita's example by living life with honour, kindness, honesty, and resilience. As Aboriginal women, I believe we need to find ways for our inner warriors to shine. We can find the strength of our ancestors through means that we never thought possible. I end with Rita's words.

WORDS ON WINGS

There are words I want to put on wings
That when I am gone, someone read
Maybe to create the emotions inside
And tell their own story, instill pride
Then their words will have wings
To create another thought, pretend
We are a chain, linking together
To span a bridge where communication scatters.

–Rita Joe (Joe and Choyce 2003, 95)

Works Cited
Joe, Rita. 1989. *Song of Eskasoni: More Poems of Rita Joe.* Halifax: Nimbus Publishing.
–. 1991. *Lnu and Indians We're Called.* Charlottetown, PEI: Ragweed Press.
–. 1996. *Song of Rita Joe: Autobiography of a Mi'kmaq Poet.* Charlottetown, PEI: Ragweed Press.
–. 1999. *We Are the Dreamers.* Wreck Cove: Ragweed Press.
Joe, Rita, and Lesley Choyce, eds. 2003. *The Mi'kmaq Anthology.* Halifax, NS: Pottersfield Press.
Mihesuah, Devon Abbott. 2003. *Indigenous American Women: Decolonization, Empowerment, Activism.* Lincoln: University of Nebraska Press.
Monture, Patricia. 1995. *Thunder in My Soul: A Mohawk Woman Speaks.* Halifax: Fernwood Publishing.
Usmian, R. 1994. *Kelisultiek: Original Women's Voices of Atlantic Canada.* Halifax: Institute of Women's Studies, Mount St. Vincent University.

14

The Graceful War Dance

Engendering American Indian Traditional Knowledge and Practice in Leadership

Annette Squetimkin-Anquoe

AS A MEMBER OF A northern plateau tribe in Washington State, I am fortunate to hold the honoured positions of mother, auntie, sister, and friend. I am also a daughter to a Cree man from Canada and an Absentee Shawnee woman from Oklahoma who, being astute about my childhood experience of removal from my family, took me into their families during my adult years. Over the years, my service to the broader urban-based American Indian community has included counselling, coordinating, managing, and directing health and social service programs to address the multitude of needs among our people. Having the privilege of providing technical assistance and training to tribal communities across the country allowed me to see firsthand how Traditional Indian Medicine (TIM) is integrated in other settings besides my own. It is no coincidence that I'm now offering my perspective on how we, as American Indian people, are holding on to our tribally based knowledge, knowledge that serves as a guide for our collective leadership as we work among our families and community.

What I learned from our people and about our people regarding traditional knowledge came from experiencing and practising our ways from young adulthood to the present. I've heard from Elders that to learn something, it must be said four times. They told me that everything happens for a reason and that everything is interconnected. My work as a traditional health liaison began after my beloved entered the spirit world ten seasons past, and it is with the utmost honour and respect that I continue the important work that he carried out since the launch of TIM services in our Seattle-based community health clinic two decades ago. Although he was a practitioner initiated into several tribal medicine societies, it would be a stretch for me to claim the same credentials. I am privileged to conduct specific cultural and traditional activities. This is what I have to offer.

Although there are several American Indian organizations in our community that I have the honour of being connected with in some capacity, I focus here on my work as an employee of a nonprofit community health care organization, an entity that espouses the integration of traditional wisdom and practices. One of the stated values at my workplace is the integration of traditional values and Western practices; we are "committed to the integration of traditional and western approaches to healing providing culturally appropriate choices for health care" (Seattle Indian Health Board n.d.). This value alone makes our health care organization unique in our area, a fact that I do not take for granted. Integrating traditional and Western approaches to healing is a challenging feat, especially when our workforce holds diverse worldviews, American Indian and non-American Indian. This diversity is even more remarkable considering that the workforce includes members of many tribes, a feature that brings its own challenges as we strive to integrate our worldviews. Suffice it to say that there is a striking difference between those who adhere to the American Indian health model and those who subscribe to the Western medical model (Hollow 1999). In the American Indian model, illness is more likely to be viewed as a message that something is out of balance, and one is challenged with an opportunity to learn about how to regain her or his balance while experiencing the illness. In contrast, under the European-based Western model, illness is more likely to be viewed as a biological problem to be overcome (Morgan and Freeman 2009).

Before I offer examples of what this difference means in practical terms, I must clarify terminology to avoid throwing everything into the pot and using words interchangeably. The concepts American Indian worldview, traditional knowledge, wisdom, and practice may carry different meanings depending on who uses them. In this chapter, *American Indian worldview* refers to the way we perceive the forces that construct our existence, the forces that moderate how we function as human beings. This worldview includes our creation stories and our philosophy about how we obtain and carry out our individual and collective purpose. Our traditional knowledge is information passed down generation after generation and includes our history, stories, findings, inventions, and languages. Our traditional wisdom is the compilation of our worldview and traditional knowledge. It is based on lived experience. Our wisdom keepers are those who have not only acquired a wealth of knowledge and experience, they are the ones who are also emulated. Their teachings are carried on because their actions mirror what is to be sustained in all areas of life. Traditional practices are the genuine acts that evolve from traditional wisdom and are exhibited in ceremonies, rituals, song, dance, prayer, and other expressions. Given that each of these terms centres on spirituality, it is also my belief that they represent interrelated parts of a greater whole. When one part shifts, all the other parts are subject to change as well. I have seen this over and over again in my own community.

Of course, this description is but one among many. It is my own interpretation of these concepts. I do not discount other views. Rather, I offer these descriptions to provide a context for communicating the ways in which traditional Indian medicine is practised by our traditional leaders as they interface with unbound realms.

The World Health Organization defines traditional medicine on its website as "the sum total of knowledge, skills, and practices based on the theories, beliefs, and experiences indigenous to different cultures, whether explicable or not, used in the maintenance of health as well as in the prevention, diagnosis, improvement, or treatment of physical and mental illness." If we imagine how American Indian health care systems might have operated prior to the generation of Westernized systems, we may be able to appreciate the value of providing treatment that integrates these two diverse models.

Life in Urban Indian Organizations

Organizations consist of a diverse group of people who bring multiple perspectives to planning, decision making, operations, and service delivery. Although it seems that most, if not all, of the urban Indian organizations in the community where I live are replications of Western-based models (our tribal organizations are structured along similar lines), our organization has certain aspects of American Indian culture that make it unique. Even though others have examined the similarities between urban Indian organizations and Western-based models (Alfred 1999), I am still fascinated and confused about how this occurred, especially since traditional Indian medicine is likely responsible for our continued existence. So, the question is, why have we based our health care systems on Western models? Perhaps we modelled our American Indian organizational systems on mainstream society, which adheres to the Western European model as a means to fit in, to gain funding, to be visible, and to be included. Whatever the cause of this phenomenon, we as a people have demonstrated our ability to make the best of what we have. So we do.

Given that our organizations operate on Westernized models, my first question might be: What makes our American Indian organizations and leadership unique? Is it that our stated values match our collective principles, which, as mentioned previously, are prioritized in a way that reflects our worldview? Is it because, as we go to work and are among other American Indian people, we experience a sense of belonging and acceptance in comparison to what we experience when we work in non-American Indian organizations and among non-American Indian people? In my experience, our uniqueness has a number of causes. Yes, I am drawn to work alongside American Indian people and for American Indian people because of our focus on culture and tradition, as well as the satisfaction of having a commonality of interests. More often than not, I observe the very essence of this shared commonality when I find myself talking with an American Indian colleague whose worldview has been challenged or, at least, who has been required to explain something to someone unfamiliar with our history or way of life today.

Leadership takes on layers of complexity as we struggle to navigate and integrate traditional and Western approaches to health care. Unfortunately, funding often takes precedence over other concerns because our services are configured within the managed care system. As well, our nonprofit status subjects us to a host of other forces. If traditional Indian medicine has funding, there are still other issues to address. What will be provided and by whom? To what extent is there a formal or informal process for providing traditional Indian medicine services? Addressing these matters entails developing budgets and procedures, identifying practitioners, and training them. I am aware of other Indigenous communities that are working to maintain their traditional practice, and I find this inspiring because it demonstrates that our ways are alive and well. More importantly, I can point to these cases to show wary colleagues that this service is desired, needed, and available among our communities.

It is reassuring to see how other groups are supporting their traditional medicine programs. For example, one model described at an international research gathering (Jones 2010) involves a group from New Zealand that provides traditional healing in their communities on a voluntary basis. Apparently, the communities take care of the health care providers by giving them a place to stay, paying for gas, and feeding them. I imagine this might have been how our health care systems operated before they were consumed within the managed care system of mainstream America. Although some suggest that our traditional Indian medicine program should be modelled after a highly formalized program in another region, I am not convinced that taking that approach would work because of the possibility of adding access barriers to services. Fortunately, I am able to consult with various decision makers to consider to what extent traditional Indian medicine services should be formalized in our community.

Organizations and those serving urban American Indians undergo soul-searching processes from time to time. Just as I might ask myself who I am and where I come from, others within our community may be asking the same questions. Members of urban Indian organizations and those we serve are people who have their own stories to tell. These people left their tribal communities and moved off their reservations or tribal communities for various reasons. Some were dislocated from their families generations ago as a result of federal policies to assimilate American Indians into mainstream society. These policies included children being forcibly placed in boarding schools, a movement to relocate American Indians to major US cities, and child welfare initiatives. Today, the urban Indian community represents a wide range of tribal members and descendants, including many residents who have never have set foot upon their own tribal land or reservations and those arriving to the city for the first time. With this diversity in mind, here are some of the questions I ask: What is the connection between the American Indian worldview and our organizations? How has traditional Indian medicine been maintained in our organizations and community? Who are the knowledge keepers? What traditional Indian medicine knowledge and practices do we need to sustain? What is the legacy that we hope to instill for our descendants to follow?

Although the community health clinic where I work serves urban Indians in addition to individuals from other ethnic groups (African Americans, Hispanics, Asians, Pacific Islanders, East Indians, and others), the focus here is Indigenous people. It is essential that all persons serving American Indian communities become aware that traditional knowledge is revered among urban American Indians, that our traditional practices are being preserved within community-based organizations. It goes without saying, however, that teaching American Indian traditions in this day and age remains a challenge because many people are too busy to learn by experience, which takes time and patience. Schedules are packed, and we are challenged to keep up with each new wave of technology. The way we communicate has changed. A question we can ask ourselves is, what story do we want our actions to convey as we carry out the responsibility of maintaining our uniqueness? I have to believe that our ancestors did not intend for future generations to lose sight of who we are and where we come from, for they made sure to share their worldview and wealth, especially their knowledge and wisdom. This strong foundation of tribal knowledge has enabled those of us who have moved to the city to rely on our own resources and to integrate healing practices into mainstream health care systems based on the Western medical model.

How Our Traditional Medicine Practitioners Lead

Our American Indian leaders have entered into all types of professions and live and work within both American Indian and non-American Indian communities. Many of these professionals have received credentials from formal educational institutions based on the Westernized value of individual self-promotion, a value that is oftentimes observed among those working in mainstream society. There is also a silent group of professionals who, by nature, do not seek out attention or recognition for their knowledge, experience, position, or service. They are our traditional practitioners. One of these practitioners who lived in our community said, "My grandparents told me that, whenever I dance, to never step backwards, because that would set me back instead of moving me forward in life. To this day, and for all good days to come, I always step forward." These words were spoken by my beloved, a traditional practitioner and leader whose life centred on prayer, spirituality, kindness, honour, and respect. He now walks beside our ancestors. As a recognized practitioner of traditional Indian medicine within our community, he was always able to meet the needs of our community when called upon. Because our clinic's facilities are not designed to accommodate traditional practices, his work took place in the homes, hospitals, or other gathering places of whomever had called in need. Although I am biased, I will say that his time, energy, and efforts were effective in healing our community.

To show how traditional knowledge and wisdom is carried on in modern Indigenous leadership, it is helpful to examine how he, one leader in the field of traditional medicine, was able to navigate between the clinic and community effectively. I watched as he followed his own set of values, which included being humble, inclusive, respectful, and kind. He used humour skillfully in his work, which, for me, is hard to do when faced with conflict and adversity. This is where our value system comes into play: it helps us address challenges at every conceivable level.

I recall a particular situation that called forth his quiet form of leadership. One day, we discovered that our sweat house, which was placed via agreement on the grounds of a fellow American Indian organization, had been bulldozed over. Many people turned to him and expressed their anger towards those responsible. My beloved listened to their expressions of outrage and just nodded his head before reaffirming that we have to move forward, not back. His actions and words are forever a reminder to me that we, as American Indian people, can get through the toughest times if we only follow his example and that of other spiritual leaders who model and live by our traditions, values, and teachings.

Integrating Traditional Medicine into a Western Model of Care
Practitioners of traditional Indian medicine take their time even when they are on call twenty-four seven. They pick up and go for as long as they are needed, and an assessment may take several visits, during which a relationship is built. Treatment may be short or lengthy, depending on the condition and initiative of the patient. I have known many practitioners who do not base treatment on the almighty dollar since they follow the teaching that helping others is more important and that payment will come in due time and in many forms. Traditional Indian medicine is about taking all areas of a person's health into consideration in relation to their physical, emotional, social, cultural, and spiritual state of being. If you were to access this type of care, the practitioner would likely ask you to provide your story, to explain who you are and where you come from. When I sought services from our traditional practitioner (or *traditional professor,* if you accept my claim that traditional knowledge keepers are equal to doctors of philosophy), he engaged me in a discussion that explicitly focused on *who I am and where I come from* as a human being. The core of the visit was me disclosing my experience and knowledge, including my worldview and background as an American Indian.

When I was a little girl, around age seven, I remember having a deep connection with Grandmother Moon, who helped to get me through the darkest times. On the many nights that I could not sleep, I would get up and just sit by the window, gazing up at the sky where my illuminated relative lived. She was so bright, so welcoming, so intriguing, and so magnificent. It was at those times that I uttered my most meaningful prayers, shedding tears amidst my grandmother and the Creator about events in my life that felt too big to endure. Mostly, I asked for understanding about my seemingly humiliating life and for a change that would help my sister and me to gain happiness. I relied on Grandmother Moon to listen, to soothe, and to watch over us until she had reached her next full cycle.

I recall listening to many animated stories about our historic American Indian leaders. I learned some of them informally from tribal relatives or friends. Others we came to learn about through formal educational systems, such as public schools. Growing up in small rural towns off the reservation since age two, I was subjected to finding out about our people through a non-American Indian lens until my teen years, when I was able to visit my family on the reservation. I eventually moved back there as a young adult.

Throughout my formative years, the topic of Indians came up mainly around Thanksgiving, a national holiday celebrated across the country, an event interpreted by my non-American Indian teachers, who explained that the pilgrims were holding their first feast and invited the Indians. Through such accounts, made by these influential educators, I was led to believe that the Indians in portraits from long ago definitely were not the key figures of this historic event. In fact, they were commonly referred to as the "friendly but uncivilized Natives." As a pre-teen, I realized that the rural town where I lived was named after one of the chiefs of my tribe, a fact that was not mentioned in the civics or history courses of the day. It was during these young years in my life that I realized that non-American Indians had deliberately rendered our tribal people invisible, leaving me to profoundly question my own identity and place in the world as an American Indian.

In an attempt to learn about who I am and where I come from, throughout grade school I began to rely on my own means of learning about our people rather than on the sparse selection of books in the libraries authored solely by non-American Indians. As an adolescent, whenever I had the chance to see my family back home, I would seek out those places where I could watch and listen to the Elders speak, which at that time happened to be at powwows. It was serious because I wanted to know exactly how our people were much more than what was depicted in the books and by outsiders. I wanted to connect the dots between those eastern Indians and present-day tribal people. Perhaps my reasons were selfish, yet they came from a place that urged me to be validated as a tribal human being. I yearned to see my tribal relatives and our leaders receiving the same recognition and signs of admiration and respect that were given to and by non-American Indians in the community. I deeply wished for words of knowledge about our people, our ways, and our leaders that spoke about our significant place in this world.

Interestingly, it was within the city – among the urban Indian community, where, according to the last census, many of our people live today – that I learned the most about who we are as a people and where we come from. Whenever I had the privilege of hearing our tribal practitioners, storytellers, historians, and leaders speak, I paid special attention and listened carefully because I knew that, collectively, we were more than the images portrayed in books.

Moving to the city is a story in itself, as I was drawn to the waters of Puget Sound from my initial visit. I've kept with the belief that things happen for a reason, especially after applying for several positions with my tribe and not being hired. I believe that I was supposed to live in the city. This was also at a period in my life when I did not expect to have children because I did not want them to live a catastrophic life. In time, that changed too. I had finished my bachelor's degree and had moved to the city because I believed I was meant to dedicate my adult life to working for our urban Indian community and to addressing the health and well-being of our people, who have made their way from tribal origins across the country.

Would a story like this be told during a visit to a Western-trained practitioner? In my experience, it never has. The integration of traditional Indian medicine into clinics based on a Western-based philosophy allows

American Indian patients to be and feel understood. The practitioner listened to my story deeply, in a way that I had never experienced before and that had far-reaching effects that touched my spiritual being. In essence, this person heard recollections that extended back to my first memories, including the effect of being in a state child welfare system, growing up in communities that were rampant with racially prejudicial attitudes and actions towards American Indians, and how it all related to my holistic (mind, body, and spiritual) health. This holistic approach, which showed my story profound respect, may be one of the most important aspects of traditional Indian medicine. It was for me. The traditional practitioner had to understand my story in order to take into consideration all aspects of life. This understanding marks the beginning of a sacred process between the one who is caring and the one who is cared for.

I relate the next chapter of my life to show how traditional Indian medicine can be integrated into our contemporary health care systems.

The kindest person I had ever met entered my life at a good point. We later became life mates, and, at the time, I knew that the change I had prayed for was being answered. I also knew that I would have the honour of being a mother. We had a traditional wedding that included providing a feast and a giveaway. Like many American Indian events, this one stayed true to our saying "Whatever happens was meant to be," for we had double the number of attendees than had been invited. Although we had a team of cooks, many brought food to share, so there was enough for everyone. Whenever I see one of our Elders, she always says, "Your wedding was the most beautiful one I've ever seen," which brings good medicine to me and others who were there.

Eventually, our family started. My experience of giving birth in a spiritual and ceremonial manner occurred at a city hospital. I found out I was with child during a visit to the doctor for an earache and double vision. Within a couple of days, I had facial paralysis, was unable to walk, and had lost my balance. According to the neurologist, the blood titers indicated that I had diphtheria. My doctor was not able to make a prognosis about whether I would gain full recovery from these conditions, and that is when a traditional practitioner led me through a series of ceremonies.

By the time my third trimester came around, I was feeling much better. I could walk and talk, and my vision had mostly returned to its normal state.

During this time, my husband and I visited an obstetrician and explained to her that we wished to have a traditional American Indian birthing based on our cultural and spiritual practices. She supported our wishes. As my due date neared, there were some medical concerns. I had gestational diabetes, which led to the labour being induced. Although I did not use pain medications because of my belief in natural childbirth, I accepted medicine for my high blood pressure. A ceremony was conducted from the point that I entered labour until the first hours of our son's exit from the womb.

Who can say why I was so ill during the first months of my pregnancy? Before that point, I had sworn off having a child with the intention of preventing another human being from having a hopeless existence. To carry a child and to give birth is more than a miracle. Besides gaining a deeper understanding about the sacredness of life, I also learned from this experience that I am strong enough to deal with whatever is handed to me and that it is with this strength that the circle continues.

My own personal story shows how traditional practices can be effectively integrated into unnatural settings such as hospitals during the most meaningful moments of our lives. My son's entry into this world means that the ways of our ancestors will be passed on to family members who have yet to come. During the summer of 2009, within the confines of an urban hospital, our newest family member was welcomed into this world with birthing songs sung by my son that will protect her from that day forward. As patients, it is important that American Indian people do things in our own way. Thus, when these opportunities come, we must take the initiative to inform our health professionals about what we envisage. We can practise our American Indian culture and traditions within the city if we educate and stand up for ourselves, our families, and our communities. Traditional Indian medicine practitioners bring from their respective tribes a span of original wisdom that serves as the foundation for living purposefully and does so in a way that will benefit the whole community. My birthing stories show that, despite historical events that have had an adverse effect on our American Indian being, we maintain a distinct worldview that stems strongly from our tribal wisdom and reflects generational longevity.

The Future Practice of Traditional Indian Medicine

When American Indian families decide to raise their children in the city, there is a concern that we will forget *who we are and where we come from.* This concern stems from the belief that our traditional knowledge and practices, which are based upon our Indigenous worldview, must be maintained in order for us to live in balance. We continue to dance and sing, have gatherings and ceremonies, and participate in community events such as potlucks and powwows to maintain our sense of belonging. Because our values are lived by being among family and traditions, we sometimes travel back home, which also allows us to reinvigorate our cultural traditions and understanding. I believe that our level of success at being in balance – from the individual to the community level – is dependent on how connected or reconnected we are to our traditional wisdom.

Not only do we learn about our American Indian ways in our homes, we also learn about other tribal ways from those who live in the city. There are many urban Indian organizations in our community, and each person within them brings a specific worldview based upon what he or she has learned from Elders and tribal communities. Collectively, we carry out our work with a broad understanding about the importance of maintaining our cultural and traditional knowledge.

To maintain our original wisdom and traditional knowledge in our work is an intensive process that requires us to consider many important questions pertaining to specific tribal protocols and other tribal perspectives. For example, we have a way to cleanse the whole mind, body, and spirit through a sweat bath. Some tribes partake in male- or female-only sweats; others allow mixed sweats. Some of us know how to build and take down the sweat house. We know where the door faces and where the fire is placed. Some of us observe the teachings about how to enter, how to participate, and how to exit the sweat house. Participating in the sweat can be a challenge in an urban setting that does not necessarily afford families their own location. We have to share community space, which opens the door to disagreements when we are faced with determining which tribal ways take precedence. Our traditional leaders figured this out, and their knowledge is reflected in their teachings: When you enter someone's home, you show respect by following their ways. The same consideration should be shown when entering someone else's sweat. I've found that before I enter a sweat led by another person, I take the time to understand how she would proceed. I then have the option to decline if I feel strongly that participation would compromise my own teachings.

Traditional ways that are passed from generation to generation are forever changing. Activities performed today are different from those performed a generation or two ago. The work of many traditional medicine practitioners involves song, and some of us believe that to sing is to bring on ceremony. Once started, the song is not to be interrupted. Our family drum, with great intention, sings certain sets of songs, depending on the occasion. We sing for several reasons, and in preparation, we enter into another realm where songs are selected. Songs are prayers that have a purpose, and each song exists to help someone. As the songs begin, the ancestors take their place around the drum circle and thus add much welcomed strength to the circle. The spirit of the four-legged and plant life that make up the physical properties of the drum are there as well. Many more teachings about singing and the drums have been passed on to us. All the while, traditions are changing, which makes me stop and wonder about what will be maintained if our traditional knowledge and teachings continue to transform.

To maintain our traditional knowledge, we will also need to bring our minds, bodies, and spirits together. It was not long ago that my beloved said that our traditional people are gone, that what is accepted today as traditional is far from what he was taught by his grandparents. Today, I spoke with my sister back home, and she described how she had been privileged to cook at a spiritual gathering led by those who follow the real old ways, in contrast to the contemporary traditions that she sees occurring on our reservation today. We may need to develop a shared vision for our community as we continue to integrate traditional Indian medicine into our practice. I expect to grapple with some big issues, including defining what *traditional* means in contemporary society. I know what I mean when I answer that question. My answer is similar to the views held by my beloved and my sister. It will be interesting to see how the community defines *tradition* and which views will have the most influence. I can only hope that as we evolve we do justice towards our ancestors, who will be watching.

As I look around our community and at our American Indian organizations, I occasionally take note of the interactions within and between each of our entities since it is a reflection of how we have prioritized our American Indian values. In some ways, we have succumbed to the forces of time and money, which results in competing for funding and puts us at risk of moving further apart from one another. In spite of that, our organizations have managed to successfully join together for common purposes, demonstrating that we are able to reach a shared vision whenever we are called upon to do so.

We need to continuously assess our American Indian worldview and what we want to carry forward. In our diverse community settings, that means conducting training that helps others see the value of integrating traditional Indian medicine and Western approaches. In particular, we need to communicate how we relate with our practitioners, a subject that we do not take lightly, for practitioners are part of our American Indian leadership and are the strongest models of our original teachings and values. It is a huge accomplishment to incorporate the practices of traditional practitioners – people who carry diverse worldviews, knowledge, and wisdom – into health care, particularly when Western-trained medical practitioners are also at the table.

Oftentimes, the efforts of traditional practitioners are overlooked because they do not call attention to themselves or their work. I have heard many practitioners say that they should not get credit when someone regains balance after undergoing treatment because they are only the helper and that the Creator is the healer. Another point made by our practitioners is that they know just a little bit, which means that we as human beings have limitations. No one person can possess all of the knowledge in the world, even if she or he lived a thousand lifetimes. The practitioners' humility is misinterpreted or lost among those who have a Westernized worldview. My role as liaison affords me the opportunity to bring these differences into focus through in-service training, by which staff and community members are introduced to our worldview – traditional knowledge, wisdom, and practices.

To engender traditional knowledge and practices in leadership requires the strength and support of others. For me, this support came from the kindness and love of those who genuinely live by principles based on our American Indian worldview and value system. As I fulfill my roles as mother, worker, and community member, I do so with the understanding that I am following teachings that originated in a time before I came into this world. As I recount who I am and where I come from, what I learned from our people and what I have to offer, and how our original wisdom will be affirmed, it is with the utmost concern that our legacy will continue in a good way.

Traditional Medicine as an Affirmation of American Indian Wisdom and Ways

I spend a great deal of time talking about family because this is the training ground for our emerging leadership. When I was young, growing up in the rural area, I used to go out and dig camas roots not only because I liked the taste of them but also because experiencing the sanctuary of nature was uplifting. It was not until I was a young adult that I found out that this root is a medicine, that our tribal feasts offer it, and that it provides sustenance for the mind, body, and spirit. I am fairly certain that if I had not reconnected with my family and met practitioners who carry our traditional wisdom and cultural knowledge with them, camas would not have the significance that it has for me today. If I had not learned about the interconnectedness of all things – mammals, plants, birds, fish, and the elements – then I would have missed out on passing this teaching to others.

Our wealth of traditional knowledge and understanding begins in the family and permeates from there into our communities. I recall when I first felt a deep desire to learn more about our people, our ways, our heritage, our history, our land, and whatever I could absorb that taught me about who I am and where I come from. I vigilantly watched our tribal Elders, who at times seemed protective of our American Indian ways, who carried our traditional knowledge with dignity and grace, and who held our tribal wisdom carefully so that it would be sustained in our traditional practices. My beloved's traditional foundation and deep wisdom encouraged him to teach our entire family about the old ways to the best of his ability. During our time together, I was given a name that translates as Winter Moon Woman Medicine. This name not only reflects our belief that everything has a purpose, it also magnifies the powerful concept that everything is connected. I strongly believe that names come to us intentionally. Wintertime has always been my favourite season, perhaps because it is the time of year when natural life slows down and is dormant. It is a time to reflect on spirituality and a time for inner self-inspection, which occurs in solitude. Earlier, I mentioned that I had formed a relationship with Grandmother Moon in childhood. This connection was meaningful for many reasons and still carries significance for me today. I am a woman, and am privileged as a life giver. Isn't it interesting that I received that name over twenty years ago and now work in traditional Indian medicine. That is what is meant when we say everything has a purpose and is connected.

Knowledge keepers have their origins in specific tribes. And as American Indian people, we all need to make sure that we have a place in our own communities. I want to continue to learn from Elders because, like our languages, the traditional practices and knowledge they hold are diminishing with each passing year. Regardless of what hat I am wearing at any given time, my work within my family and community is to be mindful and conscientious as I bring forward our traditional knowledge and ways. This process begins by reinforcing the message that our communities have traditional knowledge keepers who manoeuvre much like graceful war dancers as they promote the continuation of our original wisdom, that their vision of forever moving ahead and translating the knowledge of the ancestors will benefit all.

Will we dance forward with strength and purpose? The transformation can begin at any stage in the life cycle. I started dancing traditional plateau style as a young adult with the help of my beloved and others who encouraged me with kind words and compassion. I was taught that as I circled around the dance floor, prayers would be said. To this day, that is how I proceed. For me, dancing is an honour, one of many ways to continue what has been handed down. My son first stepped onto the floor when he was a young child, and it is no coincidence that his philosophy about American Indian traditions is so insightful. During one of our discussions, I asked him how he would teach our young people about our traditions. He thought awhile and replied that for someone to learn about our traditions, they really have to want to, so much so that they learn what they can and progress forward. He said it is like always stepping forward. That was heart-lifting.

We who live in urban areas and who come from tribes from across the country are working hard to keep our traditional knowledge alive for our families and communities. We strive to find ways of helping our people move forward in life and to maintain balance, which is best accomplished by integrating traditional Indian medicine into Western health care settings. Even though we face many challenges in our mission to help our people, some of which have been addressed here, our efforts are not lost, nor are we.

That leaders in my community and perhaps others want to see us progress is apparent in their efforts to help us carry on our practices.

Every time I attend a American Indian gathering, browse through our tribal newspaper, or surf Indian Country Today online, I am reminded that American Indian people have so much to offer when it comes to demonstrating how their wisdom and collective history has influenced their work as traditional practitioners, business entrepreneurs, attorneys, political officials, scientists, government and nonprofit executives, educators, doctors, and a host of other professions. The descendants of our ancestors, from the east to the west coast, have emerged and are visible. Their history and legacies are being documented from American Indian perspectives and worldviews, and these histories and stories are, in turn, having a real impact on our collective psyche, particularly the minds and hearts of young people who are figuring out who they are and where they come from. Five hundred years from now, portrayals of our leadership will have a positive effect on the spirit of our people because, unlike our American Indian relatives who gathered at the first thanksgiving and whose extraordinary leadership was lost in translation, we will not be mere "extras" in stories of our past. Rather, we will be visible and viable representatives of our communities, nations, and country as a whole. It is happening now, and I am proud.

Works Cited

Alfred, Taiaiake. 1999. *Peace, Power, Righteousness: An Indigenous Manifesto.* Don Mills, ON: Oxford University Press.

Hollow, Walter, B. 1999. "Traditional Indian Medicine." In *Primary Care of American Indian American Patients: Diagnosis, Therapy, and Epidemiology,* edited by J.M. Galloway, B.W. Goldberg, and J.S. Alpert, 31-38. Boston: Butterworth-Heinemann.

Jones, Hinetara. 2010. "Homai, Hoatu Traditional Health and Healing Practices by Iwi, Hapu, Whanau Practitioners Based in Turanganui a Kiwa, Aotearoa NZ." Paper presented at the Fourth Biennial Conference of the International Network of Indigenous Health Knowledge and Development, Poulsbo, Washington, 27 May 2010.

Morgan, Robert and Lyn Freeman. 2009. "The Healing of Our people: Substance Abuse and Historical Trauma." *Substance Use and Misuse* 44: 84-98.

Seattle Indian Health Board. "Mission Statement" and "Values and Commitments." http://sihb.org//about_SIHB.html.

15

Leaders Walking Backwards

Male Ex-Gang Members' Perspectives and Experiences

Alanaise Goodwill

I AM ALANAISE GOODWILL, mother of two young sons and one adult stepdaughter and grandmother to an infant granddaughter. I introduce myself in this way, at the beginning of this text, as a way to share how I see myself in the world. I am, among many things, a wife, psychotherapist, researcher, and aspiring academic. I have had these roles for only a portion of my life, but for all of my life I have been Anishinaabe, daughter to Vivian Ferguson and the late David Ferguson. Of all these things, being Anishinaabe and a mother have inspired me the most to be a researcher. I have a fierce and possessive love for all Native people, as well as for children. Let me tell you a story about a time, during 2005, when I was visiting my in-laws with my husband and children. This visit helped me to determine a research direction for my doctoral studies and relates directly to the theme of leadership in Indigenous communities.

My husband is Fabian Goodwill. His brothers and sisters and their families live on Standing Buffalo Dakota First Nation Reserve near Fort Qu'Appelle, Saskatchewan. My Dakota family is a generous one, rich in culture and knowledgeable of their impressive history, which links them to the 1862 Minnesota uprising and Sitting Bull's vision. Every year in August, Standing Buffalo Reserve hosts one of the largest outdoor competition powwows in Canada. This powwow attracts dancers, singers, family members, and spectators from all over North America. My husband's family has been gathering there to celebrate powwow singing, dancing, culture, and family for over three generations. My husband and I, along with our two sons, then aged one and six, travelled eighteen hours by car to be with our community and family during the annual powwow.

Upon entering the powwow grounds on the Friday evening of the first grand entry, we were greeted by members of the community who were valiantly serving as the security. A cardboard sign attached to a temporarily erected signpost read, "No colors, gang signs, or weapons permitted on powwow grounds." The security guards created perimeter checkpoints to conduct vehicle examination and searches. In the thirty years that I had lived in British Columbia, I had never experienced this kind of security at a family-friendly event.

Upon entering the powwow grounds, I began to understand the vigilant and protective posture of the community members at the security gates. I was enjoying the grand entry and standing in a large crowd of powwow family when a youth no older than twelve limped past me. He was bleeding from a wound somewhere on his head, covered in blood, and proceeded to stumble through the crowd unaccompanied. He walked right past where I stood. My son, in his stroller, stared at this injured boy with shock and concern as the boy disappeared behind the crowds of people and food-vending trailers. I do not know what became of this boy, but I do know he was not the only youth who experienced extreme violence that weekend. News of machete fights, swarmings, gun seizures, and violence disrupted the communal spirit and excitement of the powwow. Community culture and violence seemed to run on two separate but simultaneous tracks at the powwow. I observed that two traditional dancers competing in a dance off and two women in a brawl could equally attract a large radius of attention and awe.

The image of the boy covered in blood has never left my memory. I think about this boy's serious injuries and how I, like so many others, did not stop him to offer help, comfort, or safety. The goriest part of this experience was not the vision of a blood-covered boy, but my own experience of the bystander effect, a social psychological phenomenon that inhibits individuals from helping another during an emergency because of the presence of others (Alcock, Carment, and Sadava 2005). The bystander effect may be what caused us, community members, to watch an injured child stoically stumble alone, isolated from a culture that honours the sacredness of children (Hart 2002). The guilt and anxiety that I felt when I observed this boy's emotional and psychic segregation from the cultural kinship network that children deserve demanded that I take action in a way that could be meaningful to children who are alone, injured, bullied, and unsafe. I could see no issue more important than that of gang violence in and among our children and young adults in Indian country.

I knew that, beyond the bystander effect, First Nations communities suffer from normalized levels of violence that affect our collective ability to stand up to it (Badger and Albright 2003). Large cultural gatherings like the powwow at Standing Buffalo Reserve were becoming sites where youth could vividly express the manifestations of our cultural loss. Youth are often the first to initiate change in our communities, and youth in gangs were seeking opportunities to build their reputations in well-populated First Nations gatherings where there was a perception of low crime enforcement or security (e.g., lawlessness). The beauty, artistry, and spirituality of powwows draw many Indigenous nations together, but harmonious and loving kinship networks are often no longer intact for many Aboriginal youth (Badger and Albright 2003). As a mother, I was concerned about children hurting other children in extreme and sometimes permanent ways. As an Anishinaabe, I was concerned about the impact gang activity could have on the vitality and endurance of culture. As a researcher and aspiring academic, I could not find a more neglected area of research of concern to our First Nations people.

At the time of this visit, I was a second-year doctoral student in the University of British Columbia's Educational and Counselling Psychology and Special Education Department. I was studying counselling psychology specifically and had a private counselling practice that served First Nations clients living within Stó:lō territory. Both professionally and personally, I lean towards preserving Indigenous cultures as one of several means to heal and help those First Nations and Aboriginal peoples who present in counselling settings. Based on what the body of research stated during my literature searches, there was very little guidance on how to understand, conceptualize, and plan counselling treatment and therapy with those affected by gangs.

What I needed to know as a therapist was how to understand the variables that contribute to a person entering and then leaving gang life. I wanted to be able to recognize the turning points in a person's life that could contribute to a trajectory into gang life so I could better prevent a youth from entering this life. I also wanted to be able to recognize how those who survived gang life were able to leave it. These questions became the basis of my research project, which involved interviewing ten Aboriginal men who had successfully left gang life. These men were all asked the same two questions: What experiences did you have that got you more involved in gang life? What experiences did you have that got you less involved in gang life? Each man discussed as many different experiences as he could recall. A total of thirteen different experiences facilitated gang entry, and thirteen different experiences facilitated gang withdrawal. Seven of the ten men were Anishinaabe, one was Metis-Anishinaabe, one Cree, and one was Dakota, Ojibwa, and Cree. They ranged in age from nineteen to forty and had been out of their gangs for at least one year (Goodwill 2009).

This chapter illustrates a type of leadership in Indigenous communities. Identifying our future leaders is an important and necessary practice for all cultures, and it usually begins when adults observe some of the mannerisms and tendencies of children. An Indigenous understanding of leadership extends beyond describing power within a title or location within the hierarchy of an organizational structure (Deane, Bracken, and Morrissette 2007). I refer in particular to a leadership style that my people observe in the young children they call Baajagosuk. Baajagosuk is a nickname often given to daredevil children who instigate activity and demonstrate a fearless attitude towards playing and socializing. Quite often, boys attract this label when they appear to be willing to try anything and then encounter discipline styles and reactions to suppress rather than nurture this innate leadership quality.

I began to think of this term affectionately while conducting research interviews with the ten men who spoke about their development during their youth. These interviews were conducted between February and May 2008 in confidentiality. The names of the interviewees are withheld by mutual agreement.

> I guess I was a pretty bad boy. They used to call me "Bad Boy" back then, too. I remember that. I was pretty bad. Now, I like to share. That's what I do a lot myself. I share. Now, for instance, we have little ones that come here. We get calls to do presentations and stuff. And we even get calls from a mom, eh, sayin' her son is, wants to be a drug dealer and a gang banger. And, so, I tell her, bring him down. Maybe we can talk to him, have a smudge and talk, tell him whatever, share our lives with him.

> You know, I actually tried to start my own gang when I was younger. That's what I tried to do. I did it. I did make a little gang on the reserve, and that's when I ended up getting kicked out of school when I was fifteen. When I got kicked out, same time, same year, I got expelled from that school, and I couldn't come back there. I didn't really care because I figured, then I'll be

at home, be there with my grandpa. But then they passed away when I was sixteen. My mom and my grandpa – they passed away not even a month apart. But then that's when I got placed on independent living. That was the last step, because I was placed in boys' homes, group homes, foster homes. I kept getting kicked out of all of them.

I felt a lot of pain growing up with my mom. I was left a lot. A lot of the time I was growing up, I felt a lot of pain. I was left alone, tears. I had my two younger brothers to watch. It was kind of sad for a while. I felt good to be with my friends all the time. I was always scared, and then I'd say, "Let's go do this, go throw some rocks at some cars, tomatoes, or whatever, whatever, go throw donuts around, bumpershine." You know, I followed the ... maybe I followed myself. I felt, I would bumpershine all the way home from school. It wasn't good to bumpershine. It was bad. I used to like making people laugh, you know. I'd jump up on this bumper. I was kind of a ... I'd try to encourage people to come bumpershining, things like that. I wasn't much of a leader either growing up. I don't think, I mean, I was a silly kid. Whatever anybody'd want to go do, I'd go do. Fights? I'd go too. I'd go check out a fight, too. Things like that. When I was asked to do something, I'd go head first. I wouldn't stop to think about how it would affect me. At a young age, I was pretty healthy. I liked ... I just went for everything, whatever.

When I reread the first quote, I see how a child who carried the label "Bad Boy" actually developed a leadership style based in generosity. His "Bad Boy" nickname likely referred to his tendency to get into trouble and never fully captured his innate desire to share. In the literature on Aboriginal gang life, I discovered that those who grow up together as children and then form a gang also tend to be very generous as children. This generosity helps them (as it did the man who provided this quote) to overcome the gripping pain of hunger and loneliness. The men in my study revealed that the survival skill of sharing was also a virtue that they came into contact with again when they began to learn their cultures and traditions, something that other researchers have determined as well (Deane, Bracken, and Morrissette 2007; Badger and Albright 2003).

The second quote illustrates the leadership potential of a young man who happened to be growing up in an environment with limited opportunities. Leadership qualities become distorted in colonial spaces, such as First Nations reserves that endure the legacy of residential schools, which oppressed and traumatized our people (Lane et al. 2002). Had this person been exposed to role models who were athletes or activists, his leadership capabilities might have led him to form a sports team or a Greenpeace chapter instead of a gang. The legacy of residential schools in First Nations communities includes prevalent abuse of our most vulnerable community members. In the case of many of the men interviewed in this research, enduring childhood abuse and traumas during several important developmental stages were excruciatingly common.

The life of the person who provided the third quote illustrates the results of disrupted parenting, neglect, and living with many conditions of loss. This person speaks of his life as a boy and the means by which he escaped some of the sadness he experienced in his family life. Although he does not refer to himself as a leader, he remarks that maybe he "led himself" in the best way he knew possible. His ability to instigate action and activity and act without thinking and his impulse to create laughter in spite of his sadness are leadership qualities manifested in a ghettoized urban space. Understanding Aboriginal children's unique leadership development also includes understanding the role of the social forces acting on them, their families, and their communities. Jana Grekul and Patti Laboucane-Benson (2008) write extensively about the economic marginalization within colonized spaces that leads to the displacement of Aboriginal peoples and the creation of gangs in Aboriginal communities.

The price that we pay as Indigenous peoples is the loss of our youth to a process that leads them backwards from their potential as our future leaders. Youth end up in gang life, prison life and, sadly, for too many, the afterlife. In the case of the ten men I interviewed, their backwards walk eventually led them to their Elders and their culture and language. They encountered a cultural kinship network in which they could lead in a good way.

The ten male survivors of gang life shared details about their family and social relationships that encapsulated their notions of kinship and the importance of family and relationships during their adolescence. Cousins, uncles, siblings, peers, parents, and extended family provided the social capital in the early lives of the men. Role-modelling was a particularly powerful leadership mechanism that served as a catalyst for gang entry. The largest proportion of their statements paid tribute to the role of relationships in causing them to either enter or exit gang life.

Showing others, kind of like role-modelling to other little gang bangers, like, "If you wanna be like me ... If you wanna be in the gang like me ..." I just told 'em, "I got my buddy. Just like my buddy come and brought me into the gang, come and sit around, see how it goes." And say, "This is why I'm out all weekend. This is why you don't see me, 'cause this is what I'm doing. So, come and chill with me for a few days, and see what I do." Kind of like, "You wanna be like me? Be straight up, man. Don't fuck up. Don't get fucked up, whatever." I'm, like, bringing my buddies in, like, "I'll introduce you to my boys." What I'm doing is, "I'm the one introducing you. So, if you fuck up, it makes me look bad, 'cause, you're fucking up, and you're under my name." It was my brother.

I was thirteen, fourteen, younger even, like ten-ish, 'cause, like I said, I grew up with older people. I'd see my cousins wearing rags and stuff. Just stuff like that. Not even really hustling. I seen them with their cell phones, like, why are they always answering their cell phones? Stuff like that. Saying, "I'll be there in ten minutes." It made me want to be like that. My cousins used to always hook me up, like, come to my school and bring me lunch and shit like that. I said, you know, I wanna do that for someone one day, like, be a good role model, like a role model, gangster role model. Because you don't know what to think. You're like ten. Everyone has role models and stuff.

Yeah, seeing that star on someone [an uncle] I look up to. If I had that star, nobody could touch me. That's what I thought. I kept that to myself. No one would have known I was thinking that. I just looked at that tattoo. I just wanted that star to be on me. But I thought that, if he had that star, no one could touch him.

Although these three quotes include the perspective of being either the leader or follower, two of their themes are important to our understanding of leadership: (1) role-modelling and mentoring are powerful mechanisms for activating group membership, and (2) children are driven by the desire and opportunity to obtain family protection and mentoring, regardless of the social context. One possible way to view gang affiliation is in terms of children's attempts to fill the empty space where Indigenous kinship systems used to exist in community life. If gangs are the dominant system in which children seek validation, focus their dedication, and enhance their learning, then the cultural implication is that we must revitalize Indigenous kinship systems to compete with gang systems for the leadership of our kids.

Many of the men I interviewed expressed a dedication to helping others stay out of or move out of gang life. This dedication has parallels in one of the Teachings of the Seven Grandfathers (also known as the Seven Grandfathers or the Seven Teachings), that of love or *zhaagiitoonan*. This Anishinaabe teaching urges us to love others in a way that lays claim and is protective, to express compassion and commitment to our people in the spirit of service. Doing so takes bravery or *zhogiitawin*. It means having a strong heart and the courage to make a difference in one's own community and to stick with the agenda of preventing the growth of gangs. Here's an example of love and bravery in action within a leadership context:

> It's more like, the Native, the culture, nobody's racist, they're all Crees, Ojibways, and Saulteaux. So, back in the day, the cultures used to think they were better than each other. Like, the Blackfoots, the Sioux. You know what I mean? And the Ojibways. The Crees. Everybody's thinking they're better, and all that. But it's all one race. It's the traditional race. I wanted to come here [workplace] because of my background, and I see a lot of other brothers and sisters that need help. And they come. Out of my experience, I help them. I direct them to a different kind of path. Like don't go through what I went through, because I've been through a lot throughout the years.

Another of the Seven Grandfathers focuses on humility, or *daabaazan-dizowin*. It is a very important teaching about levelling oneself and not talking down to others. Many of the men spoke about the significance of ceremony and described the process of entering a circle where no one person was elevated above another, where the teaching of daabaazan-dizowin is embodied. They related how humility incited feelings of responsibility for others in the circle and in their families:

> Opening prayers and traditions, and they are said in the Native tongue. Language is very important. Ceremonial practice, the spiritual ethics. It's like saying you can't touch that drum because something bad will happen to you unless you're using the right type of medicine, unless you have the right type of tobacco, or unless you have the right type of methods of relating. Because, if you don't, that drum can backfire on you, and something can happen to you or your family. You can't break any rules. That respect is there, those principles – trust, loyalty, respect, honour, sincerity – through culture.

The social nature of experiencing gang life is an expression of the social values shared by the men. Trust, loyalty, respect, and sharing are all central to the lure of gang life. They are what children long for and need to develop, but they are also present within the practices of Aboriginal culture and tradition. The Seven Grandfathers were also reflected in some of the ways in which the men learned how to hone their leadership capabilities. The Seven Teachings are meant to be enacted at the same time, or their effects will be reversed. For example, you cannot be really *courageous* in gang life and earn *respect* if you lack the necessary *honesty, humility, truth, love,* and *wisdom* to go with it. In fact, if the other five teachings are not observed, the outcome will be not respect, but disrespect and fear. Just as the improper use of medicines will backfire in the circle, incomplete cultural guidance will cause the development of the leader to backfire. Men who could be powerful leaders get led backwards. They will keep moving backwards until they find their cultural kinship community, which provides the security, direction, and structure needed for forward-moving leadership. It was not until all of the Seven Teachings were learned and identifiable in the leadership of the men that the effects of the teachings could be realized.

I want to return to the term *Baajagosuk* to examine how it can be interpreted within the context of understanding the lives of the men I interviewed. Of the ten men interviewed, eight reported that they had been apprehended by child and family services, and half disclosed that they had had multiple family members in gangs. Only one had graduated from the provincial school system. Half had experienced childhood traumas and abuse, seven had mental health or addictions problems, half were orphans, and all had been incarcerated as young men or youths. Many of them had learned Anishnaabemowin (Ojibway) as adults or while incarcerated.

It was apparent that, even with such a small group of participants, there were several significant psychosocial factors to take into consideration, especially when working to understand a group so profoundly affected by Canada's institutions. The instigating quality and leadership capabilities of these perceived "Bad Boys" could not be allowed to blossom in the context of institutional powerlessness and childhood vulnerability. To the credit of the men who agreed to be interviewed, none of them attributed their choices to their poor, impoverished, or abusive childhoods. Many of them were wise to recognize their past and how it affected them, but none of them used this as an excuse for hurting others with their gang activities. However, it was their ability to create action, lead "play," and set the pattern for others to follow that became apparent as they described their lives after leaving gangs:

All the presentations I've done ... mostly, when I succeeded in one – when I did one for probation services – it was for youths, youths getting involved in gang activities and criminal activities. And they were having problems at home and stuff, and then a lot of them I was able to relate to. There was about four or five young guys. There was a group of twenty. It was good. Yeah, because a lot of times, when I go to presentations, there's always the younger ones. They ask me questions. I notice a lot of times, I talk about something, it reflects on them, too. I'm able to talk about myself and, you know, a lot of people kind of, nowadays, that, you know, like me, for I had a hard time trying to admit to the fact that I'd been sexually abused when I was a kid. Like a lot of guys, you know, they can't talk about that. A lot of them can't talk about it because it gets them mad, embarrassed, and it's too hard to talk about it. A lot of them just hide it. And then, you know, you'd be surprised how many kids out there – like, out of all the presentations I've done, they've come up and talked to me about that. Like, I don't know how to, I try not to get myself angry because I'm hearing someone else talk about it, eh? Sometimes I ... that's how I know it gets through to kids when I talk to them.

I can also do gang awareness presentations. I go to schools, banquets, assemblies of nations, and banquets, uh, auditoriums, schools, agencies, one-on-ones. I do it for all communities that have gang issues in their neighbourhoods. It doesn't matter if they're pink, yellow, black, or white. Don't matter. I just do those things. It helps me feel a lot more better about myself. It helps me really look at myself in a leadership way. It makes me feel real good inside knowing that someone is exceeding [sic] out there, that someone is doing something positive with their lives and that they're going somewhere instead of nowhere. Like me.

I felt humbled by the extent to which these men shared their lives with me for the purposes of helping others understand their complex realities. Many people speak of gang members with disgust and disdain. As a mother, I have always been acutely aware of the times when we send double messages to our children, when we say things such as "Everyone deserves love and is equal" but follow it up with "If you are in a gang, you are not lovable any more. In fact, you are disgusting and worthy only of rejection." When children experience this type of rejection, they will do anything to rid themselves of the negative feelings and thoughts associated with this type of attack. When we attack the emotional well-being of children, we abandon them and lose the opportunity to mentor them into their rightful positions as our future leaders. The most important lesson that I learned from the ten men was that, if we want to develop pro-social leadership in our communities for future generations, gangs cannot be more accessible to children than Indigenous kinship structures. If these structures are for some reason unavailable to Aboriginal children, then it should become the task of our people as community members to instill knowledge and awareness of these structures in children so they can recognize the difference between gang leadership and cultural leadership.

I conducted this research project out of love for my people. As an Anishinaabe woman, reaching out to my relations who are affected by violence is very meaningful to me. Clöe Maddanes, in a speech presented at the 2005 "Evolution of Psychotherapy Conference," states, "It is very easy to have compassion for the victims, but it is even more important to have compassion for the offenders. If we are to change the violence in our world, that is where our work and compassion should be pointed." I was inspired by this statement and continue to hold on to her words in my work as a clinician and as a researcher. I learned from this process that it is easier than I thought to appreciate those who are initially hard to love. I have a great deal of respect for the efforts and achievements of the men and women who have lived in a way that is hard for us to understand. I am grateful that some shared their stories with us. Miigwetch.

Works Cited

Alcock, J., D. Carment, and S. Sadava. 2005. *A Textbook of Social Psychology*. 6th ed. Toronto: Pearson Prentice-Hall.

Badger, G., and C. Albright. 2003. *Alter-Natives to Non-Violence Report: Aboriginal Youth Gangs Exploration: A Community Development Process*. Saskatoon, SK: Federation of Saskatchewan Indian Nations.

Deane, Lawrence, Dennis Bracken, and Larry Morrissette. 2007. "Desistance within an Urban Aboriginal Gang." *Probation Journal* 54, 2: 125-41.

Goodwill, A. 2009. "In and Out of Aboriginal Gang Life: Perspectives of Aboriginal Ex-Gang Members." PhD diss., University of British Columbia.

Grekul, Jana, and Patti La Boucane-Benson. 2008. "Aboriginal Gangs and Their (Dis) placement: Contextualizing Recruitment, Membership, and Status." *Canadian Journal of Criminology and Criminal Justice* 50, 1: 59-82.

Hart, Michael. 2002. *Seeking Mino-Pimatisiwin: An Aboriginal Approach to Helping*. Halifax: Fernwod Publishing.

Lane, Phil, Michael Bopp, Judie Bopp, and Julian Norris. 2002. *Mapping the Healing Journey: The Final Report of a First Nation Research Project on Healing in Canadian Aboriginal Communities*. Ottawa: Aboriginal Peoples Collection.

Contributors

Michelle Archuleta is a member of the Lone Pine Paiute Shoshone Tribe. She shares an ancestry with the San Juan Pueblo (Tewa) and is also of German and Irish heritage. She is the health promotion consultant for the Bemidji Area Indian Health Service in northern Minnesota. She is passionate about working with collaborative processes that draw from the wisdom of community narratives. She is a doctoral student in the Antioch University PhD in Leadership and Change program.

Gail Cheney was born and raised in Kake, Alaska. She is a part of both the Tlinget and Haida Tribes in Alaska. On the Tlingit side, she is of the Raven Moiety and a member of the Fresh Water Marked Sockeye House. On the Haida side, she is Eagle Moiety and a member of the Hummingbird House. Gail is currently completing her PhD at Antioch University in the Leadership and Change program. Her work focuses on creating effective, culturally appropriate businesses and organizations in Alaska Native communities.

Patricia Doyle-Bedwell, BA (HONS.), LLB, LLM, Shidoshiho, is a Mi'kmaq woman originally from Maine and Chapel Island, Nova Scotia. She is an associate professor and directs the Transition Year Program at Dalhousie University. Patricia has researched and published work on Aboriginal women's issues. She is married with one son. She is also an instructor in the Bujinkan Doyle-Bedwell Dojo in Halifax, Nova Scotia, and has a fourth-degree black belt.

Stelómethet Ethel B. Gardner, BED (UBC), MED (UBC), EDM (HARVARD), PHD (SFU), is a Stó:lō member of the Skwah First Nation in British Columbia.

She is currently associate professor of education at the University of Alberta. She was previously chair of Aboriginal Education and associate professor at Lakehead University (2006-10) and assistant professor at Simon Fraser University (2002-06). She has a passion for Indigenous language revitalization and is engaged in a number of major research projects, including the "E-Master-Apprentice Pedagogy for Critically Endangered Languages" and "Language Planning for Anishinaabemowin Revitalization in Treaty #3."

Tina Ngaroimata Fraser, PhD, is a Māori scholar who works at the University of Northern British Columbia. She is a research and scholarship fellow with Massey University in New Zealand and an assistant professor (School of Education) and adjunct professor (School of Nursing and First Nations Studies) at the University of Northern British Columbia. She has lived among the Dakelth people and on their traditional territories for over thirty-five years.

Alanaise Goodwill, PhD, is an assistant professor in Brandon University's Indigenous Health and Human Services program, where she teaches courses on Indigenous approaches to healing and psychotherapy. She also works as a psychotherapist in Indigenous communities and is a member of the Sandy Bay Ojibway First Nation.

Raquel D. Gutiérrez, PhD, is passionate about strengthening the lifetime efforts of leaders working for inclusive and sustainable social justice. She is a private consultant who specializes in leadership development and the transformation of nonprofit culture. Her expertise includes assisting individuals and organizations to develop coherency between their values and their actions to realize social justice. For over twenty years, she has dedicated herself to working with those who have the courage to take care of themselves so they may better engage in their commitment to social justice.

Michelle M. Jacob, PhD, is an associate professor of ethnic studies at the University of San Diego. Her areas of interest include Indigenous health, gender, and education. She enjoys collaborating on community-based wellness projects with Indigenous communities in San Diego as well as in her home reservation community, the Yakama Nation, in Washington

State. In all of her work, inside and outside the academy, she seeks to help empower Indigenous communities to heal the wounds of colonialism.

Carolyn Kenny, PhD, is a professor of human development and Indigenous studies in the Antioch University PhD in Leadership and Change program. She has two adult children and four grandchildren. She has worked as a music therapist since 1969. She has Choctaw and Ukrainian ancestry and was adopted into the Haida Nation as the daughter of Dorothy Bell in 2000. She was a professor of First Nations education in the Faculty of Education at Simon Fraser University. She currently lives in Santa Barbara, California.

Yvonne G. McLeod (née Anaquod), PhD (in Educational Administration), is a Saulteaux Cree from Peepeekisis First Nation in Saskatchewan. Alfred McLeod is her husband of forty years. They have two children, Rachel and Gilbert. She is proud to name her six grandchildren: Vincent Desnomie, Rylan Hardisty, Deidra Desnomie, Tristan McLeod, Thaddeus McLeod, and Tyson McLeod. She is the executive director of the Kwayaciiwin Education Resource Centre, in Sioux Lookout, Ontario. She works collaboratively with twenty-four First Nation communities in northern Ontario by supervising the provision of second-level educational services.

Michelle Pidgeon, PhD, is an assistant professor in the Faculty of Education at Simon Fraser University. Her family and ancestry is from Newfoundland and Labrador. She teaches in the area of educational leadership, and her research focuses on indigeneity in higher education, Aboriginal student recruitment and retention within student affairs and services, and Indigenous methodologies.

Annette Squetimkin-Anquoe, a member of the Colville Confederated Tribes, works with the Seattle Indian Health Board in traditional Indian medicine. Trained with a master's degree in psychology, her experience among the urban Indian community – providing chemical addiction and mental health treatment, substance abuse prevention, and mental health services – has led her to direct programs, oversee special projects, and offer training and consultation on the health and social issues faced by American Indians. As a doctoral student in the Antioch University PhD in Leadership and Change program, she is interested in mobilizing culturally effective ways of addressing health disparities within the urban Indian community at the local level.

Evelyn Steinhauer, PhD, is a member of the Saddle Lake Cree Nation in northeastern Alberta. A visionary, an academic, and a committed lifelong learner, she is an agent for change in the advancement of First Nations education. She completed her undergraduate degree at Athabasca University and her MEd and PhD at the University of Alberta (Department of Educational Policy Studies), where she specialized in Indigenous peoples' education. She has a dual role in the Faculty of Education at the University of Alberta. She is an assistant professor in the Department of Educational Policy Studies and also the director of the Aboriginal Teacher Education Program (ATEP).

Alannah Young Leon is an Anishinaabe Nehiyaw Muskego from the Opaskwayak Cree Nation and a PhD candidate in the Faculty of Educational Studies, University of British Columbia. Her areas of interest are Indigenous leadership education, Indigenous knowledge, and place-based education.

Index

Printed and bound in Canada by Friesens

Set in Galliard and New Baskerville by Artegraphica Design Co. Ltd.

Copy editor: Lesley Erickson

Proofreader: Jean Wilson

Indexer: Shannon Venable